SCOUNDRELS VILLAINS & KNAVES

by FOXX NOLTE

INKLINGWOOD PRESS

© 2024 Foxx Nolte

FIRST EDITION
Published by Inklingwood Press

No part of this publication may be reproduced, distributed, or transmitted in any form or by any means, including photocopying, recording, or other electronic or mechanic methods, without the prior written permission of the publisher, except for brief quotations for critical, educational, and non-commercial uses permitted by copyright law.

This book is not associated with The Walt Disney Company. Quotations and images used throughout this book either have permission to be used or are used under Fair Use for educational and research purposes. Various nomenclature including theme park names, land names, attraction names, and intellectual property is copyright its respective owner.

Although every precaution has been taken to verify the accuracy of the information contained herein, no responsibility is assumed for any errors or omissions, and no liability is assumed for damages that may result from the use of this information.

"The pirate show lasts a quarter of an hour (but you lose any sense of time, it could be ten minutes or thirty); you enter a series of caves, carried in boats over the surface of the water, you first see abandoned treasures, a captain's skeleton in a sumptuous bed of moldy brocade, pendant cobwebs, bodies of executed men devoured by ravens, while the skeleton addresses menacing admonitions at you.

Then you navigate an inlet, passing through the crossfire of a galleon and the cannon of a fort, while the chief corsair shouts taunting challenges at the beleaguered garrison; then, as if along a river, you go by an invaded city which is being sacked, with the rape of the women, theft of jewels, torture of the mayor; the city burns like a match, drunken pirates sprawled on piles of kegs sing obscene songs; some, completely out of their heads, shoot at visitors; the scene degenerates, everything collapses in flames, slowly the last songs die away, you emerge into the sunlight.

Everything you have seen was on a human scale, the vault of the caves became confused with that of the sky... the boundary of this underground world was that of the universe and it was impossible to glimpse its limits."

- Umberto Eco

Contents

Foreword by Tom Morris 1
Charting the Course 5
Part One: Lost Down Pirate Alley 9
    I. The Spanish Main 11
    II. Pirates of Fact and Fancy 12
    III. The Gothic Pirate: Father Red-Cap and Billy Bones 28
    IV. The Romantic Pirate: Errol Flynn and Company 39
Part Two: Pirates in Walt's Utopia 51
    V. The Uncertain Forties 53
    VI. Treasure Hunt in Cornwall 60
    VII. Assembling the Rogue's Gallery 71
    VIII. Pirates of the Caribbean at Disneyland 91
Part Three: Exotic Ports of Call 161
    IX. Pirates of the Caribbean at Walt Disney World 162
    X. The Pirates Sack Asia and Europe 202
Part Four: On Stranger Tides 231
    XI. Pirates 'R' Good Enough 233
    XII. Weight Watchers of the Caribbean 249
    XIII. Raiders of the Cursed Genre 263
    XIV. July 2006: Rechristening 280
    XV. Captain Jack Goes Down With the Ship 290
    XVI. Pirates Across the Horizon 300
Notes 313
Bibliography 331

FOREWORD BY TOM MORRIS

Sometime in May, 1967...

Dad: "Disneyland just opened up a new ride called Pirates of the Caribbean."
Me: "What's that?"
Dad: "You go around in a boat and see pirates."
Me: "Like in Small World?"
Dad: "Yes, but with pirates, and you go down a waterfall."
Me: "But what about the Haunted Mansion?"

When Pirates of the Caribbean opened its nondescript French doors to the public on April 19, 1967, no one knew it would soon set the gold standard by which other attractions for decades would be measured, nor that it was about to propel the art and commerce of the theme park industry to the next level. Certainly no one expected it to someday become a cultural icon. The recognition built slowly.
    In those days, Disneyland generally did not place advertisements on TV as it relied on the weekly Disney prime time series to cover that base, but the episode hailing the latest Disneyland attractions including Pirates would not air for several more months. Word-of-mouth regarding the spectacular new Disneyland adventure rippled slowly through Southern California and eventually across the country, thanks to positive coverage in newspapers and magazines. By summer, the word was out: "The Pirates Are Here!" and by year's end, the attraction's popularity helped boost the attendance to record levels at Disneyland as well as surrounding local attractions; a similar jump was experienced in hotel occupancy rates followed by a steady increase in additional rooms - not just in Anaheim but across surrounding Orange County. Attendance levels never looked back.
    Yet, in those pre-internet days, this 1967 Disneyland "boom" was not a high-profile event. Years later, my boss and mentor at the time, Marty Sklar, relayed to me that Buzz Price (Disney Legend and esteemed president of Economic Research Associates) had remarked

on several occasions that Disneyland's "Summer of 1967" was a seminal moment in theme park history, one at which the combined art, technology and business pillars of the theme park industry reached a new maturity level, with Disneyland at the epicenter. The summer's new attraction lineup also included an all new, "great big beautiful" Tomorrowland, and along with the pirates, delivered an impactful one-two punch, generating great excitement throughout the region. Tomorrowland's many new attractions were mostly free, paid for on behalf of corporate sponsors, and as such were side dishes to the swashbuckling entrée on the other side of the park; it was the pirates that people were talking about. Soon, "Pirates of the Caribbean" would enter the local lexicon, serving as a descriptor of a particular kind of place or experience: "We saw fireflies... like in Pirates of the Caribbean."

It may have caught Walt Disney Productions by surprise, sailing for the first time without its founder and captain of the ship. Before the attraction's opening, the on-and-off construction over a 5-year time frame, from first shovel to opening day, was surely considered by management to be a nuisance, leaving a "big hole" (as Walt was fond of calling it) where pedestrian traffic needed to be, not to mention the headache and rising expense of rearranging retaining walls and heavy steel beams in order to accommodate changing requirements of the show and surrounding facilities.

Adding to the corporate angst must have been some ambiguity surrounding what exactly the attraction was going to be and whether people would actually ride it. Had Walt finally gone off his rocker before checking out? Would families really want to embark on a slow-moving boat ride through the marauding escapades of drunken 18th-century buccaneers - essentially criminals of the high seas? The general public, unless they were paying close attention, were oblivious to the forthcoming underground spectacle. Consequently, there was little pre-opening anticipation for this, the biggest E Ticket attraction yet. Unlike the similarly delayed Haunted Mansion, which was an easy and irresistible concept to grasp, the subject matter of Pirates was less of a slam dunk. When the attraction eventually opened, the public was so unaware of its debut that there were virtually no lines for it initially, and cast members had to beckon guests inside its unlikely-looking baroque "municipal building" facade.

Those growing pains between 1962 and 1967 probably left enough of a bitter taste in the mouths of Disney executives and Imagineering leaders that when the decision was made to build a second version of the attraction at Walt Disney World's Magic Kingdom a few years later, a desire to shorten the attraction (and therefore simplify the process) won out. This curious misstep was perhaps the first example of Walt's heirs not quite understanding the public the way that Walt did; that part of the attraction's appeal and mystique was a byproduct of its convoluted and collaborative history, a process that manifested itself in the physical layout, long trip time, and dream-like sequencing of the extraordinary attraction.

Future Imagineers, magicians, and filmmakers took note.

By the time the Disneyland Paris version was launched in the late 1980s it was now in the hands of those who grew up with, and loved, the original.

I know because I watched it develop, vicariously, as my fellow Show Producer on the Paris project, Chris Tietz, along with his capable team fashioned a new version of the show. Composed partly of favorite moments from the original, partly of "never built" scenes from the brushstrokes of Disney Legends Marc Davis and Herb Ryman, and partly from the imagination of Tietz himself, the Adventureland team blended the old and the new with a fresh sequencing that was as effective in its own way as the original. I looked on enviously, almost tempted to trade in my castle assignment for a chance to work on 12-year-old-me's dream job!

For those Disney aficionados who are familiar with the 75c Pirates of the Caribbean "Souvenir Booklet" once sold in the parks, as well as Jason Surrell's comprehensive Pirates of the Caribbean: From the Magic Kingdom to the Movies, and are still thirsting for more, here is the deep dive addendum you've been waiting for! Travel now through time and across the globe to soak up the all-important "rest of the story" of this epic attraction's origins and evolution, from the 1957 notion of a "Wax Museum" to the incredible, state-of-the-art version presented in Shanghai Disneyland.

Now hold on tight, with both hands if you please...

A Disneyland fan from an early age, Tom Morris went on to have a long career at Walt Disney Imagineering. His credits include Journey Into Imagination, Splash Mountain, Fantasyland at Disneyland Paris, DisneyQuest and Hong Kong Disneyland. He is currently writing a book on the first 20 years of Walt Disney Imagineering tentatively entitled "Imagineering - In the Beginning."

CHARTING THE COURSE

This book is already a little too long, and therefore I shall not detain this buccaneer cruise at port for any longer than is necessary. There are waterfalls to descend and towns to plunder and chickens to chase, after all. The length was probably unavoidable and could have been still longer, despite your author's best attempts to produce a book shorter than their first. I failed.

The process of writing it began before my first book *Boundless Realm* had been released; I was musing with my publisher David Younger that an interesting story could be told of how Disney came to single-handedly corner the cultural market on pirates. I threw myself instantly into research and discovered that the story was indeed interesting, but in order to tell it the scope of the book widened, and widened, and widened yet more.

So in the end this book embraces it all; I'm covering three centuries of popular culture and practically every incarnation of the concept of high seas piracy. My approach is interdisciplinary - the books, the plays, the movies, the video games - I've tried to include them all in an effort to understand and illuminate our culture's relationship with these greedy little opportunists. All of this has hopefully been harnessed to better answer the question of why this a boat ride at Disneyland has remained culturally relevant for a half century.

This means that this new book is quite different in character from my first. I feel that these differences are due to the nature of the two rides. Pirates of the Caribbean is grand but contemplative; and what really is Haunted Mansion but a bunch of weird little things to look at? This means that while I have to cover a lot of weird little things while discussing Haunted Mansion, Pirates presents the opportunities for big concepts and sprawling panoramas. As such this book has *sprawled*.

I truly believe if you read this book from start to finish every piece will have "fit together" by the end. I've tried to only include relevant examples of pirating that will occur again at some later point.

This book seeks to present the best, shortest path to our modern-day concept of pirates.

However, as a researcher I know that I often don't have time to read every book from cover to cover. As a result, as a reader you should not be afraid to use this book in the same way. You can choose to read the history in a linear fashion, or you can pick and choose the sections that strike your fancy and jump around as the mood suits. I hope sometimes you'll read this book one way and sometimes you'll read it the other way. I want my books to be useful reference material as well as entertaining histories, and the way they are laid out was done with intention.

Looking over this book in its finished form I can't help but express satisfaction that this truly was a job well done, the full and nuanced history that this attraction demanded. I think it's a significant upgrade over *Boundless Realm* and should better serve those who wanted more of a complete narrative from that book. It certainly satisfies me.

It would have been impossible to write this book in the same way without the support of my parents, Bill and Dorenda, as well as my best friend Brandon, co-conspirators Steven, Brice, and Michael, and publisher David.

Much of Part I of this book is indebted to Neil Rennie's *Treasure Neverland*, an excellent cultural overview of pirate literature which runs out of material in the 20th century because the author doesn't seem to be willing to follow the Disney ride down the cultural rabbit hole. I was pleased to be able to complete that story. There was also significant help extended by Tom Morris, Martin Smith, Chris Merritt, the Orlando Public Library, and Ted at DisneyDocs.

Thanks finally to my readers, who supported a niche book by a new author and made possible more. May the wind forever fill your sails.

Part One
LOST DOWN PIRATE ALLEY

I. THE SPANISH MAIN

In 1493 the Pope gifted the New World, which had just been discovered the year before by Christopher Columbus, to the Spanish crown. For about two decades following, the discovery and charting of this vast region was very much a background activity of the European continent.

But things changed in 1521. That's when Hernán Cortez managed to topple the Aztec empire. Acting now as Governor of Mexico, Cortez sent newly-enslaved native peoples to work in mines extracting wealth from the central American topography. The results could scarcely be believed. A steady stream of silver and gold was now sailing across the Atlantic back to Spain, enriching what was already Europe's most formidable military power - the United States of its day.

This stream of wealth multiplied with the conquest of Panama in 1533. The stretch through the Gulf of Mexico, across the isthmus of Panama, and down across the north reaches of South America became known as the Spanish Main - the treasure pot of the known world.

France, Holland, and England stewed in their resentment. Each nation would fund their own tardy New World expeditions, snatching up whatever Spain had either failed to claim or neglected in absence.

As a result, mongrels and riffraff the world over descended on the Americas to stake a claim to this fortune. You are probably related to some of them. Policing was spotty in this wild west atmosphere, and the New World filled up with misfits, criminals, bandits, and those willing to risk it all for the almighty Peso. As in the Yukon Gold Rush... or the internet in later times... the barrier to entry was low and the potential rewards huge. As historian Neal Rennie put it, "*The New World that turned the Old World upside down was the stimulus, the basis, for the revolution on the ocean.*"

In times of war, these opportunists were known as Privateers. In peacetime, they were declared enemies of mankind.

Today, we just call them Pirates.

II. PIRATES OF FACT AND FANCY

"LAFITTE'S ANCHOR - Said to be from a pirate ship commanded by Jean Lafitte in the Battle of New Orleans, January 8, 1815
It is also said that Lafitte's privateering ships left a wake of blood from the mainland to Barataria Bay But don't believe everything you read."
  - Plaque located in Disneyland

In New Orleans' French Quarter, there is a small side street called Pirates Alley. It runs from Jackson Square (where once the colonial government reigned), ducks down beside St. Louis Cathedral, and connects to Royal Street. French Quarter tour guides inform us that the residents of New Orleans were so grateful to privateer Jean Lafitte for helping defend the city in the Battle of New Orleans that they renamed "Orleans Alley South" in his honor.

From the Gorillas Don't Blog Collection

Except that can't be true, because the street was actually renamed in 1964[1], although the sign labeling it "*Pirates Al.*" had been hanging there for a long time before that. Times-Picayune writer Mike Scott, who investigated all of this, couldn't find any references to the term "Pirate(s) Alley" predating 1924, when it appeared advertising The Pirate's Chest Gift Shop.

Others counter that the alley used to be a hideout for the pirates of Barataria, except a bunch of pirates hiding between a church and the front door of the city courthouse makes absolutely no sense. There isn't even full agreement on what to call the thing - is it Pirate's Alley, Pirates' Alley, Pirates Alley or simply Pirate Alley?

Yet in another sense this confusion is absolutely accurate, because the minute you set out to prove anything historical about pirates - anything at all! - your history collapses into fantasy and dust. Researching pirates is like some historical version of one of those pointillist paintings where the closer you get to the canvas, the less you can see the image. Get too close, and you eventually have to concede that even the most basic facts about pirates - where they were born, what their names were, what happened to them - cannot be decisively proven. This is because pirates, in the sense that you and I know them - in the sense that we mean when we speak of pirates - are not real and *never have been.*

To be sure, there once were men and women who sailed the open seas with names like Captain Kidd, and Edward Teach, and Mary Read, and Barthlomew Roberts, and they did indeed pillage, plunder, rifle and loot. But these crimes are merely a starting point to their cultural relevance. Because to study piracy means to study historical crimes, ship navigation, early international trade and law enforcement, and this is not really what you and I mean when we speak of pirates. When you and I speak of pirates, we speak of a romantic idea which has descended from these historical crimes and woven itself into the fabric of the culture of the English-speaking world - not pirates, but **Pirates.**

Now, in the United States in particular, we are pirate traditionalists. We treasure our pirate myths as an outgrowth of American individualism, and we like our pirates to be as evil and gruesome as possible. We even flatter our preconceptions of pirates by couching these notions in some deference to historical fact.

But this is not actually true - our ideas of pirates come much more from books and movies than we like to think. The pirate is an archetype by which we understand ourselves, very much like superheroes or cowboys. And uncovering the history of this archetype is the aim of this book... where it came from, how it developed, what it means to us, and how those meanings have changed as our culture has. It's the story of the Disneyland ride, yes, but we simply cannot tell that story without telling the story of all pirates... real, or imagined.

But in order to recognize mythology, we first must try to understand the truth, and in this case our story does indeed start in historical record. Thankfully, we really only need to take the merest dip into these deep waters on our way to broader horizons. We need to focus only on three key pirates here, the big three who made the reputation of all the rest.

Conveniently for your author, their stories also slot neatly into periods at the start, the middle, and the end of what historians call *The Golden Age of Piracy*, allowing our overview to take in most of the really obligatory ground. So let's cast off into these choppy waters and see what we find.

We must begin, as so many books before us have, with Captain Henry Every.

For a man so enormously famous in his own time to have been dubbed "The King of the Pirates", very little historic information is known about him. We first discover Every some 40 years old aboard the ship *Charles II* in 1693. The *Charles II* was a privateering boat acting under the command of the King of Spain, but with an English crew and command.

This requires some explication. The difference between "Privateering" and "Pirating" in those days was largely one of opinion and perspective, with the shifting sands of political alliances determining whether one was an authorized privateer or acting entirely outside the laws.

Privateers were generally licensed to capture foreign goods from enemy vessels during times of war, and were supposed to carry documents demonstrating that they were acting on behalf of some European government - although of course before mass communication said documents could be rendered quickly meaningless by events on the Continent. The ship *Charles II* didn't have her documents, nor had her crew been paid. They did, however, have a habitually drunk captain.[2]

When the crew mutinied, Every was elected Captain and disposed of the former captain by putting him in a boat headed for shore. The *Charles II* was renamed the *Fancy*, and set out a-pirating along the coast of Africa.

Captain Every plundered numerous ships along the way, and with each plunder his crew swelled in size. Merchant sailors were easy to persuade to join a pirate crew, given the comparatively relaxed lifestyle - unlike merchants, pirates had no incentive to keep costs low and trips quick, meaning the work of running the vessel was spread amongst a much greater number of sailors. Whereas merchant crews of sailors topped out at about twenty, pirate crews of a hundred were not unheard-of.

By 1695, Every had rounded the southern tip of Africa and stopped off at Madagascar to re-supply. As a convenient stop between the slave coasts of Africa and the Indian Ocean, Madagascar was dotted with a few under-the-radar ports where those engaging in less than official maritime activities could drop anchor. His next stop was Perim, at the mouth of the Red Sea, where he had a rendezvous with five other pirate captains. Elected leader of the six-boat flotilla, Every now commanded nearly 450 pirates.

Their shared objective was a caravan of boats traveling from Mecca across the Arabian Sea to India. This yearly pilgrimage was undertaken by the Grand Mughal of India and his family, and the "Treasure Fleet" was famous for its abundance of wealth. This caravan of vessels consisted of a gigantic treasure-laden warship and a smaller consort ship owned by a wealthy merchant. The pirates gave chase, picked off the consort ship, and after a week successfully overtook the treasure ship.

What the pirates did then is up for debate.

There may or may not have been a relative of the royal family on board, and there certainly would have been numerous wealthy individuals loaded down with their most prized possessions. It is very likely that the passengers were subjected to an extended campaign of terror and rape as the criminals sought to extract every last item of value before setting the ship back on its way.

The plunder from this ship is literally incalculable, and while subsequent events may have caused the actual value to be overstated, a conservative estimate puts its value at a modern equivalent of $200 million. This single raid was one of the two or three most profitable thefts in history.

When the ship finally reached India, outrage spread quickly. India had just fought England in the first of numerous wars for trade on the subcontinent, and relations were strained. Citizens rioted; the Indian government responded by arresting English citizens living in the on-site East India Trading Company factories. Word reached London quickly; Parliament declared Captain Every to be an enemy of the state and placed a bounty on his head.

Most astonishingly of all, after a short attempt to extract a pardon from a colonial governor in the Caribbean, Henry Every disbanded his crew and vanished. He was never located and the East India Trading Company repaid the Mughal King for his losses. Perhaps the most successful pirate of all time got away scot-free.

In London, it was rumored that Every had eloped with a Mughal princess he had encountered aboard the treasure ship and was living a life of luxury on Madagascar in a pirate utopia. Are pirates bad guys? That depends on who you ask and when, and in the London of the early eighteenth century, Every was something of a hero. He had struck at an enemy of England in a place outside the law, like the Lone Ranger, and was said to be fabulously wealthy. Broadsides and ballads were printed, stories were told, and the legend became the basis for a 1712 play called *The Successful Pirate*.

The astonishing size of his treasure haul and the near total failure of the government to apprehend him inspired other young sailors in those dockside taverns who had grown up hearing the stories. It was the crime that launched a thousand pirate ships, the most influential pirate in history... and the true start of the Golden Age of Piracy.

At almost exactly the same time that Every was raiding a Mughal treasure ship on the other side of the world, Captain William Kidd was setting sail on a quest to rid the ocean of pirates. You read that right.

Kidd had been a decorated privateer defending New England during King William's War, and was hired by the newly appointed Governor of Massachusetts - Richard Coote, 1st Earl of Bellomont - to attack pirates as a growing threat on the open seas. Kidd was given documents authorizing him to plunder French ships and sent on his way aboard his specially constructed ship, the *Adventure Galley*.

Kidd was spectacularly unsuccessful.

He cruised the coast of Africa and found nothing. He rounded the Cape of Good Hope and sailed for Madagascar - then supposed to be teeming with pirates - and found nothing. This was a problem.

Privateer boats operated on a "no prey, no pay" scheme, and by now his crew was growing mutinous. One insubordinate crew member was struck by Kidd with an iron bucket and killed. Kidd began picking off merchant vessels belonging to England and America simply to recoup the significant investment of his voyage. By the time he reached the Indian Ocean, his bait-and-switch scheme was to fly the French flag while approaching merchant vessels. These ships often had numerous passes aboard, and if the merchant captain produced a French pass, he would raid the ship.

Word of all of this was circulating in England and her colonies, but thanks to Captain Every, the situation surrounding piracy was now quite different. Parliament had been passing more and more laws designed to curb piracy[3], but the political chaos provoked by Every in

Captain Kidd burying his bible seen in The Pirate's Own Book by Charles Ellms, Library of Congress

India and London and the subsequent international manhunt was still ongoing. By the time Kidd limped his way back to the Caribbean in a different boat and with only the fraction of his crew, he must have known that he was a marked man.

Kidd made his way north to New York in a bid to negotiate with Bellomont, sailing lesser frequented channels. His next action would ensure his immortality, as he stopped off at Gardiners Island at the tip of Long Island to hide some treasure. Burying valuable items for later retrieval was a common emergency tactic of the day; during the London Fire, wealthy individuals buried their valuables before evacuating. In doing this Kidd was attempting to give himself a stronger bargaining position; none of the investors in his voyage would be paid if only he knew where his treasure was located.

Lord Bellomont, meanwhile, had realized that he would be implicated in piracy when Kidd was captured, and extended an offer of clemency to lure the captain in.

Kidd fell for it, and he was arrested, shipped off to London, tried and hung in 1701. To the very last he maintained his innocence. His body was hung in chains at Tilbury Point on the River Thames for three years as a warning to sailors.

Before Kidd, the idea of buried pirate treasure was already common, as demonstrated in this Parliamentary tract suggesting that pirates be pardoned, not prosecuted:

> "... [The Treasure] now lies buried or useless in or near the Island of Madagascar; it's much better [that the pirates] should be permitted to bring it to England with safety, where it may do good, than let it remain where it is (as useless and unprofitable as the earth that covers it)."[4]

Remember that this was an assumption by a politician attempting to curb piracy - in reality most plundered wealth was spent on whores or liquor, pirates generally having no expectation of seeing old age in the first place. But it was Captain Kidd who would turn this popular conception into a tradition.

Authorities were able to retrieve Kidd's treasure, but this did nothing to reduce the rumors that more of his treasure was buried in various locations up and down the Eastern seaboard.

And so it is today there is hardly any town from Boston to Charleston that does not claim to be the potential hiding place of pirate plunder. The search for pirate gold has been ongoing for three hundred years and counting.

Fifteen years later, Edward Teach was already a legend in his own time, the first truly legendary pirate since Every. He was known far and wide as Blackbeard.

His career was both spectacular and spectacularly short. We first hear of him in 1716; by 1717 he had captured a French slave ship off the coast of St. Vincent. This he fitted with 40 cannons and renamed the *Queen Anne's Revenge*, the largest pirate ship of its day, with a crew of 300 (!).

Pirating in the Caribbean with a flotilla of up to three ships, Teach was legendary for his behavior intended to terrify his prey into submission. This is one case where the stories really do seem to be true; with his huge black beard tied up in ribbons and burning fuses under his hat, commanding a ship capable of obliterating all but the largest man-of-war on the ocean. The terribleness of his crimes in the popular imagination grew to epic proportions.

One such fanciful example of his ruthlessness has the captain wagering his crew:

> *"...being one Day at Sea, and a little flushed with drink; "Come," says he, "let us make a Hell of our own, and try how long we can bear it." Accordingly he, with two or three others, went down into the Hold, and closing up all the Hatches, filled several Pots full of Brimstone, and other combustible Matter, and set it on Fire, and so continued till they were almost suffocated, when some of the Men cried out for Air; at length he opened the Hatches, not a little pleased that he held out the longest."*[5]

Teach's most famous action was the blockading of Charleston, South Carolina. An entirely opportunistic act of piracy, the city's sea port was accessed through a narrow sand bar and Teach anchored his flotilla at the entrance, picking off loot as the ships entered. After about a week of this, he managed to capture a handful of citizens and ransomed them to the colonial government for barrels of medicine for his men.

Now to be fair to Teach, he both upheld his side of the bargain and granted the government additional time after their expected supply boat capsized. This did not, of course, prevent him from insisting that if the colonial officers did not comply, he would behead his prisoners and burn all of the ships he had captured! The classical pirates relied more on terror than brute force and the vast majority of their victims would capitulate without struggle. That is indeed the entire point of flying flags emblazoned with skulls, bloody hearts, or hourglasses.

If genuine facts about Blackbeard's short career are scarce on the ground, it can perhaps be said that, as Shakespeare put it, "nothing in his life became him like the leaving of it". Although Teach accepted a pardon from the government of North Carolina, after several months of laying low he was back at it. Teach was reported carousing with such pirate contemporaries as Calico Jack - in whose crew was Mary Read and Anne Bonny. If true, to contemporary pirate historians that would have been an eye-watering sight.

Within a few months, the governments of Pennsylvania and Virginia had issued warrants for Teach's arrest. The governor of Virginia - one Alexander Spotswood - overrode the pardon issued by North Carolina because Teach represented such a threat to Virginia's profitable shipping ports. Lieutenant Robert Maynard was awarded the resources to capture Blackbeard.

Surprising the pirate off Ocracoke Island along the outer banks of North Carolina, what followed was one of the most exciting and (probably) grossly exaggerated pieces of pirate lore in history. As the fleet drew nearer, Blackbeard is said to have appeared on the deck of his sloop, toasting Maynard and bellowing:

> *"Damnation seize my Soul if I give you Quarters, or take any from you. In Answer to which, Mr. Maynard told him, That he expected no Quarters from him, nor should he give him any."* [6]

Blackbeard as depicted in *The General History of Pirates*, Wikimedia

In the resulting fray, Blackbeard was reportedly shot a half dozen times and sustained some twenty lashes from swords before he lay dead on the deck of his ship. One popular newspaper account of the day[7] includes the unlikely detail of a colorful Scotsman bounding out of the fracas and lopping off Teach's head at a stroke. Maynard returned with the head to claim his reward and, as Charles Johnson wrote:

> *"Here was an end of that courageous Brute, who might have passed in the world for a hero, had he been employed in a good cause."*

But to Americans, North Carolinians, and fantasists of all eras and times, Blackbeard has remained a hero of a sort.

Almost instantly folklore spread of Blackbeard having buried treasure up and down the colonial seacoast, from Florida to as far north as New Hampshire. On New England's Isles of Shoals, he's said to have secreted bars of silver and left some of his reported fifteen wives (!!) behind to guard the treasure.[8] In this sense we can already see Blackbeard bleeding together with Captain Kidd and other pirates in the popular imagination, to create a composite, ideal pirate.[9]

To be sure there were pirates who were more successful, as in Henry Every, and pirates who were more dashing and romantic, like Roberts; there were even pirates who were more brutal, like Ned Low. But the fact that we have to peer through such a thicket of fantasy written even while Edward Teach's corpse was still warm gets to the core of the reason why Blackbeard has remained beloved; he was history's most picturesque pirate. A man against the world, wind in his hair, screaming defiantly even as death descended upon him from all directions. As a criminal he may have been underwhelming but as an idea he was instantly iconic, the pirate to beat all others.

Blackbeard's defeat came in the midst of a turning point in the Crown's war on piracy; in 1722, Bartholomew Roberts' flotilla of three vessels were engaged off the coast of Africa, Roberts killed, and his captured crew sold into slavery or hung. Ned Low's flotilla was defeated in Delaware Bay in 1723; although Low escaped, his ability to operate as a pirate was permanently compromised and his final fate is unknown.

Once the crown expanded the rights of the colonies to try and execute sailors for piracy, the executions ramped up to between 40 and 80 hangings per year. As historian David Cordingly estimates the total number of pirates operating in the Atlantic circa 1720 at around 2000[10], it's easy to see how the widely publicized atrocities, trials and executions helped bring the Golden Age of Piracy to a quick end.

And right at that end point, in 1724, a London book seller published *A General History of the Pyrates*, written by the pseudonymous "Captain Charles Johnson". This is the point where pirates peel away from historical reality and start to become literary anti-heroes, the point where our story really begins.

It's important to understand that the eighteenth century was a time before the concept of a historical text, written by specialists from primary sources, had really taken hold. Whoever wrote the *General History* was primarily a generous storyteller. Indeed, even three hundred years later, it's hard not to be impressed by the apparent authority of the text.

Whomever wrote it gives the appearance of having been an ocean-going man; his descriptions of such exotic ports as Madagascar, Brazil, and St. Thomas are compelling and do not seem to be fabrications.

He has plunged into legal documents and prints letters, pronouncements, and legal arguments pertaining to the pirates in question. All of this seems to legitimize the obvious places where the author has spun fantasy to connect the facts... although this may simply represent folklore of the era.

For instance, the *General History* has Henry Every destitute in England as of 1724, his enormous plunder having been stolen from him by merchants — far too poetical a punishment to be true.

II. PIRATES OF FACT AND FANCY

Much of Johnson's account of Edward Teach is entirely invented and has effectively created Blackbeard as a character in the public imagination. Let's read Johnson publishing what he claims is a "recovered" ship's log in Teach's own hand:

> "*Such a Day, Rum all out:—Our Company somewhat sober:—A damn'd Confusion amongst us!—Rogues a plotting;—great Talk of Separation.—So I look'd sharp for a Prize [...] Such a Day, took one, with a great deal of Liquor on Board, so kept the Company hot, damned hot, then all Things went well again.*"

But Johnson *really* goes full-on fan fiction while discussing Mary Read and Anne Bonny, two female pirates who were indeed actually tried in Jamaica and reprieved from execution on account of being pregnant.

Here Johnson goes totally off the deep end, inventing such absurdities as mothers who dressed both of them as boys, a love triangle with the captain, and a "meet cute" where Bonny attempted to seduce Read, believing her to be a boy! Johnson winkingly admits to this in his Preface, where he insists on the accuracy of his romantic fable even while cueing the astute reader to read between the lines:

> "*If there are some incidents and turns in their stories, which may give them a little the Air of a Novel, they are not invented or contrived for that purpose; it is a kind of reading this Author is but little acquainted with.*"

A novel? *What's a novel?*?

Again, those inter weavings of fact and fiction, right from the start. Henry Every was a king on Madagascar, a region so much supposed to be overrun with pirates that Captain Kidd actually wasted time going there. Blackbeard was perpetually roaring drunk. Calico Jack sailed with two disguised lesbians. No wonder Londoners ate it up; even today, it makes for some gripping reading.

But, as Disneyland reminds us, don't believe everything you read.

If we now leap forward in time a hundred years, we shall see what the distance of antiquity has done to the pirates.

Let's look at *The Pirate's Own Book* by Charles Ellms, printed in Boston in 1837. Despite its gutter press associations, throughout the *General History*, Captain Johnson is continually aware of his subjects as contemporary criminals; the start of the *General History* is an outline of the causes and potential cures for piracy, and its final chapter is an abstract summary of the current laws concerning piracy. Each chapter on the life of a notorious pirate seems at pains to emphasize their pitiful, ignoble deaths.

Ellms has no such concerns, regarding his subject from the vantage of nearly one hundred and twenty years. Which means that *The Pirate's Own Book* is even more sensationalistic and bloodthirsty than was the *General History*.

Nearly every one of the numerous woodcuts in the book is of some outrageous crime: men being hewn limb from limb with axes or priests being ridden around the quarter-deck and flogged like animals. Ellms repeats and paraphrases long sections of the *General History*, but adds his own material concerning more recent pirates, as well as folklore.

Where Johnson is at pains to describe the causes of piracy as an immediate threat to trade in his introduction, Ellms assures readers of the millions to be uncovered in buried pirate gold and finds his subject at rest on Crusoe-esque tropical isle:

> "*Thus his hours of relaxation are passed in wild and extravagant frolics amongst the lofty forests of palms and spicy groves of the Torrid Zone, and amidst the aromatic and beautiful flowering*

vegetable productions of that region. He has fruits delicious to taste, and as companions, the unsophisticated daughters of Africa and the Indies."

In other words, by the start of the nineteenth century we find our rather squalid little opportunists now fully at home in their native environment of fiction.

And it is here - in fiction - that the pirate will grow to be one of the English-speaking world's favorite archetypes.

*Low presenting a **Pistol** and **Bowl** of **Punch**.*

Typical Illustration from The Pirate's Own Book, Library of Congress

III. THE GOTHIC PIRATE: FATHER RED-CAP AND BILLY BONES

When Washington Irving died in 1859, the outpouring of affection for the United States' first celebrity author was so intense that mourners visiting Irving's gravesite began to shave off parts of his monument. According to the cemetery, the stone has had to be replaced twice since then.

Irving is best remembered for *The Legend of Sleepy Hollow*, although his influence on the nascent country's mythologizing of itself was so profound as to be difficult to understand today. Starting with *Knickerbocker's History of New York* in 1809, Irving took a nation that was still little else but ornery independence and a lot of natural resources and gave it back to Americans as a place of fascination and myth.

For instance. Irving, writing for a Manhattan society magazine, gave New York its first nickname - Gotham - and popularized the figure of Saint Nicholas, patron saint of the Netherlands, as a figure for New Yorkers. Later, in his *Sketch-Book of Geoffrey Crayon*, he introduced and promoted the celebration of Christmas at a time when some states still banned the holiday. Irving's mash-up of Saint Nicholas - native New Yorker - with the English character of Father Christmas created the American Santa Claus decades before Charles Dickens had even conceived of Ebenezer Scrooge.

The fame of Irving's writings compelled North Tarrytown to finally make Irving's nickname "Sleepy Hollow" the official town name in 1996. Irving is even the deep source for the oft-repeated New York myth, told everywhere from Charlestown to Boston, that the infuriating network of roads were laid atop cow paths.

If there's an antebellum American tradition that's still spoken of, Washington Irving is probably lurking somewhere in the background with a smirk on his face.

All of this requires some explanation.

Irving's fame and fortune was immediately made with *Knickerbocker's History*. That book was a satiric diatribe aimed at

III. The Gothic Pirate

Entrance to the Irving family plot in Sleepy Hollow, New York. Taken by the author in October 2022.

such targets at economic development, high society, historical societies, and Thomas Jefferson, but it was instantly adopted by New Yorkers as a symbol of local identity.

Irving actually wrote the history in character as Deitrich Knickerbocker, a tedious bore of an author who never once let a fact get in the way of a good story. According to Knickerbocker, everything great, terrible, or just weird about Manhattan can be traced directly back to its period as New Amsterdam. *Knickerbocker* invented not only the New York story, but a whole invented cosmos of history to go with it. And then as now, if it made it there... it could make it anywhere.

Over the next fifteen years, Irving published yet more material, always including a story or two "by Knickerbocker", relating to one aspect or another of Americanness while it was yet in the process of being invented. These Knickerbocker stories generally hone in on the differences between Dutch-ancestry Americans and English-ancestry Americans.

Rip Van Winkle, who wanders into the enchanted Catskills and sleeps for 20 years, is a contrast to the characteristic American restless bustle which already was part of the national character. Ichabod Crane is a Connecticut Yankee with his eye on the local burgher's estate who is chased out of town by the sleepy Dutch locals with no time for his new ideas about money and property[11].

All of these ideas combine in Irving's final Knickerbocker novel of any length, *The Money-Diggers*. A fascinating moral fable about the allure of ill-gained wealth, *The Money-Diggers* is as wonderfully imaginative and compulsively readable as anything in 19th century literature. It is also the first pirate novel of significance, and so we must dive deeper into it.

The Money-Diggers begins with Dietrich Knickerbocker in the company of an uneventful fishing party bobbing about Manhattan's East River. Knickerbocker describes a real part of the river known as "Hell Gate" where, when he was a youth, the wrecked remains of a ship - said to be a pirate sloop - could be seen stranded on the rocks. This recollection begins a series of interlocking stories told by the members of the fishing party, both on the boat and after

III. THE GOTHIC PIRATE

they land to have lunch. What follows is a complex, multi-faceted look at the notion of buried treasure as a national preoccupation, folding in Captain Kidd, the devil himself, usury, inheritance, and gold fever.

The key section is *Wolfert Webber; or, Golden Dreams*, in which Wolfert is the heir of a Dutch cabbage farm which he has allowed to go to ruin in his obsessive preoccupation with digging up pirate gold.

Webber is shocked when the local inn is suddenly host to an actual pirate, a terrifying, thundering man with a huge cleft in his face. After bullying and horrifying the local Dutch burghers with his bloodthirsty tales of life on the open sea, the pirate vanishes into the night with his sea chest. The locals see - or *think* they see - the buccaneer dragged to a watery grave by the contents of his chest.

Later, Webber sets out with an old fisherman who claims to have witnessed the burial of treasure and they row out to what is now New Rochelle to uncover the cache. But the area is said to be haunted by the ghost of a seaman called Father Red-Cap, who may or may not have been the pirate Webber saw in the inn...

In *The Money-Diggers*, Irving mashes up local and invented history with characteristic brilliance. Hell Gate was a stretch of the East River that bedeviled navigation so much that the city took to dynamiting boulders out of the water around the turn of the 20th century.

Just up the river from there, rumors still swirl in the villages of Mt. Vernon and New Rochelle of buried gold, and the climax of the book seems to be based around an authentic location known as Kidd's Ledge (although the only corroborating evidence I can find of this are newspaper articles post-dating the novel which suspiciously repeat some of its key plot points). We just seeming can't stop mashing up real and invented history when it comes to pirates.

But it's Irving's conception of the pirate treasure plagued by devils that really matters here. Popular tradition has it that Captain Kidd stopped on his privateering mission to bury his bible in the sand, aligning himself eternally with demonic powers. In one of Irving's stories, a certain sealed pot of treasure will re-bury itself in the earth if

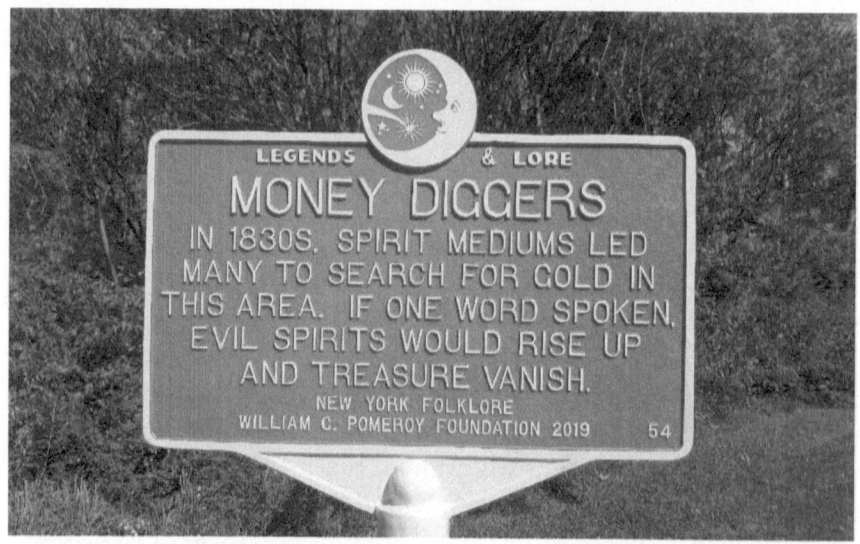

"Historical marker" repeating details from Irving's book in upstate New York, Courtesy William G. Pomeroy Foundation.

any of its unlucky finders so much as speak while unearthing it - I've come across that story repeated as local folklore in nineteenth century newspapers, demonstrating how quickly this fable took hold of the popular imagination. Washington Irving essentially invented the pirate ghost, and with it, the entire genre of Pirate Gothic.

If there was a great, classically American writer after Washington Irving but before Mark Twain, it was certainly Edgar Allan Poe, and in 1843 Poe published his own riff on unearthing pirate treasure - *The Gold-Bug*.

Poe had recently caused a small sensation in a Baltimore newspaper by writing on cyphers, and the centerpiece of his story - the reason for its great success - was in the demonstration of how a cypher can be decoded. But while Irving was writing of money diggers, *The Gold-Bug* gives its readers money *finders*, considerably increasing the thrill of the story.

III. THE GOTHIC PIRATE

Set on a stretch of coast in the Carolinas where Poe had been stationed in the army, *The Gold-Bug* is at its most inventive when coming up with complex ways to uncover hidden gold. A certain tree must be located by sitting on a specific rock, facing a certain direction, and looking through a telescope. You see, inside the tree is a skull nailed to a branch, and a weight dropped through the left eye socket of the skull will mark a heading on the ground...

All of this is a little similar to Poe's detective stories, *The Murders in the Rue Morgue* and *The Purloined Letter*, and the *Gold-Bug* is sometimes grouped with them. But the emphasis in *The Gold-Bug* is totally different - more interior - and the exact method of finding the treasure is only revealed in small snatches. The central section, the revealing of the cypher, takes up much more space than the rest of the treasure hunt, and there are other aspects of the story that make it difficult for modern audiences to enjoy. But in 1840, *The Gold-Bug* was hugely successful, selling hundreds of millions of copies and launching Poe's literary fortune in Europe. It was second only to *The Raven* in popularity during his lifetime.

But in terms of importance, it's the morbid elements of the story which have endured. There's the skull nailed up in a tree, with its face out so that "*the crows can get at the eyes good*". Furthermore upon unearthing the treasure, the three money-diggers find some skeletons, and a chest buried in a wooden sarcophagus "subjected to some mineralizing process". As Poe's laconic hero Legrand notes casually in the final paragraph of the story:

> "*It is clear that Kidd --if Kidd indeed secreted this treasure, which I doubt not -- it is clear that he must have had assistance in the labor. But, the worst of this labor concluded, he may have thought it expedient to remove all participants in his secret. Perhaps a couple of blows with a mattock were sufficient, while his coadjutors were busy in the pit; perhaps it required a dozen --who shall tell?*"

I have come across no previous precedents for this gruesome bit of pirate lore, meaning we probably have the authors of *The Legend of Sleepy Hollow* and *The Pit and the Pendulum* to thank for inventing the deathless genre of the pirate ghost.

John Quidor's painting of the climax of The Money-Diggers - note Father Red-Cap peering over the ledge in the upper right. Wikimedia Foundation and the Google Art Project

III. THE GOTHIC PIRATE

Pirates pop up in popular literature here and there for the rest of the 19th century. They provide a memorable Deus ex Machina in R. M. Ballantyne's *The Coral Island*, a deserted island adventure which remained popular for nearly 100 years. Mark Twain's Tom Sawyer and Huck Finn pretend to be pirates, where Tom asserts brightly that pirates "*take ships and burn them, and get the money and bury it in awful places in their island where there's ghosts and things to watch it, and kill everybody in the ships—make 'em walk a plank.*" This bit of childlike hokum transmutes into reality, for you will recall that at the end of the novel, Tom does indeed find treasure - lifted from the depths of the caverns in which Injun Joe hides.

Something had happened in the culture to turn these terroristic opportunists into figures of childlike fantasy; really, several somethings. The great reign of high seas piracy had been thoroughly crushed by the middle of the eighteenth century; later bandits, like Jean Lafitte operating in the Gulf, were already being labeled as pirates in a more romantic sense.

But really, the invention of the steamboat and the railroad in the nineteenth century led to the decline of sail as the economic engine of the entire world, meaning the social threat represented by pirates was largely contained safely in the past. The ascent of steam and the decline of wind power meant that the pictorial and romantic value of the golden age of sail was now apparent; it is no coincidence that the nineteenth century saw an explosion of ocean-going epics like *Billy Budd* and *Captains Courageous*.

Pirates, the scoundrels of this vanished world, benefitted from the association, their pictorial and dramatic value heightened by the long shadow of Romantic fiction. In the same way that modern-day Americans are much more willing to have fun with Depression-era gangsters, pirates joined such diverse figures as highwaymen and Robin Hood as figures of danger now safely and romantically preserved in amber.

By the end of the century, the whole notion of pirates had spread widely enough to be parodied in Gilbert and Sullivan's *Pirates of Penzance*, where the pirate crew also will stand for the Queen. The joke is that every character acts as though the pirates are terrifying, although they're about as intimidating as children play-acting.

This conception of pirates as being basically goofy and harmless would not change until a young, broke author named Robert Louis Stevenson would pick up his pen one dreary summer and start dashing off a "boy's own adventure" yarn of his own.

If you're reading this book I have to assume you're familiar with *Treasure Island*, one of the foundational novels in the Western canon. It's one of the most filmed and remade adventure stories ever, by a wide margin. Even if you've never read the book you almost certainly have seen one of the dozens of adaptations. Therefore, unlike with the obscure *Money-Diggers*, I see little point in re-litigating

Arthur Rackham's *1935 illustration of Captain Kidd dispatching the crew in* The Gold Bug. *Wikimedia Foundation.*

its excellence or summarizing its plot. You know *Treasure Island*, one way or another.

The book begins with the old ritualistic assertion of being a reminiscence of actual events, but events which happened over 150 years ago — pirate myths are created by the 19th century fantasizing about the 18th century. This ritual gesture towards "history" remains a key component of the pirate mythos, the door that opens to allow us, the audience, to accept even the most outrageous of plot machinations.

The opening section of *Treasure Island* at the Benbow Inn is lifted nearly directly from *The Money-Diggers*, with the frightening drunk sailor thundering about a seaside tavern. Stevenson also lifted the evocative phrase "Dead Man's Chest" from a travel book by Charles Kingsley called "*At Last: a Christmas in the West Indies*". Stevenson emphasizes the horrible difference of the pirates, with their missing legs, missing fingers, and missing eyes. Even if you haven't read the book, you will recognize their names as the names of pirates: Billy Bones, Israel Hands, Black Dog, Blind Pew. The story is laid out to allow most of the exciting bullet points common to pirate yarns to unfold in rapid succession: there is an ocean voyage, a mutiny, an escape, battles, and finally a treasure hunt with a surprise twist. The skeletons of Poe's *The Gold-Bug* reappear, there is an island castaway *à la* Crusoe, and the whole thing has a happy ending.

Blackbeard would have to wait nearly 150 years before a character as compelling would challenge his title for the ultimate pirate, but Long John Silver is that character. He has both a wooden leg and a parrot, which counts as some sort of pirate hat-trick. Stevenson's story sidesteps the narrative contortions required of many such tales by making his protagonist a young boy, allowing Jim Hawkins to operate with honor amongst both the pirate crew and the wealthy patrons who finance the expedition.

But the true secret sauce that makes *Treasure Island* work is that it is the coming-of-age story that so many others in the adventure genre aspire to be. Jim Hawkins' feckless father dies in the Admiral Benbow at the start of the story, and amongst his adventures with the pirates he obtains multiple surrogate fathers, but none quite so compelling as Long John Silver. Despite his villainy and treachery, Silver is the bad dad at the heart of the story, out for no one but himself but still managing to save Jim from a mutinous pirate crew. He may not be a hero, but readers come to love him.

Stevenson's aim was to create a novel for young boys, full of adventure and excitement. Aided by both his father and stepson, three generations of boys poured incident, intrigue, and adventure into a framework designed to be as exciting as possible. But perhaps most importantly, *Treasure Island* was an original, drawing bits and pieces from previous stories, yes, but couched much more in myth and folklore. It is the ultimate pirate story, starring the ultimate pirate.

During the writing of the novel Stevenson apparently asked his publisher for a copy of the best history on piracy, and was accordingly sent Johnson's *General History*. What is striking is that he used almost nothing from the book; drawing a few incidents mentioned in passing by Silver during the apple barrel scene, and the name Israel Hands from Blackbeard's crew.

This is important, because generally the ideas about pirates that have survived - those that have been consistently "voted" upon by being repeated and passed to the next generation - have next to no basis in historical fact. Irving, Poe, and Stevenson used pirates as identifiable figures in tales which truly are about something else.

And those are the pirate stories which have survived to remain relevant to us today, long after the economic importance of seafaring has ended. We have received pirates not as actual criminals, but metaphors for something indomitable about the human spirit in the untamed regions of the world.

The pirate joined the cowboy and the bandit as our culture's way of expressing and exploring notions of difference, independence, greed, and fate.

IV. THE ROMANTIC PIRATE: ERROL FLYNN AND COMPANY

See now Douglas Fairbanks as he leaps through the rigging of the mainmasts. Somehow resembling a fusion of Burt Reynolds and Jackie Chan, his body is a blur of tawny flesh amidst the glory of primitive Technicolor - which makes everything look like an old Polaroid left out in the sun. The year is 1926.

Fairbanks plays the Duke of Arnaldo, a nobleman whose ship is looted and destroyed by pirates. Burying his fallen father on a desert island, the Duke swears to revenge his death. To affect this he joins the pirate crew as the anonymous Black Pirate. He kills the pirate captain in a duel, which delights the crew. To prove his worth, Fairbanks boards and captures a Spanish Galleon single-handed, zipping through the rigging like a monkey, and descending each sail by dragging his knife through it to reach the deck below.

It is a stunt that will burn itself into the memory of cinema.

Are pirates bad guys? To a world where there was no such thing as an anti-hero, no truly heroic character could also be a murderer and a thief... therefore a pirate could never be a hero. This presented a conundrum to those who wished to write pirate tales, because their heroes could not engage in piracy, making the whole exercise moot. But what if there was another way? What if there could be a pirate who fights... *for honor*?

This was Lord Byron's idea. He produced a wildly popular 1814 poem - *The Corsair* - in which his titular Mediterranean pirate broods moodily while rescuing a Princess from a Turkish castle. It's not exactly gothic, but it made ladies swoon heartily on both sides of the Atlantic. This was bad news for Father Red-Cap.

Then, Sir Walter Scott published *The Pirate* in 1822, based on an old woman's recollection he heard while touring the northern isles of Scotland. Scott pasted together his romantic pablum with a bit of Johnson's account of John Gow and thus was a hit novel born. In *The Pirate*, the notorious pirate Captain Cleveland woos the daughters of a wealthy noble; his rival for their affections is a monstrous aristocrat. *Who shall she marry?*, wept a million silk handkerchiefs.

There is a great deal of dramatic tire-spinning regarding Cleveland's identity and social status; in the end, documents proving that he is the half-brother of his rival - and therefore of good breeding - are found in the sea-chest he carries with him. Recovered family honor takes the place of plundered treasure in the pirate cosmos.

Inspired by Scott's landlocked pirate drama, James Fenimore Cooper took up his pen in an attempt to produce ocean going tales more acceptable to those with experience on the waves. Now, if Cooper is discussed at all today, it is for his novel *The Last of the Mohicans*, a sort of proto-western set in the deep frontiers of, um, New York State. It's rough sledding for anybody making the attempt today, but Cooper was a beloved writer of adventure tales during the 19th century. He's even called out by Robert Louis Stevenson in the preface to Treasure Island; when he evokes "*The Cooper of the wind and waves*".[13]

Cooper's famous pirate novel is *The Red Rover*, a ludicrous muddle of mistaken identities, secret brotherhood, and a prophetic pirate who believes that the American colonies will one day form their own nation. It was of course wildly successful in its day, and both it and Scott's *The Pirate* were performed on stage repeatedly during the 19th century.

Even further down the scale of respectability is Ned Buntline, a dime novelist and promoter who had not yet discovered William Cody and re-christened him Buffalo Bill.

Buntline produced pulp novels with such titles as *The Black Avenger of the Spanish Main* and *The Red Revenger*. But the lineage is clear; the Romantic pirate trope is a sort of ocean-going cowboy whose identity, like Bruce Wayne's, must remain a secret. In other words The Romantic Pirate was not a pirate at all; Scott's Cleveland sails the oceans doing good deeds and recovering stolen property. Byron's *The Corsair* broods below a red flag on the Mediterranean, but will not lift his sword to steal a farthing.

Noblemen, angry poets, and lost twin brothers can all be pirates who sail for valor, so long as their identities as noblemen are eventually revealed. This dramatic construction tickled the fancies of the early 19th century, who preferred their heroes moody, romantic, and chivalrous. Just as Gothic novels center on matters of family paternity dressed up with a lot of crumbling old castles, the Pirate-Who-Isn't-A-Pirate - the Romantic Pirate - begat an entire raft of imitators, enough to count as a full-on counterpoint to the Gothic Pirate.

Library of Congress

One hundred years after Scott published *The Pirate*, another industry was much in need of a plot construct which would allow their heroes to perform daring deeds and dangerous escapes while not succumbing to base villainy.

Motion Pictures had sprung up from urban centers catering to illiterates and foreigners during the first decade of the 20th century; this alone had been enough to send certain social critics wagging their fingers after it from the start. As early as 1909, coalitions had formed to shut down motion picture theaters or institute government censorship - and this was *before* the salaries and budgets of film stars had very publicly ballooned to absurd proportions in the years following World War I. A series of public scandals had rocked the film industry in 1920 and led to the formation of a central, voluntary censorship office. Movies were about to do a lot of minding their Ps and Qs and their heroes needed to be squeaky clean.

Of the rough lot, Douglas Fairbanks had graduated from comedies to costume adventures quickly. Noted for his trim figure and athletic energy, Fairbanks was one of the few film stars to finance his own pictures. His gamble on an opulent costume picture - *The Mark of Zorro* - launched him into the stratosphere of fame, inventing the screen action hero along the way. Although Fairbanks' pictures are more overtly fantastical than modern tastes demand, they pioneered the specific blend of modern pop culture touches and lavish period setting that modern action blockbusters still use today.

Building on the success of *Zorro*, Fairbanks next embarked on *The Three Musketeers* and then *Robin Hood* - had the term swashbuckling not existed prior to Douglas Fairbanks, it would have been invented to describe him. Unlike previous costume and adventure films, Fairbanks used every aspect of motion picture production - stage design, editing, special effects - to create sequences of excitement which build upon each other, which left 1920s audiences breathless and elated.

This chain of remarkable blockbusters climaxed in *The Thief of Bagdad* in 1924, which remains one of the most gorgeous fantasy films ever put on screen - none of the remakes, including that one by Disney, can even remotely compare.

It was becoming increasingly difficult for Fairbanks to "top" each previous picture, so for *The Black Pirate* in 1926, he went in a different direction. *The Black Pirate* would aim for straightforward action instead of pictorial effect, but with an important new addition - color!

The color look of *The Black Pirate* is unlikely to impress modern viewers, but the lavish *scale* of the film remains top notch. The film's enormous buccaneer crew perches in the masts and rigging of their ship like birds in an apple tree, cheering Fairbanks as he captures an entire merchant ship singlehandedly. Modern audiences still cheer.

But the narrative really is only there as an excuse for fabulous action, signaled to the audience by an opening title card:

> *"Being an account of Buccaneers & the Spanish Main, the Jolly Roger, Golden Galleons, bleached skulls, Buried Treasure, the Plank, dirks & cutlasses, Scuttled Ships, Marooning, Desperate Deeds, Desperate Men, and - even on this dark soil -* **romance.** *"*

Which really does say it all. Douglas Fairbanks took the existing, recognized figure of the Romantic Pirate as given to us by Lord Byron and Sir Walter Scott and smashed him together with his movie action heroes to gift posterity the Swashbuckling Pirate. All others hence have descended from this original.

Fairbanks called it quits in motion pictures shortly after the ascendancy of sound, as did his wife Mary Pickford. That was in 1934. But in 1935, the screen would choose its next action hero.

Captain Blood had been made once before, by Vitagraph in 1924. Lavishly produced and photographed, it was based on a then-current bestseller by Rafael Sabatini - *Captain Blood: His Odyssey.*

The title *Captain Blood* perhaps oversells the actual pirate content of this story, which follows Peter Blood, a noble doctor accused of treason and sold into slavery. Escaping during a Spanish raid, Blood turns pirate and sails across the Caribbean attacking Spanish ships until his eventual pardon by a new king of England and appointment to the governor of Jamaica.

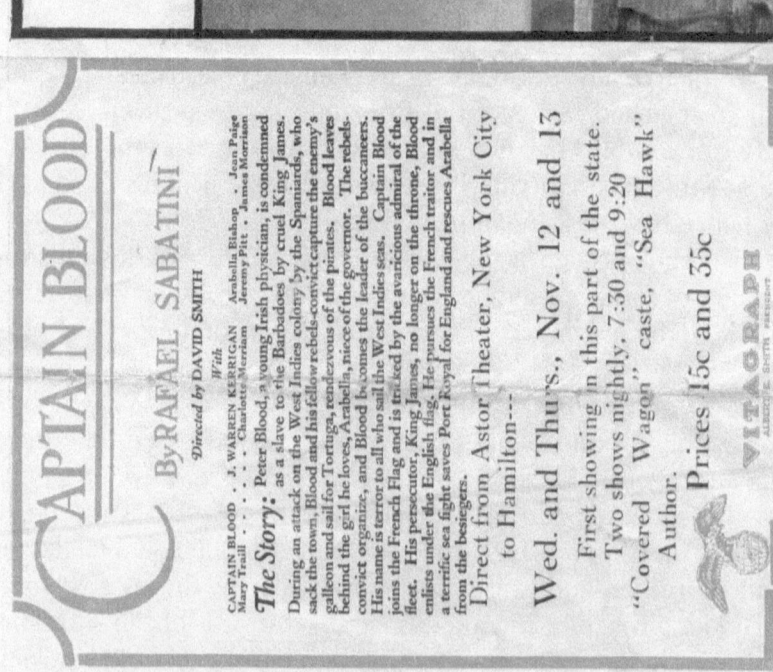

Souvenir Program from the 1924 version of Captain Blood, Author's Collection

This is the old Scott formula of the nobleman turned pirate, with extra layers of detail concerning politics of insurrection during the reign of James II. Since we meet Peter Blood attempting to hide an injured rebel against an unjust ruler, his moral code and upstanding nature is never seriously in question. In the end his detour through slavery and the criminal classes serves to elevate him even higher in the social structure of 18th century England, winning him a bride in the process. It's much more of a costume drama than a pirate story.

The 1924 film proper is a lost item. What remains is a roughly 30-minute condensed version, sold by Pathe for home projection on a now-obscure 9.5mm film format. For what we can see of it it's handsomely mounted, with miniature ships and galleons ablaze. Warner Brothers purchased Vitagraph outright in 1925, allowing the rights to pass to Warners for their 1935 remake.

The remake was directed by Hungarian emigre Michael Curtiz, who was brought to Hollywood to direct Warners' special effects extravaganza *Noah's Ark* (1926). Curtiz's dictatorial style and unstable mastery of English made him few friends on the set, but as a studio filmmaker his brisk pace and polished style elevated many a studio production, making Curtiz one of the most consistently excellent filmmakers to ever have worked in Hollywood's golden age. Curtiz gifted to a grateful world such classics as *Casablanca, Angels With Dirty Faces, Yankee Doodle Dandy, Mildred Pierce, White Christmas,* and even Elvis in *King Creole.*

Upon failure to retain the acting services of Ronald Coleman, Warner Brothers producer Hal Wallis set out on a casting jubilee, eventually landing on unknown Australian Errol Flynn as Captain Blood. Supported by Olivia deHaviliand, Lionel Atwill and Basil Rathbone, Flynn became an overnight success, moving on to *The Charge of the Light Brigade* and, eventually, the immortal 1938 *The Adventures of Robin Hood.*

Wallis, Flynn, and Curtiz would strike gold again with *The Sea Hawk* in 1940, with a magisterial soundtrack by Erich Wolfgang Korngold that looks ahead to *Star Wars.* Supposedly based on another Sabatini novel, *The Sea Hawk* wanders far afield of its source, this time using the 16th century Spanish military as a metaphor for Nazi Germany's assault on Europe.

This time Warners built two large-scale ships on stage in a studio water tank, and the visual results are staggering, a real high point of cinematic ocean-going combat. Flynn's patriotic privateer wages war on the Spanish armada of 1598, while Queen Elizabeth delivers a rousing speech on the defense of liberty in the face of tyranny.

Joining *Captain Blood* and *The Sea Hawk* was another contender for the Douglas Fairbanks sweepstakes, Tyrone Power, in 20th Century-Fox's *The Black Swan*. Based on still another Sabatini novel, *The Black Swan* is a brisk and exciting chase picture. It is the easiest of the three 1940s pirate romances to recommend to modern audiences, ticking most of the key boxes for ocean-going piratical excitement - and the main characters are genuine pirates, fighting now for England. Making a big contribution is a clever script by Ben Hecht:

> *Captain Morgan: How do you stand on that, lads?*
> *Are you ready to do a little law-abiding killing for king and country?*
> *Tommy Blue: It's better than none!*

Tyrone Power's Captain Jaime is introduced romantically bare chested being stretched on the rack. Within minutes he has turned the tide on his inquisitor and is stretching *him* on the rack; moments later Maureen O'Sullivan enters with a gun, Power knocks the pistol out of her hand and kisses her, and she bites his face! The film proceeds in this manner for a brisk 100 minutes.

Much of the film is devoted to the rough romantic interplay between Power and O'Sullivan. In another scene, O'Sullivan lulls Power into a reminisce about his childhood before bashing him on the head with a rock and fleeing. Modern audiences will raise their eyebrows at these antics, but recall that *The Black Swan* was made for the same popular culture that considered Rhett Butler dragging Scarlett O'Hara upstairs kicking and screaming the height of romance.

IV. THE ROMANTIC PIRATE

Tyrone Power in The Black Swan, Author's Collection

The onset of World War II in 1941 effectively halved the possible market for Hollywood pictures, and productions were scaled back across the entire industry - no more lavish spectacles on the scale of *The Sea Hawk* or *Gone With the Wind*. Although the late 40s were a high point for attendance at the movies, the looming specter of television and the Supreme Court's 1948 decision that Hollywood Studios must divest themselves of their vertically integrated theater chains changed the business forever. Rising costs and lowering attendance figures no longer made gigantic films feasible to produce, and by the time Hollywood got back on the spectacle bandwagon in the 60s audience tastes had changed.

The romantic pirate has remained persona non grata since, known only through tribute and parody. The enduringly popular example is the Dread Pirate Roberts in *The Princess Bride,* the gentleman pirate who is no pirate at all.

But another one of those pivotal pirates was on the horizon, and his appearance on the scene would give us a *pirate of pirates*, a pirate for the ages. Robert Louis Stevenson's man with one leg was coming back to movie screens reclaim his crown as the definitive seadog.

"In the pirates' cave, more than anywhere else, [the Audio-Animatronic technique] demonstrates all its miraculous efficacy. Humans could do no better, and would cost more, but the important thing is precisely the fact that these are not humans and we know they're not. The pleasure of imitation, as the ancients knew, is one of the most innate in the human spirit; but here we not only enjoy a perfect imitation, we also enjoy the conviction that imitation has reached its apex and afterwards reality will always be inferior."

- Umberto Eco, *Travels in Hyperreality*

Part Two
PIRATES in WALT'S UTOPIA

V. THE UNCERTAIN FORTIES

"Walt Disney recently returned from Europe, and a photographer was on hand to meet him. Referring to Disney's next movie venture Treasure Island, which will be produced entirely without cartoons, the photographer said, "I hear you're working with people now, Mr. Disney." "Yes," said the great cartoonist with a twinkle, "it's quite a come-down."
- Swing Magazine, March 1950

Walt Disney had a big problem.

It's hard to say exactly when Disney realized that his film business was going to have to change. Most likely it was a slow process, kicked into overdrive by the onset of his studio's animation strike and the box office failure of *Fantasia*. His two previous experiments with live action - the host segments of *Fantasia* and the war lecture *Victory Thru Air Power* - had been shot on the studio's lone soundstage. This building - Stage D - was infamous for not having been sound proofed, requiring filming at night to avoid disruptions from the nearby Lockheed air base.[1]

During production of *The Three Caballeros*, experimentation by Ub Iwerks and Technicolor cameraman Ray Rennahan had expanded the possibilities for the interaction of animation and live action, leading to the invention of the double optical printer. The resulting visual effects were head and shoulders above any previous attempts to integrate animation and live actors onscreen, and they were in color, too![2]

Yet costs of producing animation had risen steadily since *Snow White and the Seven Dwarfs*, and despite efforts to scale back costs, the Studio had produced a string of films of limited to moderate success. Perhaps, then, it was time to make a proper live action picture and put to use the techniques pioneered on *The Three Caballeros*. Walt Disney chose as his first venture into this unknown territory the tales of Uncle Remus. The film would eventually be released as *Song of the South*.

Disney commissioned Dalton Reymond, who had been "technical advisor" on Warners' costume potboiler *Jezebel*, to adapt the Remus stories into a screen treatment for live action in June 1944[3]. The cost of soundproofing Stage D proved to be cost prohibitive, so instead Disney reached out to Samuel Goldwyn. Goldwyn agreed to lease Disney his cinematographer Gregg Toland, fresh off William Wyler's *The Best Years of Our Lives*. Disney could also make use of Goldwyn soundstages and facilities... total cost: $400,000.

To produce and direct his first full hybrid motion picture, Walt tapped Percival C. Pearce. According to Didier Ghez and George Grant[4], Pearce was an ambitious story man who had succeeded in getting Walt's attention during meetings with a crazy routine with his pipe:

> *"...Pearce would interrupt himself at a crucial phase by producing a kitchen match, lighting it, and resuming his monologue. Just when it was about to burn his fingers, Pearce would apply it to his pipe and take a few puffs before going on, then the pipe would go out and he'd repeat the whole performance. [...] [Walt] would sit hypnotized by the pipe routine and the W. C. Fields voice. The result was that Pearce received every sign of Walt's favor, including the chance to work as a sequence director on Snow White. From apprentice to director in two years speaks well for nicotine addiction."*[5]

Some of the best sequences in *Snow White* were overseen by Pearce, including the legendary "dark forest" chase. Pearce then went on to direct the *Sorcerer's Apprentice* section of *Fantasia*, and head up the *Bambi* unit. By 1944, Perce Pearce was a Walt Disney confidant who could be trusted to look after Walt's interests.

Walt Disney placed child actor Bobby Driscoll in the lead role and brought in comic stage actor James Baskett to play Uncle Remus. Hattie MacDaniel, the first black actor to win an Academy Award, appeared in the film and sang one of its best songs. Walt sought the advice of both Baskett and MacDaniel in the film's pre-production, and brought back Hall Johnson, amongst the most respected black songwriters of his era, to perform with his choir in the film. It was all very earnest and respectful, Disney tried to do everything right, and the film turned out just awful.

Song of the South is today vastly more famous than it was in 1946, and far in excess of its actual merit. To modern eyes, child star Bobby Driscoll is dreadful, and the film is only interesting when James Baskett, Hattie McDaniel, or their cartoon co-stars appear on screen. The 25 minutes of animation directed by Wilfred Jackson are as funny, lively and colorful as anything in the Disney canon... but the rest of the film nearly capsizes the whole production.

There is of course the fact that the film glamorizes the whole old south milieu, but this is hardly a unique or controversial narrative device in the 1940s; it's popular-culture-of-the-time problem, not a Walt Disney problem. It's curious to consider why exactly this sentiment began to percolate in the zeitgeist in the 30s and 40s, because it was never unique to *Song of the South*. Perhaps simply that generation of filmmakers had grown up listening to the stories told by their grandparents and associated America's bloodiest war with a distant era of valor. Still, we can set this aside because *Song of the South* has plenty wrong with it above and beyond moonlight and magnolias. Perce Pearce turned out to be incompetent as a director.

Walt Disney had a habit of picking employees seemingly at random to take on enormously complex tasks with no preparation; when this gambit worked, the results could be marvelous. For example, writer Bill Walsh ran into Walt Disney one day in 1950. Walt bellowed: *"You! You be the producer of my TV show!"* Walsh replied he had no experience as a television producer, but his boss simply responded *"Who does?"* and walked away. The resulting television show, *One Hour in Wonderland*, was a smash and Walsh would go on to produce most of the company's best live action films. It would appear that Walt gambled in the same way on Perce as a motion picture director - gambled, and lost. The defeat was total - Perce Pearce isn't even afforded a director's credit on the film.

Cinematographer Gregg Toland, who six years earlier had taken young Orson Welles under his wing for the production of *Citizen Kane*, did not extend the favor to Pearce. We can guess why based on events told later in this chapter. When viewed in the context of films from 1946, *Song of the South* is dull, languid, and surprisingly colorless. Viewed as an overall product and taking into account the high degree of sophistication attained by the Hollywood studio system during the 1940s, *Song of the South* may be the single least accomplished film to go out into theaters bearing Walt Disney's name since the silent era.

The Walt Disney of the post-war was sliding into a slump, stretching out in any direction at all to find something new to inspire him, and *Song of the South* really shows it. The contemporary animated films *Fun and Fancy Free* and *Melody Time* are full of freewheeling invention but are surprisingly uneven - the highs are higher, but the lows are frequent. Walt was paying less and less attention to his animation staff.

Baffling his employees, Walt purchased reels and reels of nature documentary footage shot by Alfred and Elma Milotte and released the result as *Seal Island*, a 30-minute featurette which won an Academy Award. But now that Walt had Bobby Driscoll and Luanna Patten under contract, and had produced a film largely made up of live action material, he was fulfilling his long-held dream of creating Hollywood motion pictures. Walt recalled: "*When I came to Hollywood, I was fed up with cartoons. I was discouraged and everything. My ambition at that time was to be a director.*"[7]

Regardless, *Song of the South* was a success and warranted a sequel. After much foot-dragging, Walt landed on a Sterling North novel called *Midnight and Jeremiah* and sent Perce Pearce off to Indiana to soak up the rural atmosphere of the book.

The resulting film, *So Dear To My Heart*, manages to be a better film than *Song of the South* but overall has less in it to recommend. Having apparently learned his lesson, this time Walt brought over an actual director: Harold Schuster arrived from 20th Century-Fox, where he had directed *My Friend Flicka*. Having been delivered an actual director to work with, Bobby Driscoll is vastly improved in this film. He's backed up by Burl Ives and Beulah Bondi in the supporting cast, playing lovable eccentrics. The result is a charming, if slight, excursion into Americana.

Truthfully, it's a little hard to see exactly what Walt saw in this project, but the fact remains that *So Dear* was a very important picture to him personally. In the course of restructuring the novel, Walt added a prologue where the young boy Jeremiah briefly sees his hero, legendary racehorse Dan Patch, whose train (with attached private boxcar!) stops in his small-town depot.

Carrying the idea forward, Jeremiah's black sheep is named Danny, and at the end of the picture the cycle comes full circle as Danny, having won an "Award of Special Merit" at the fair, is paraded through the depot just as Dan Patch was. Walt Disney told a reporter later in life: "*So Dear was especially close to me. Why, that was the life my brother and I grew up with as kids in Missouri. The great racehorse, Dan Patch, was a hero to us. We had Dan Patch's grandson on my father's farm.*"[8]

For the production, an Indiana small town was rebuilt in the San Joaquin Valley, a location Walt visited frequently. Director Schuster recalled:

> "*Some of the interior sets were built on the location in conjunction with the exteriors, mostly because there was only one small stage at the studio. [Burl Ives' hardware store] was one of those. They found an old, and I mean old, hardware store near the town of Portersville. It was closed, and the various wares inside were bought Lock, Stock, and Barrel, and moved into the Grundy store. Both the barn and granny's house were built on location. The railroad station was already there as were the railroad tracks. We rented the old engine and cars from Paramount, who had used them on Union Pacific.*"[9]

This 1949 lobby card from RKO is emblematic of the difficulty in marketing So Dear To My Heart. Christie's Auctions.

Suddenly, Walt Disney could go on location and step into a virtual recreation of his childhood; it's hard not to see the idea of Disneyland forming there in his head along the railroad tracks in Tulare County. The wooden depot would be rebuilt in Disneyland as the Frontierland train station; Walt rebuilt the red barn from the film to serve as his own backyard railroad workshop.

But the spark of *So Dear To My Heart* had not left him. Within a few years he had gone to his friend, animator Ken Anderson, and said:

> "I'm tired of having everybody around here do the drawing and painting; I'm going to do something creative myself. I'm going to put you on my personal payroll⁹, and I want you to draw twenty-four scenes of life in an old Western town."

V. THE UNCERTAIN FORTIES

Then I'll carve the figures and make the scenes in miniature."[11]

Walt built a miniature of Granny's Cabin from *So Dear to My Heart* before the project fizzled out, although he didn't give up on the idea so easily. Early concept art postcards for Disneyland show a "Frontierland Miniature Museum" just to the left of the area's entrance; time and money meant that this building opened as the "Davy Crockett Arcade".

So Dear To My Heart was a tough sell to RKO and Walt tinkered with it in editing for over a year - as publicist Card Walker later remarked, "He knew he had a problem."[12]

In the end, new animated sections were created and inserted throughout the film. Some of these, like the dreamy opening where lace cutouts and old postcards come to life in a boy's scrapbook, are among the most enchanting in the Disney canon. Others, starring a wise owl and an animated version of Danny the Sheep, come off as weird distractions. As Disney later remarked to Fortune Magazine on this period in his life; "*I struggled with it. I kept playing around. I couldn't decide what kind of live action I should do.*" Neither *Song of the South* nor *So Dear To My Heart* offered a way forward out of Disney's financial and creative doldrums, but as it so often does, suddenly real life intervened.

VI. TREASURE HUNT IN CORNWALL

The end of World War II had boosted the American economy, but much of Europe was still reeling from the economic and literal devastation brought about by the conflict. And so the Anglo-American Loan was negotiated in 1946, which extended billions of dollars to the United Kingdom - so many that it was not fully repaid until 2006(!). Modern viewers can well imagine the political resentment such a pact would inspire today, and one of the most prominent local products being squeezed by American imports was the film industry. Would Britain simply lay down and let America steal their film industry out from underneath them?

And so it came to pass that Robert Boothby, conservative Parliament member, stood up in session and announced with calculated fanfare: "*If I have to choose between Bogart and bacon, I am afraid that the decision must, for the time being, be in favor of bacon.*"[13]

For once the popular press and the government were in synch here and the United Kingdom placed a 75% levy on the profits from American films, effectively freezing the money in Europe and away from the clutching hands of Hollywood. Hollywood screamed; they protested; they got Congress to pass tit-for-tat laws; — they gave in almost immediately.

As a result similar laws were passed in France, Italy, and Argentina. The result was a flowering of Hollywood productions in Europe - especially in England and Italy - where American crews could use local film production resources and unfreeze their overseas money to produce films inexpensively. This gave rise to the legendary "Hollywood on the Tiber" period, immortalized by such films as *Roman Holiday*, *To Catch A Thief*, *Ben-Hur*, and *Two Weeks In Another Town*.

For the Disney Studio, these frozen assets apparently exceeded $1 million,[15] making the necessity of finding some way to spend the money in England urgent. Larry Watkin - the man who had accidentally invented the nature documentary by writing the narration for *Seal Island* - was still knocking around the Disney Studio on the payroll and had found the Story Department vaults, where he discovered that Disney owned the rights to Treasure Island. Watkin produced a treatment which caught Walt's eye. Director Byron Haskin relates how this came about, apparently having learned the details from Watkin:

> "Walt had always been in love with Mark Twain's Tom Sawyer. There was an agreement among the major producers for story material in the public domain. If a company was the first in line with a claim, they were given priority. Each year they must maintain a certain amount of expense for story development, securing the rights. It was an agreement among the major producers. Walt had always wanted Tom Sawyer in the worst way. David Selznick had prior rights as producer for MGM. MGM also had the rights to Treasure Island as well as a lot of other things. Walt put in a kind of shotgun claim for all material either not claimed, or delinquent. MGM carefully maintained rights to Tom Sawyer, but one year they slipped and didn't develop Treasure Island. Suddenly Disney becomes the possessor! "What the hell do I do with this?", he asked. "I want Tom Sawyer, not Treasure Island!" They threw it in the vault."
>
> "I'll tell you what we'll do,", said Roy Disney. "We've got a subject almost prepared, with a sixty-page treatment. Put Watkin on a screenplay. Do it in England, with those frozen pounds in our company over there..." [...] So Treasure Island got underway."[16]

Nothing like this story appears in either of the official Walt Disney biographies, although many details of it track with demonstrable facts about both Walt Disney and Hollywood studio film production of the era. Walt *did* obtain rights for properties as diverse as *The Wind in the Willows* and *Peter Pan* following the success of *Snow White*, and of course he would get to do his own version of *Tom Sawyer* at Disneyland.

There also appears to be been some story development done on *Treasure Island* in 1948, including an idea for an animated segment where Hawkins would appear as a fox[17]. This was a bad idea in more ways than one. As Haskin later told an English newspaper: "*Trouble with Walt's hybrid mixtures of live action and animation is that the public is too partisan - the live actors simply haven't a chance*".[18]

But Haskin has a real axe to grind with Disney, so his stories can be approached with caution. He barked to Joe Adamson in 1984: "*You could go on the* [Disney] *lot at any time and you couldn't understand what was going on. Guys were playing baseball, other recreational activities. Any time you wanted to talk with Walt, go in the toilet — he's usually hanging out in there.*" (!)

Byron Haskin had arrived in Hollywood in 1919 when the town - and the industry - was still a wide-open place. An avid photographer, he worked his way up the ladder as a cameraman through the 1920s, in that distant time when Douglas Fairbanks and Mary Pickford still cavorted through those green hills.

Haskin met Jack Warner at a party, told him he wanted to work for him... and Jack agreed, beginning a 21-year association. Haskin worked in the Warner effects department, heading up everything from basic process shots to the ethereal, gorgeous special effects for the 1935 *A Midsummer Nights' Dream*. Haskin's department had created the opticals for *The Sea Hawk* and an astonishing bar fight for *Dodge City*, until finally Haskin left Warner Brothers in a pay dispute in the late 40s. He struck out on his own as a director for hire.

In 1949 Haskin made *Too Late For Tears*, a film noir potboiler starring Don DeFore[19] which Walt Disney had seen. Says Haskin: "[Walt] *equated* Treasure Island *with a kind of gangster movie. By some quirk of fate, he'd recently seen my latest film,* Too Late For Tears. *He liked the action and the aura of gangsters. He said,*

VI. TREASURE HUNT IN CORNWALL

"That's the kind of stuff we need for Treasure Island" - which only Disney could put together."[20]

Walt's logic may have been loopy, but it's impossible to say that his choice didn't pan out in the end. Byron Haskin was the first live action film director to work for Disney who can truly be called talented. Walt Disney didn't really work with great directors - the 1930s had taught him that many truly talented creators could just as easily leave his orbit and ply their trade elsewhere, as he waged endless battles with Ub Iwerks, Carl Stalling, Pinto Colvig, and Grim Natwick. His relationship with Byron Haskin would be no less tumultuous.

Disney's Treasure Island tax shelter was off to a good start, but a good director can only get you so far. The picture wouldn't truly develop its sea-legs until they cast Long John Silver.

Byron Haskin never explicitly took credit for the casting of Robert Newton, an actor then best known for playing toughs and thugs. Newton hadn't been in *Too Late For Tears*, but he could have been. Robert Newton had appeared in Laurence Olivier's surprise hit film *Henry V*, which had played both sides of the Atlantic to great acclaim. Newton, as Ancient Pistol, is a very amusing low life with a funny voice and bug eye, the sort of amusing turn in a wildly creative movie that could have stuck in Walt Disney's mind. Whoever made the call, bringing Newton onboard saved *Treasure Island.*

Newton was a well-connected actor on both stage and screen, and with the Disney prerequisites of Perce Pearce and Bobby Driscoll in tow, Haskin enlisted Newton to begin casting the picture. Newton even acted as a location scout, suggesting the Fal River in Cornwall. He had good reasons as well as personal reasons to want the film shot in that area. Cornwall had been the center of the English sailing industry, containing such legendary ports as Plymouth.

Newton had a hardscrabble childhood in Cornwall, and he played Long John Silver based on his memories of old-timers from the area. The voice and accent of Cornwall would become, through Newton, the sound of pirates around the world.

Trouble began almost immediately. Haskin hated Pearce, whom he regarded as incompetent.

> "Pearce had this big wide brim brown felt hat. It wasn't a cowboy type hat, just a hat whose brim was too wide. It snapped down in front. There was a big bullet hole through the middle of the crown - in one side, out the other. [...] Walt would look at him with that hat on, and slap his leg and laugh. A regular guffaw. That was Perce's function at the Studio, to wander by with that hat on when Walt was in low spirits."[21]

To make matters worse, Bobby Driscoll was almost immediately dragged into court by the Ministry of Labour upon the start of shooting in England. He didn't have a work permit, and being a minor was not allowed to get one. The Disney Studio and RKO issued pleas; he was given six weeks to "prepare a defense."

Haskin threw the kid in front of the cameras at once. "*If it hadn't been for my technical ingenuity, I'm sure the picture would have been a mess; God knows what would have happened to it. As it was, a certain smoothness of characterization and dimension was missing, I thought.*"

Haskin apparently finished the shooting of Driscoll's close-ups just in time for the actor to be summarily deported at the end of the six weeks. And that was the end of Bobby Driscoll's involvement with the movie.

Local youngsters would fill in for Driscoll in over the shoulder shots for the remainder of the shoot. The major set piece of the film, the sailing vessel Hispaniola, was created out of a three masted schooner built in 1887, fitted with concealed diesel motors, and sailed around the southern coast of Cornwall into location[22].

The film crew brought an air of glamor and celebrity to the sleepy Cornish small towns, with production resources filling hotel rooms and pubs in the picturesque village of Flushing. Not everyone was duly impressed, however; local fishermen complained that the simulated cannon fire of the vessel had frightened off the fish, and were paid off by the production for their silence on this matter with five-pound notes.[23]

As for Walt Disney, he seems to have been barely involved in what English newspapers described as his "all human" movie.

Once production moved back to Denham Studios outside of London, Walt visited the set occasionally, and took the onset of production as an excuse to take a European vacation with his family. Otherwise he stayed away. It's possible that Walt simply trusted Haskin and Pearce; later collaborators would report on Walt's reticence to give them guidance when he saw nothing worth correcting. Haskin, in particular, took it all very badly, venting to Joe Adamson years later, "*Where was the magic?*"

In the end, however, the film would prove to be a boon to all involved. 1950 turned out be the year that the Disney Studio's fortunes would finally turn around, thanks to the monster smash *Cinderella* and the lesser but still significant success of *Treasure Island*. To promote the film, RKO organized a nationwide "treasure hunt", playing out in 51 cities as the movie worked its way through the country throughout the summer of 1950 (remember this was before nationwide movie premieres were a thing).

RKO's promotional scheme gave away some $500,000 dollars in prizes - mostly frivolous items, but the prize packages always managed to include both a television and a refrigerator. Newspapers distributed paper keys, which participants carried down to the local department store to see if any of their keys would unlock one of three treasure chests. The prize vouchers inside were, of course, to be redeemed at the local movie theater showing *Treasure Island*.[24]

Treasure Island is a very good film - not superlative, but head and shoulders above Walt's previous live action efforts. Its quality perhaps reflects Walt's ability to learn how to pull back and let his chosen team do what they do best. It helps that this is a case where his team really knew what they were doing. Besides Haskin's stylish direction, the film is a buffet of marvelous turns by British character actors, largely unknown in the States but the backbone of the English film production community. This time, Driscoll is very good, and only occasionally wears that "shocked face" expression which seems

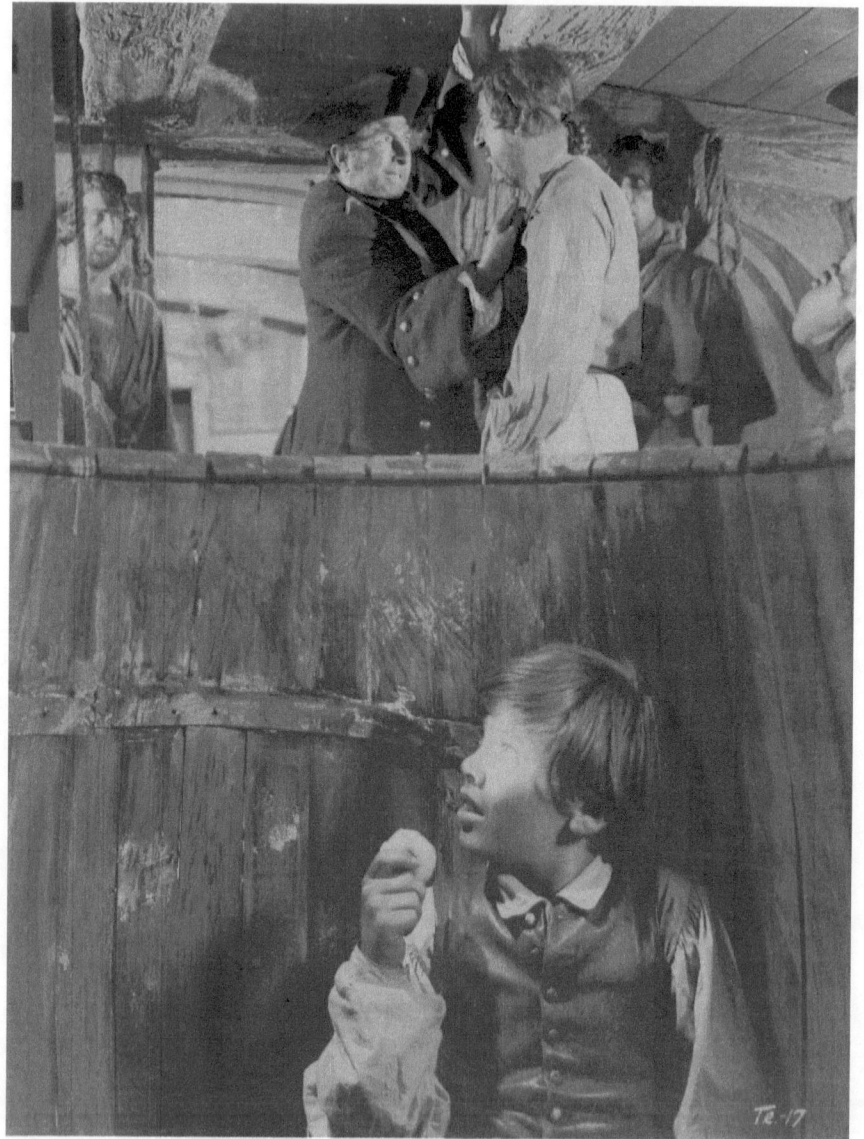

Treasure Island, vintage RKO Publicity still, Author's Collection.

permanently glued on in *Song of the South*. Whether it be the presence of Haskin, his older age, or the comparative absence of Walt Disney, this is Driscoll's best on-screen performance for Disney.

VI. TREASURE HUNT IN CORNWALL

Larry Watkin's screenplay is smartly structured to drop the fat and simply *go*; the film hits the ground running and only slows down once the complex series of negotiations begin surrounding Flint's block-house. All possible fat is stripped out, with clever touches seeded throughout the screenplay which help track character beats and reversals.

The film begins with a shady pirate wandering into an old stone inn on the coast of England; readers of the book will immediately assume this is Billy Bones, but we are surprised... it's Black Dog, neatly dispensing with a full chapter of material. Billy Bones never gets any further than the staircase to his room before he dies; Squire Trelawney arrives in the coach with Doctor Livesey and they make their plans at the inn that very night, thus dispensing with another location and moving the story along as quickly as possible.

In other places, Watkin reorganizes material to clarify character growth and relationships. At their first meeting, Silver gives Hawkins a silver pistol, the same gun Jim uses to defend himself against Israel Hands in the crow's nest. At the end of the film, Silver snatches the gun away from Hawkins and uses it to affect his escape.

The shipboard apple barrel is set up in Long John Silver's tavern, carries through to multiple scenes of Hawkins and other crew members eating apples, and finally is tied together in a scene where a crew member is teaching Jim navigation and describing the depleting crew rations. This serves the double purpose of motivating Jim to climb into the apple barrel - in the book he's simply already there when he overhears the crew plotting mutiny - but helps make better sense of his later plan to set the Hispaniola adrift. These changes may seem simple, but they help enormously.

Best of all is the handling of the final scene between Jim and Silver. In Stevenson's book, Silver simply escapes overnight with a small chest of jewels, reported only after the fact. All filmed versions of *Treasure Island* change this, most often by having Jim come across Silver in the course of casting off. The only previous sound version of *Treasure Island* was made by MGM in 1934, and follows this track[25]. The 1934 version does a lot of shuffling around and expanding of scenes to give more screen time to stars Jackie Cooper and Wallace

Beery. The MGM version turns the scene mawkish; Silver gives Hawkins his parrot and tearfully rows away as Hawkins cries out that he'll never forget him. Watkin had the respect to keep Silver true to his character to the end.

Watkin's newly devised ending plays out like this: being rowed back to the Hispaniola to be put in irons and stand trial, Silver steals the gun he gave to Hawkins and tosses Squire Trewlaney out of the boat. At gunpoint Silver forces Hawkins to man the keel and set him on a course out of the secluded inlet towards the open ocean with the intention of allowing Hawkins to disembark on the spit of land at the mouth of the cove. Hawkins instead drives the boat into the sand bar and jumps out. Silver demands that Hawkins push the beached boat off the sand bar and threatens to shoot him, but on the point of pulling the trigger finally cannot. Hawkins finally pushes the boat off, and he and Doctor Livesey watch Silver running up a sail and heading off into the horizon with some of the treasure.

This forces Jim to make an active choice, not simply choose to allow Silver to escape, but to actually aid him. Gone is the complicated business of Silver escaping from the brig, lifting some treasure, and setting out unseen; each character is finally forced to make a choice and just as Silver is unable to harm the boy, the boy cannot allow Silver to be harmed, and they part ways.

Readers unfamiliar with the book may miss these subtleties entirely, but this is screenwriting of a higher order. Walt would repeatedly bring back Watkin to write for him again, including the marvelous screenplay for *Darby O'Gill and the Little People*.

And the film *looks* just fabulous. Production designer Tom Morahan had worked with Alfred Hitchcock on *Jamaica Inn*, then again on the lesser Hitch curiosities *The Paradine Case* and *Under Capricorn*. Cinematographer Freddie Young brings out terrific atmosphere, especially in the early parts of film set on the English coast - Young would go on to film some of the most indelible images in screen history in *Lawrence of Arabia*.

Haskin's labors to disguise Cornwall as a tropical island mostly pan out better than similar pictures of the era, although in one wide shot of the Hispaniola at the supposed deserted tropical isle we can see tilled fields! On the location they seem to have had some vines, bamboo and tropical ferns to place in the foreground, and it mostly comes off well. In fact, it's hard to remember to keep looking for those body doubles for the absent Bobby Driscoll, so fast and lively does the film move.

But it's the wide shots, on the island and in the port where Silver's tavern lies not far from the docks, where the contributions of matte painter Peter Ellenshaw really save the day.

Ellenshaw had worked on the astonishing visual effects in such English A rank pictures as *The Thief of Bagdad* (the 1940 version) and *Black Narcissus*, and he would be instantly poached by Disney. Ellenshaw is of course now famous for his masterpiece, the dreamy and sooty London of *Mary Poppins*. My favorite Ellenshaw creation, and appropriate for this book, is the surreal jumbled-up pirate's inn from *Blackbeard's Ghost*.

When the picture was finished, Haskin apparently had one last row with Pearce, over the final cut of the film, of which Haskin exclaimed, "*I never saw a worse massacre in my life*".

He goes on: "I *took Larry Watkin and a copy of the script into a cutting room with the picture. The trims were still in England, so we unglued the whole damn thing, putting the rolls in the rack. Laboriously, we put it back together the way it was written and shot. [...] That was my final association with Walt. Perce was my enemy.*"[26]

Another wild story from Byron Haskin? I don't think so. The completed film has some unusual fades on action to end scenes, as well as several moments where the film has been step-printed - a process where frames are printed repeatedly to stretch out action, giving action an odd juttering movement. These would seem to confirm Haskin's story.

In the end, Percival Pearce stayed loyal to Walt, and Walt Disney stayed loyal to Percival Pearce. Following the success of *Treasure Island*, Walt set Perce up as Producer of further pictures in England - *Robin Hood and His Merrie Men* (1952), *The Sword and the Rose* (1953), and *Rob Roy* (1953).

To provide a bit of Haskin counter-programming, here's Ken Annakin, the English director on those first two pictures, who would be brought back by Walt to film *The Third Man on the Mountain* and *Swiss Family Robinson*: *"I saw coming towards me a genial-looking man with sandy hair and a droopy mustache. He reached out his hand and said "Perce Pearce of Walt Disney Productions". He smiled like Walter Houston, like the devil in* The Devil and Daniel Webster... *he was a lovable, persuasive character."*[27]

Perce kept working for Walt right to the end. Dick Huemer recalled: "*On the opening day of Disneyland in 1955, we got word that poor Perce had suddenly dropped dead of a heart attack at our London office. He just sat down at his desk and died.*"[28] *Treasure Island* lives on today, as perhaps the best place to see the contributions of Pierce Pearce and Bobby Driscoll to the Disney canon.

But it's Newton as Long John Silver that really has ensured the film's immortality, because it is Newton's Silver who has become the ideal pirate of the popular imagination.

With his crutch, peaked cap, parrot, billowing red coat, and drawled "ar"s and "ayes", it is the definitive version of a pirate performance in the definitive pirate character. Newton as Silver is a cultural icon; he has transcended a good actor in a good role to become a touchstone. Just as the novel's Long John Silver synthesized and surpassed Edward Teach as our culture's ideal pirate, it is Newton who has **become** the character, and furthermore become all pirates, everywhere.

Every year, when the English-speaking world observes "Talk Like A Pirate Day" and participants drawl out their "arrs", speak in gravely tones, squint one eye, and cock their eyebrows, they are imitating Robert Newton.

Other definitive pirates will join he and Blackbeard, but only far in the future - our course must be set for other ports of call first. For now let's stand there with Jim Hawkins and Doctor Livesey, watching Newton-as-Silver vanish into the horizon in his skiff.

As Livesy observes, "*I could almost find it in my heart to hope he makes it.*"

VII. ASSEMBLING THE ROGUE'S GALLERY

"[Disneyland] seems to build the very structure of myths, with themes from the very depths of American consciousness, sinuously intertwined... we are swept away in the American myth."
- *Vincent Scully, Building the Dream*

In the 1950s, Walt Disney got a bad rep that has never entirely lifted.

Fact is, dear reader, you and I live in a world where Walt Disney Productions films have remained in the cultural conversation 50, 60, and 70 years past their original releases. Disney as an institution has, with various bumps and stalls and starts, continued to capture the public imagination to this very day, a fact evident by the book you hold in your hand now.

So we both have the luxury of looking back on the Disney production pipeline of the 1940s as a period of wild creativity and experimentation, resting secure in our knowledge that masterpieces like *Sleeping Beauty* and *Mary Poppins* are still in the future. But viewers of the 40s and 50s did not have that luxury; they saw the late 40s Disney films as a betrayal of the promise of *Snow White* and *Pinocchio*.

And then there's the fact that starting after the war Walt Disney began to accumulate a reputation as, as one newspaper of the day put it, an arch-reactionary.[29]

This may be giving him a bit too much credit. Walt was never too much of an intellectual in the sense that his creations were intended to be understood as *signifiers*; he worked with his emotions and memories in a way that was wholly instinctive.

Walt Disney was a guy who laid it all out on the surface. He liked old fashioned towns, Abraham Lincoln, horses and buggies, Uncle Remus tales, steam trains, and Dan Patch in about the same way when he was sixty as he did when he was nine. These things reminded him of being a boy, and in the shattered postwar environment of America in 1946, it's hard to blame him for longing for those bygone days.

Around the time of *So Dear To My Heart*, suspicions inside of the studio were running high that Walt Disney was bored and out of ideas; that he was heading off to Chicago with animator Ward Kimball to look at model trains, or rebuilding Granny's Cabin from *So Dear To My Heart* instead of working hard on *Cinderella* as a sign of creative bankruptcy. There was no conception that he was slowly building up a new idea that had nothing at all to do with movies.

These assumptions also stem from the innate but unspoken assumption that Walt Disney was a motion picture producer pure and simple.

These assumptions fundamentally misunderstand Walt Disney.

Disney was a cross-media artist willing to go where his inspiration took him. Since those days in the San Joaquin Valley stepping onto his first large scale movie set and finding himself in a simulation of his childhood, something was brewing inside him.

So Dear To My Heart, so important to him personally, did not resonate with the public. *If only they could have seen what he saw...* and perhaps motion pictures are not the way to convey that concept.

That new concept, his new creative lead, was nostalgia. After the war you can see Walt Disney going in and attacking the notion of nostalgia the same way he attacked previous creative challenges, such as what can be done with a color in animation. He may have been occasionally defeated, but always he leapt back into the challenge, enervated to try again. The result, Disneyland, is as central to the American identity as Mount Rushmore.

Walt's experience reliving an idealized form of his childhood on the set of *So Dear To My Heart* had led him to study amusement parks, city parks, national parks, a rail fair in Chicago and Henry Ford's Greenfield Village. He put a lot of these ideas into a concept he had for a vacant plot of land across from the Disney Studio, a place he called Mickey Mouse Park.

VII. ASSEMBLING THE ROGUE'S GALLERY

Almost perversely, there was no Mickey Mouse in it - instead, there was the train, a small town, the family farm from *So Dear To My Heart*, and a riverboat and river that could have dropped out of *Song of the South* by way of Mark Twain and Tom Sawyer. There was a turn of the century town that he allowed designer Harper Goff to pattern on his own boyhood town and was not yet called Main Street USA. And there were rides for the children.

But the **other** side of the coin, the secret angle that helps to explain all of this is that Mickey Mouse Park was intended to be at least partially a movie studio backlot. There was often a double motive with Walt Disney, and he was honed in on building an "Old West" town and a "turn of the century" town because those Americana stories are the sort he was interested in filming. *So Dear To My Heart's* milieu is recognizable as the basis for so much later Disney product, including Disneyland.

This backlot idea lingered in the background until the park in Anaheim opened in 1955 and turned into its own thing, despite early marketing playing up the idea of it being a "behind the scenes at the movies" experience. In the end nothing for Zorro or Mickey Mouse Club was shot at Disneyland, and in 1959 Disney bought Golden Oak Ranch outside of Santa Clarita for use as a location. Over the years this aspect of Disneyland has been gradually phased out of the mythology of the park but it helps explain how Walt's deepening financial stake in live action filmmaking feeds into and informs Disneyland.

But it was **also** that need to capture, simplify, and harness the past, to build a childhood that was better than his own had been, that would collide with the post-war amusement park boom and really make Disneyland stick. Many competitors would attempt to replicate the physical features of Disneyland, but none ever quite captured the simple honesty of the original.

Cinderella had been a huge hit for the Walt Disney Studio, but by 1951 Walt was so entrenched in the Mickey Mouse Park that he barely paid any attention to *Alice in Wonderland*, a decision he would come to regret. But the 1953 *Peter Pan* was another success, righting the ship and proving to Walt that the creative team he had placed in animation could produce good work with minimal guidance. This would be important because animation would never again command his attention the way it had in the 30s. When Walt Disney was creatively engaged, his attention was total.

Part of Walt's disenchantment with animation can be tied directly to his loss of total control over the studio in the 1940s. A deadly combination of the arrival of war in Europe and the box office results of *Fantasia* and *Pinocchio* led to the Disney studio making a public stock offering and taking out a new loan with Bank of America; this effectively gave the bank veto power over the Disneys. The bank leveraged this power to stop production on all feature films; a round of layoffs resulted in the remaining staff being given a larger workload. This eventually boiled over into a bitter strike which would haunt Walt for the rest of his life. He could be a genial boss, but he always insisted on total authority over his studio, and the betrayal rankled his pride.

Once the dust settled with the Studio on firmer financial ground in the early 50s, Walt's response was to get new ideas and start up a new company, which ended up being called WED Enterprises. It began in a bungalow on the back lot - a building moved from the studio's Hyperion days - but quickly grew and spread to become its own business unit separate from Disneyland and Walt Disney Productions. This was a business unit Walt owned and operated - and hired and paid everyone personally. He then went through and cherry picked the people from his Studio he wanted to work with, and set them back to work on Disneyland. Walt was rebuilding that sense of community he'd felt he lost in the 1940s. As pirate sculptor Blaine Gibson told The E Ticket,

> *"[For Walt], it was a rekindling of the excitement and involvement he felt working on Snow White in the thirties. I wasn't there, because I came in later in 1939, but I heard [Marc Davis] say that he was seeing Walt participate with the same enthusiasm he had shown in the earlier days of Snow White."*[30]

VII. ASSEMBLING THE ROGUE'S GALLERY

Walt poached talent from his animation studio left and right. This was supposedly to get the park opened on time, but in actuality his choices were very deliberate.

Claude Coats was a brilliant background painter who had worked briefly for MGM's art department and who pioneered gouache paint techniques for *Pinocchio*'s backdrops. He had built models to photograph at low angles for the appropriate dog-sized perspectives in *Lady and the Tramp*; model maker Walt had noticed.

Disney asked Coats to translate art by fellow former MGM artist Ken Anderson into model-sized layouts for Disneyland's Fantasyland dark rides, which they did using the new ultraviolet light paints. Ken and Claude were engaged in this task when Walt walked in on the pair and said: "*Grosh Scenic Studio says they can't finish Mr. Toad for opening day... you guys do it.*"[31] They did it.

Disneyland opened with a small stretch of New Orleans architecture laid out near to the big bend in the river, acting as the food court for the whole West side of the park. It constituted a line of shops: Casa de Fritos, Aunt Jemima Pancake House, and the Swift Plantation House[32]. This setup was essentially repeated from the Chicago Railroad Fair that Walt and Ward Kimball saw in 1948; the Illinois Central Railroad had a New Orleans themed restaurant and streetscape which opened into an umbrella-lined courtyard. Driving the point home, the exhibit next door at the rail fair included cowboys doing rodeo tricks and a tiny replica of Old Faithful. The direct juxtaposition of cowboys and New Orleans scenes still visible today at Disneyland descends directly from this Chicago Railroad Fair.

We aren't certain exactly when Disney began to consider pirates as inhabitants of his New Orleans street; we know that former MGM artist Herbert Ryman produced a few drawings for the pirate hideout in Adventureland[33] while the park was still under construction.[34]

But Disneyland did open with a pirate ship, out behind the Carousel in Fantasyland. Bobby Driscoll made his last appearance for Disney standing on the deck of the ship during the televised opening festivities of Disneyland, neatly drawing a line from *Treasure Island* through *Peter Pan* to *Disneyland*. The pirate ship is one of the features of Disneyland which was consistent through every iteration of the concept, and it materialized on opening day, straight back behind the castle pretty much where Herb Ryman had drawn it in his first aerial overview of the park. Bill Martin, the art director responsible for much of the opening day Fantasyland, oversaw the project based on a design by Don DaGradi. There was not sufficient time to finish the boat for opening day, and so only the side facing the walkway was painted.

Despite early proposals confusingly calling it "*The Long John Silver and Captain Hook Incorporated Pirate Ship*", Walt's anchored galley ended up housing a restaurant sponsored by Chicken of the Sea with piers extending from the mainland to the boat and out the other side. Inside, tuna sandwiches, salads, and "tuna burgers" were issued forth while the upstairs decks were open for exploration.

The Pirate Ship Restaurant was one of the most popular areas at Disneyland in the early years, and in 1960 it was the first Disneyland restaurant to expand significantly. Behind the vessel rose a shaded tropical grotto with splashing waterfalls and a large skull designed by Ken Anderson - Skull Rock. At night the eyes of the skull lit up green. By day the little seating area had a small pirate band while the decks of the Pirate Ship Restaurant were patrolled by a peg-legged buccaneer and his parrot. The pirate apparently didn't last long, as John Hench told Charlie Haas in 1978: "*He wasn't quite the guy you would want to have around kids. They didn't quite understand what the pirate was there for, so we took him away.*"

Although not nearly on the same level of ambition, it is possible to see this area and its success with the public as a prototype of a more elaborate pirate experience at Disneyland. As Jack Jensen once put it in The E Ticket, the pirate ship was "*the best fantasy in Fantasyland*".

VII. Assembling the Rogue's Gallery

As early as 1956, WED Enterprises was working on designs to extend the New Orleans Street in Frontierland to a more elaborate series of experiences, including a haunted house and a "Rogue's Gallery" of pirates.

In these early days design work on Disneyland was still very much a side activity of the movie studio, and the distance of time combined with the Disney organization's tendency to prioritize a good story over an accurate one makes it hard to know who exactly did what. Ken Anderson and Sam McKim are usually credited, though Sam McKim may have simply been working on a later pirate-themed arcade which has been conflated with the early attraction. Early Disneyland designer Bruce Bushman was almost certainly involved. The team produced a line art map - which looks like the work of Bushman to this author - in which visitors walked the decks of an anchored pirate ship and peered in the windows of a dockside shanty at rabble-rousing in the tavern. Other scenes in the tour included the pillaging and burning of a city and the Battle of New Orleans.

Work on this embryonic wax museum proceeded only in fits and starts. Ken Anderson returned to animation for *Sleeping Beauty* in 1957, and Bushman left Disney in 1958, which may be why credit for his early work on the project has been obscured. The pirate show lay dormant until Marc Davis was put on the assignment upon his arrival at WED in 1960.

Marc Davis was the brilliant animator behind Tinkerbell and Maleficent, and he was brought over to WED for his strong background in anatomy - a background needed because WED was now trying to build a mechanical man. While Mr. Lincoln awaited his moment of glory, pirates could fill the time.

Marc and his assistant Ken O'Brien produced two impressive overhead renderings of the expanded Wax Museum, carrying over the large central ship and burning city diorama, and adding in atmospheric city streets, grog shops, a storm-tossed landscape, and dim caverns where the treasure is buried. In the interim Walt had added a third attraction to the New Orleans area, a "Thieves' Market" set in a gloomy moonlit bayou based on Jean Laffitte's Barataria smuggling operation.

At this point Marc Davis was in deep researching pirate lore and processing the mass of historical material into comic - but not too comic - tableau of pirate life: the shanghaiing of a sailor, bawdy behavior in a seaside tavern, burying treasure, and so on. Marc told The E Ticket in 1999:

> *"I was taking the pirates that were real from history, like Morgan, Captain Kidd, and Blackbeard. These guys would shanghai somebody and force them to become a member of the crew. They would have to sign the articles with their own blood. [...] Most pirates died of venereal disease that they got in bawdy houses in various coastal towns. I was sorry to read that because it took a lot of the glamor out of these characters. So at first I wanted to explore the possibility of using real pirates in the show, but later I decided that that wasn't the way to go."*

Another problem was the format: Disneyland's unprecedented attractions, built in-house by Disney artists - an industry first, I hasten to add - had revolutionized the public perception of amusement rides and sent established park operators scrambling to install similar experiences. After the elaborate scenery of the Jungle Cruise and Peter Pan's Flight, regressing to stationary tableaux could be seen as a disappointment. Yet the technology to develop convincing human figures was at the moment beyond the capabilities of WED Enterprises. Walt had a secret project to build Abraham Lincoln underway in a back room at the WED Machine Shop, but the prototype figure was getting nowhere fast.

So Marc did the best that could be done with the existing technology and added a minimally animated "narrator" figure to each tableau. In an enclosed chamber off to the side of the main display, these characters behind glass had a dynamic pose which naturally suggested the telling of a tale. As the tale unfolded, lights would blink on in the main scene with limited animation suggesting action. Characters would be posed for maximum storytelling impact with limited movement, an exercise that would influence Marc's work at Disneyland for years to come.

This was also a good opportunity for Marc to use some of the historical characters he had researched - and rejected - as his narrators. Captain Henry Every sat in a chair with a pet monkey below a cross stitch motto reading "Dead Men Tell No Tales". Blackbeard was slumped over drunk, with a parrot on his shoulder narrating the scene!

But the problem, again, was the format. As Walt's Imagineers would say to anybody who would listen later in life: *walkthroughs don't work*. Disneyland actually had a lot of walkthroughs in the 1950s: a Davy Crockett Museum in Frontierland, a Sleeping Beauty peep-in attraction inside the castle, and the bulk of Tomorrowland attractions were experienced on foot.

In the 1950s Anderson had devoted a huge amount of time and effort in the development of the Ghost House attraction, including running timing tests with walking groups in the Disney soundstages. The numbers never quite jelled. Disney's ambitions - and more importantly, the capacity needs of a growing theme park - were running up against what was feasible. And so in 1962, WED began reconceptualizing the attraction as a boat ride.

A test flume was built alongside one of the Disney Studio soundstages, and rides were conducted. Nobody must have very much liked what they experienced on that mock-up, given that this minor detail has managed to have been conveniently forgotten in the official histories. The flume stood for years on the Disney lot, making no progress. The trouble is that the Disney people were artists, not ride engineers, and they really needed to bring in somebody who knew what they were doing.

Thankfully, Walt Disney knew two somebodies.

And now our story jumps north to Mountain View, California. Today this area is part of Silicon Valley, bestrode by colossi of modern industry: Google, Amazon, Microsoft, Apple, and more. In the early 1950s it was just a quiet area south of San Fransisco. This is how Walt Disney saw it when he arrived at Arrow Development in 1954.

Arrow was a small company owned by Karl Bacon and Ed Morgan. Their specialty at the time was the Antique Car Ride, a self-propelled vehicle that carried riders along a paved track with a central guide rail. Disney had come on a tour of amusement ride fabricators, which was a boom industry in the early 50s. Walt was unimpressed with these scrappy startups, but those early Imagineers on the Disneyland project knew that Disney could not produce the needed attraction vehicle systems in-house. Arrow was very near the end of the Disney national tour of possibilities. Walt was running out of options.

That Antique Car Ride turned out to be Karl and Ed's ticket to the big time. Fantasyland ride designer Bruce Bushman persuaded Walt that one of the vehicles could be modified into the car he had designed for Mr. Toad's Wild Ride.[35]

Eventually, Arrow got the contract to provide six ride systems for Disneyland: Mr. Toad cars, Snow White mine carts, Dumbo's Flying Elephants, the Mad Tea Party, the Carrousel, and the Casey Jr Circus Train.

This Disneyland connection turned Arrow Development overnight from a small-time operation into the premier builder of theme rides in the country. Disney fired Disneyland President C.V. Wood in 1956; Wood turned around and formed Marco Engineering and built cost-reduced versions of Disneyland elsewhere in the country. Arrow Development inevitably provided the ride systems for these ventures, building up their volume of experience and expertise.[36]

And then one day Bud Hurlbut came to his friends Karl and Ed with an idea.

Hurlbut was one of those remarkable do-it-yourselfers that the entertainment industry seems to attract. Hurlbut built rides and owned rides. He began his career in the amusement business building

VII. ASSEMBLING THE ROGUE'S GALLERY

The Pirates test flume standing alongside the Ventura Freeway on the Disney lot in Burbank in 1964. Historic Aerials.

miniature trains; his masterpiece is the Calico Mine Ride at Knott's Berry Farm.[37] In short, he was the kind of guy you listened to when he said he had a new idea for a ride.

Bud wanted to simulate riding a log through a flume chute just as the California loggers had done in myth and legend. His original idea was a steel tube roller coaster riding along a submerged track, but Ed and Karl convinced him that a floating fiberglass log would be better. Intending to install the new ride at Knott's Berry Farm, Bud was unable to acquire permission from the Knott family to move forward on construction. So Arrow went ahead on production of the flume concept and sold the ride to Six Flags Over Texas. The resulting attraction was called El Aserradero and it was a runaway success.

When Disney reached out to Arrow to devise a boat system for the Pirates of the Caribbean, Arrow modified their log flume attraction to meet the needs of a gentler show.[38]

The Arrow log flume was strictly run by gravity, with water flowing through gently inclined troughs to keep the logs zipping along. For Pirates, Arrow developed a forced-jet water system to keep the boats in motion. Eight submerged wheels keep each boat centered inside a metal channel, with the channel cutting a path through a very shallow pool. The guide rails hide below the water line while still allowing the vessels to be sent down chutes. Exactly as in the Arrow Log Flume, the drops are basically spill-ways, with each vehicle rolling down ramps thanks to wheels along the bottom of the boats.[39]

But most importantly, Arrow's flat-bottomed boats determined the tone of the final attraction. Riding through Pirates of the Caribbean in a log, jostling and bouncing around the flume, would make the attraction into a thrill ride. But Arrow's smooth, quiet ride system creates a contemplative mood... positively brooding. Arrow's boat system favors atmosphere which sets a keynote of mystery and suspense, and these moods would become the hallmarks of the Pirates of the Caribbean.

> **A NOTE ON NOMENCLATURE**: as a former Pirates Cast Member, I will be adopting the internal terms for the pirates attraction's waterfall features in this book. The terms are "Downramp" and "Upramp"; for example Pirates at Disneyland has "Downramp 1", "Downramp 2", and the "Upramp". The terms may be inelegant but they are correct, in the sense that the drops aren't really waterfalls so much as ramps that the boats roll down on their way downstairs. Sometimes simple really is best.

VII. Assembling the Rogue's Gallery

Arrow log flume ride vehicle from the Kennywood Log Jammer, photographed at auction after that attraction's closure.

The last few years of Walt Disney's life blur into a frenzy of activity with so many overlapping projects that it can be hard to imagine that he somehow kept all of these plates spinning in such a short amount of time. He somehow oversaw the production of four technologically groundbreaking shows for the New York World's Fair while scouting and purchasing land in Florida and dashing off *Mary Poppins*, the final masterpiece filmed under his watch. Then he pushed forward on the most ambitious ride through attraction ever built and challenged his team at WED to redesign the entirety of Tomorrowland from the ground up while fighting off crazed reporters looking for scoops on the Florida project.

Finally, he became obsessed with city planning and quite out of nowhere began promoting his new Florida theme park as some kind of city of the future, dazzling and confounding Florida politicians from Tallahassee to Miami.

In the middle of all of this, with precise timing, he died.

Work had begun on New Orleans Square in 1962, with a basement dug and the Swift Chicken Plantation torn down. By late 1962, a stately southern mansion - one day to house some ghosts - had appeared along the river. The nearby train station was ready, but the rest of the area was a hole in the ground with a green fence around it.

In the halls of WED the new Arrow designed boat system at It's A Small World was something of a breakthrough, recalibrating the minds of those at Disneyland. The 1964 World's Fair forced WED to invent the concept of a "people eater" attraction, one that moved effortlessly and, most importantly, consistently.

The Carousel of Progress remains one of the most efficient attractions ever created, as it spun on and on and effortlessly churned paying customers through its turnstiles, into the revolving theater, up to the second floor and out to the post-show area. The Ford Magic Skyway resolved the old problem of slowpokes taking their sweet time by forcing riders onto moving platforms and into the ride car, creating a subliminal sense of urgency that put a pep in the step of even the most lackadaisical pedestrian.

Marty Sklar remembered: "*When we went to the New York World's Fair, for the first time we were able to develop ways of moving people with huge capacity. Before the World's Fair, if you could get 1,500 people an hour, that was a lot. Small World was over 3,000 people an hour.*"[40]

WED was riding the lightning, pushing Disneyland rapidly away from the old start and stop guided tour format and into the 21st century.

Now reborn as a boat attraction, Walt smashed his two pirate attractions together into one. The plan always was to have the Thieves' Market on the street level and the pirate wax museum below it, but now the boat conveyance would unite both into one experience, with the boats improving the atmosphere of the bayou on their way to the pirate show below.

Very soon it became apparent that there was not enough room below the bayou to house the intended attraction; the main show graduated to a new building outside the railroad tracks. Blaine Gibson recalled: "*We flew out to [Disneyland] to observe where this pirate ride was going to be, and they were already tearing out the first go-around on it! [...] Walt, when he saw a better way to do something, he said: discard the old way! It'll pay back when you do it right.*"[41]

VII. Assembling the Rogue's Gallery

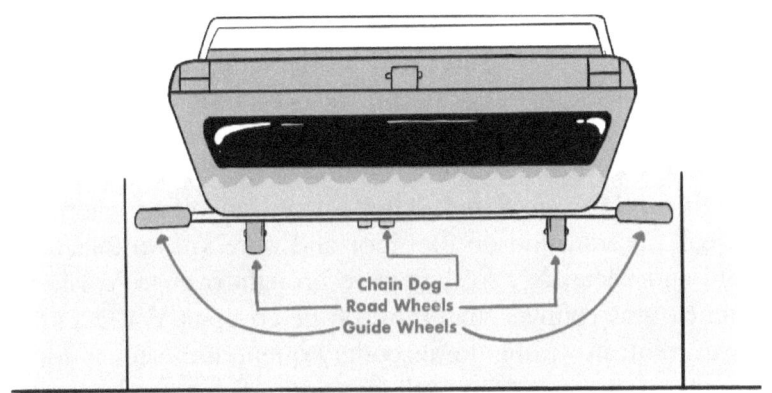

Pirates of the Caribbean, 1967

It was full speed ahead on the pirate show. Claude Coats was placed in charge of the overall attraction, expertly blending superb staging with the creative contributions of dozens of different artists.

The mutating shape of the ride building and its basement would force a radical redesign of the supporting New Orleans area. This was originally intended to be laid out in a wide rectangle - the New Orleans "Square" suggested by the name, and carried over more or less direct from Illinois Central Railroad's New Orleans pavilion in Chicago back in 1948. The massive boomerang oblong shape of the new ride path forced WED designers to create a meandering series of discovery spaces - as Charles Moore observed, the real French Quarter is "laid out in a rigid grid plan, while this is as irregular as a medieval village".[42] The result, resplendent in live jazz and torpid romance, is for 1966 the most detail rich and gorgeous themed area ever attempted. It turned out so well that Walt Disney planned to live there, in a series of beautifully appointed apartments sitting above the entrance to Pirates of the Caribbean. It's hard to blame him.

By March 1965, a continuity script by Marty Sklar had all of the attraction's scenes more or less in correct order. At this point Walt reached out to animator X Atencio, then working with Claude Coats on the Primeval World installation alongside the Disneyland Railroad, to write a script for the attraction. *"I had never done any scripting* before, and the notion was a little bit strange to me, but I said, if Walt thinks I can do it, then I probably can."⁴³

The choice of X was inspired. For several years Atencio and Bill Justice had been messing around with eccentric assignments for the animation studio, producing the stop-motion segments of *Mary Poppins* and the (truly weird!) Ludwig von Drake cartoon *A Symposium on Popular Songs*. They shared an office where they knocked golf balls around on the floor and were known together as "Dirty Bill and Clean X", so they were brought over to WED as a team. Atencio was younger than most of the group at WED and was a little irreverent; in writing the legendary queue tombstones for the Haunted Mansion, he gave himself "no time off for good behavior" for good reason.

But it's that wild, dangerous creative edge that the show needed; after creating a draft for the Well scene, X worked up dialogue for the entire show. "*When we finished with the script, I think at the final meeting, I suggested to Walt that maybe we ought to have a song in there that would run through the show... so that's how I became a songwriter.*"

Atencio was partnered with George Bruns, a wild talent who had worked as a musician for the inventive short cartoons produced by UPA in the early 50s. Bruns' claim to Disney fame was knocking out the theme song for Walt's *Davy Crockett* television show, a song which sold some ten million records. Along with arranger Walter Sheets, the team hashed out a cyclical sea shanty which ran through the action of the attraction.

X recalled: "*I got out my Roget's Thesaurus, and I'd say 'How about extort?' We used all the synonyms for one particular word, and it worked out into a nice little lyric.*" By early 1966 the attraction soundtrack had been recorded. Bruns' moody score is one of the best ever created for an attraction - somehow both leisurely and strident, with percussive bongos and reedy flute in the "Overture".⁴⁴

But especially in the haunted caverns, where Bruns' "*Scare Me Music*" is heard, the effect is truly sublime, with off-kilter sustained notes and swirling harp strings. The sound of the horns is strangled, discordant, but also reminiscent of a farcical march, like what could possibly accompany a squadron of ants marching upon a picnic. The sea shanty tune proceeds in erratic fits and starts, like a skeleton marching band that keeps falling apart. Atencio's clever wordplay and Bruns' just-right score really help put over the tone - rollicking but also a little deranged - unifying what could have been a bunch of brilliant but disconnected pirate gags into a truly cinematic experience.

Wathel Rogers' joystick rig that he used to animate the entire Enchanted Tiki Room. Jack and Leon Jensen Collection.

Speaking of those pirate gags, they were brewing up no end of trouble for the design team.

Pirates was arguably the first full-bore test of the animatronics system, which was still an awkward and new thing. It took the significant capital investment from General Electric (the Google of its day) for the Carousel of Progress show to really start to refine and standardize the machining and process for putting a human character together. This process reached its climax with Great Moments For Mr. Lincoln, the most sophisticated animated figure to date. As Marc later recalled, "*[Lincoln] was the one where you really would sweat blood.*"

Programming wiz Wathel Rogers had invented a crazy harness system to record motion for the figures by moving his body, except the harness could only record a tiny fraction of the motion possible by a human.[45] Something new was needed.

As Pirates animator Bill Justice wrote; "*The system I inherited for Pirates was only slightly less crude than the harness. The figures had two types of movement - digital and analog. Both types were programmed by altering black cardboard disks - about the same size as a 78-rpm record - and reading the alterations by shining lights through the disks into photoelectric cells. Only one analog function could be programmed per disk. This is what made the Auctioneer so complicated - there were 28 functions.*"

Justice had to rough in his motions by cutting material away from the cardboard disks around their diameter; no change would be zero motion, all the way down to the core of the record would be 100% motion. "*When I was finally satisfied, it was time to make disks which could withstand the rigors of hundreds of revolutions per day. Everybody was encouraged to bring in their old 78 records. These were stripped to their aluminum cores, cut to match my cardboard discs, and anodized black.*"[46]

Reading accounts of the creation of the attraction, the tight-knit atmosphere created by Walt at WED in those days is striking. Justice recalls: "*One day I was programming the pirate who sits on the bridge just above the waterway and swings his leg over the edge. Since he is so close to the boats everyone was taking extra care pains to make him as lifelike as possible. A talented craftsman named Ken O'Brien had just laboriously inserted hairs into the fellow's leg and smeared his bare foot with mud. I was about to make one final check on the motion when a secretary came in. She was captivated by that figure. "He looks so lifelike," she muttered as she moved closer. At that instant I sneaked over and nudged the control, and the leg twitched! Only the laundry knew how frightened she really was.*"

Harriet Burns recalled that Disney had arranged for Fred Joerger, who was overseeing the construction of the attraction's huge show sets, to be flown each morning - for nine months - from the airport in Glendale to the airport in Orange County to be driven to Disneyland. "*Walt came in early and Fred had come back early at 3 o'clock to get something. So Walt said 'Oh, you're back early - how was the plane today?' and Fred said, 'Well, I was in a hurry, so I drove!' [laughs] That hurt Walt's feelings, and he said, 'That's not the point, Fred! You're supposed to get on that plane, drink your coffee, read the paper, relax! Don't take the freeway!*"

Justice again: "*While Pirates of the Caribbean was being installed at Disneyland, the entire crew piled into a company station wagon each day and headed for the park. Work went surprisingly smoothly but there were a few tense moments. Marc Davis and I worked late once and found ourselves locked in. We were almost at the end of the attraction, by the jail scene where the inmates are trying to lure the dog holding the key, and the only exit in that area was closed. The only way out was the guest entrance and the waterway was filled. Fortunately the boats were also in the waterway. We had to step from one boat to the other all the way back.*"

You may have noticed the odd detail that Bill and Marc were programming figures with a filled ride flume. WED Enterprises simply could not build the things fast enough; a planned June 1966 debut slipped to December, then to April the next year.[46] All of this pushed the opening date until after Walt Disney's death.[47]

Truthfully, perhaps the most amazing thing about Pirates of the Caribbean is that the entire concept of an immersive ride thru experience - a concept which hardly existed in 1954 - produced its masterpiece as quickly as it did. Generally new media formats take quite a while to begin scaling up in ambition; consider the 23-year gap between Steve Russell's *Spacewar!* in 1962 and Nintendo's *Super Mario Brothers* in 1985.

But that's simply the way Walt Disney did things in the white heat of inspiration. The only really comparable evolution is the one spearheaded by the same man in the area of animated films in the 30s. Consider that in the late 20s cartoons were crude things where funny animals bonked each other with hammers to the tinkling of a silent film pianist. A universe away, in 1937 *Snow White and the Seven*

Dwarfs had lush musical numbers, sophisticated color designs, and production details which had raided fine artists from across Europe.

Pirates of the Caribbean is a masterpiece, and it is Walt Disney's final masterpiece, a 20-minute submersion in a lucid dream world. Fifty years on, themed design experiences have innovated in other areas, especially in terms of audience interaction and integration of filmed media, but Pirates remains the high-water mark, a cultural touchstone and an experience of remarkable power. As Charles Moore succinctly put it, "*its idiom, which falls somewhere between the creation of a setting and the telling of a story, is so superbly handled that the lack of narrative content seems scant bother.*"

At the 1965 WED Open House, Walt Disney pulled Marc Davis' wife Alice aside and told her: "*Marc is a genius - I haven't used him the way I should. But we are going to do some great things together*".[49] Alas, what could have been. The tragedy is that we will never know how many more ride-through masterpieces Walt would have produced had he lived even five years longer.

VIII. PIRATES OF THE CARIBBEAN AT DISNEYLAND

Pirates of the Caribbean in 1968; Amateur Slide; Author's Collection

i. Overture to Adventure

> *"[Walt Disney] didn't like the idea of telling stories in this medium. It's not a story telling medium. But it does give you experiences. You experience the idea of pirates."* - Marc Davis

It was an overcast day on April 19, 1967 – one of those Los Angeles spring days where the marine layer never quite burns off and spits rain every so often over the southland. A contingent of press men boarded the Disneyland Columbia that morning and the boat cast off, only to be intercepted by pirates in a dingy with a mounted cannon - buccaneers can't have everything, it seems.

Within minutes the pirate crew had boarded the vessel, crossed swords with the crew, and disposed of the captain over the side rail. At this point Pirate Captain Wally Boag, the star performer of the Golden Horseshoe Revue and the Enchanted Tiki Room,[50] broke open a barrel of rum punch with the pommel of his cutlass and the festivities began. A pirate band was summoned from below decks, and pirate wenches entertained the buttoned-down press boys.

Disembarking back in Frontierland, the pirates and press marched upon the new Pirates of the Caribbean attraction, overwhelmed some armed guards, and battered down the front door. Some $15 million invested over the course of four years - a span including a World's Fair, land buyout in Florida, and the death of Walt Disney - and Pirates of the Caribbean had finally opened.

What those crowds descending in 1967 saw was a three-story pink stone building resting placidly alongside the fiery red artificial foliage of the Swiss Family Treehouse. A smooth green concrete slurry walkway sloped gently up to the three entrance doors, above which hung a plain marquee. It all looks so unassuming. The front facade, designed by art director Ted Rich, is reminiscent of the Cabildo in New Orleans,[51] although it is not directly based on anything in particular - rather being, like all of New Orleans Square itself, a very imaginative pastiche.

The Pirates of the Caribbean attraction opened near the start of a stretch where WED began to design their attraction exteriors to increasingly elaborate standards, starting with the Enchanted Tiki Room in 1963 and climaxing with the raft of attractions which opened at Disneyland Paris in 1992. In these more mature works the walk up to the loading platform is often just as elaborate and richly detailed as anything seen once inside the ride. But Disneyland mostly shies away from this approach, with simple, outdoor queues bordering the main pedestrian thoroughfares, very much like the amusement parks of old.

Magic Kingdom, built just a few years later, does a lot more with their attraction entrances and having grown up with that model of Disneyland-style park, I was amused and kind of surprised that the entrance to the most elaborate attraction at Disneyland was just three doors set in a wall. But I think this accounts for some of the power of this attraction, that it really gives no hint to the depth or complexity of

VIII. Pirates of the Caribbean at Disneyland

the experience found inside. Pirates is alright playing coy for the moment - it has plenty of surprises in store.

Once inside and through the doors, the first impression one gets is of a small, plain room.

The plastered walls and tile floors are decorated with painted portraits of famous pirates through history. Much of the room is filled with an incongruous brick lined trench through which we see the attraction boats floating back to the unload area, with wrought iron scrollwork and hanging lanterns carrying forward the French Quarter design motifs.

The single touch that prepares us for the adventure ahead is a small sandy beach up past the boats.

On the beach is a treasure chest, shovels, and a pirate flag. All of this is placed before a leafy curtain of branches that subtly recalls a stage curtain. Later generations of Imagineers have spruced this scene up considerably with hanging lanterns, an animatronic parrot, and a treasure map,[52] but in overall effect this very much resembles a shop window display. Or perhaps, more to the point, the entrance lobby of a museum exhibit.

Boats aside, it's easy to imagine that this is very much what the entrance of the walk-through version of the attraction would have looked like had it come to be; indeed the connection may have once been even stronger. Dan Olson recalls that this room originally had little signs facing the queue with capsule history of each pirate - probably the very same paragraphs penned by Marc in his conceptual drawings of these pirates while he was pouring over Ellms' *The Pirate's Own Book* in 1960.[53]

But the entrance foyer is mostly preparation for what's ahead; although it's interesting in that it reflects the attraction's genesis as a walk-through wax museum experience. Painted portraits of Charles Gibbs and Sir Francis Verney situate us in a historical reality that the attraction which follows will owe very little to; indeed it will reshape piracy into its own image.

The forward flow of the boats guides us ahead and to the left, and after passing some lace-hung windows we step through a brick-lined arch, the curtain rises, and the play begins.

All at once the decor changes as if we have passed through the stage curtain, and what was once indoors is outside — although a dreamy, impossible, twilight outdoors that only ever existed in the imagination of Hollywood art directors.

Dim blue light peeks over a painted horizon and cypress and willow overhang the inky water of a bayou. Later versions of Pirates of the Caribbean would be more circumspect in plunking you into a night raid on a seaport, with Florida and Paris winding you gradually through dark dungeons and torch lit corridors before situating you "outside" seated deep in the fantasy. Disneyland just uses an arch; over here, it's night, over there, its day, and indeed one can still see daylight streaming in through the windows 20 feet behind us. Like much of Disneyland the bold confidence of its showmanship *carries* a concept that would have been easy to botch.

And so we are sorted and enter our boats, and just about everybody at this point looks straight up and reads a sign hanging above the ride channel: Laffite's Landing. I'm not aware of any other attraction that bothers to name its load area, and it's a curious touch, one that lingers in the mind long after our boats have departed from it. It's a nice little alliteration, one that, like us in our boats, will return. But for now, let's consider exactly what it's doing there.

For those who have not been there, it's worth knowing that while New Orleans is indeed a port city, it is not located directly off the Gulf due to the marshy land surrounding it. South of the city there's thirty miles of bayou and marshland stretching off into the Gulf of Mexico, a stretch which even today is only sparsely settled. It is in this relatively remote area that Jean Laffite operated.

Jean Laffite is famous as a pirate, although it's worth keeping in mind that he was active over one hundred years after the era when such characters as Blackbeard and Calico Jack were operating. It's sort of like calling John Wayne a cowboy; the hat does fit, but the context and era is totally different. Jean Lafitte may be the first man in history to be called a pirate and the term was intended to be a compliment.

What Lafitte really was is best described as a smuggler; he operated out of an area known as Barataria, far south of the long arm of the law. He operated as a go-between in the trade of stolen goods in the Caribbean, paying for cargos of questionable or legally barred ships and loading these contents into small boats to be sailed up through the bayous where they could be sold profitably in New Orleans.

The background to all of this is that Thomas Jefferson had curtailed American trade with England and France due to the ongoing Napoleonic Wars, and since Napoleon had successfully conquered much of the European continent, this was a real problem. The merchant classes, in particular, no longer had access to such goods as fine textiles with which to ply their trades, creating an opportunity for Laffite to profit handsomely by the situation.

Laffite himself was French, and this combined with the situation in Europe began to spell trouble for his operations in the run-up to the War of 1812. In exchange for an official pardon, Laffite agreed to use his fleet of vessels - apparently quite substantial by that date - as gunships under General Andrew Jackson and was officially recognized for his role in the Battle of New Orleans. This turned the brigand into a national hero, whereupon he relocated his operations to Galveston Island in Texas and continued to plunder Central American naval traffic until his death.

As part of the development for New Orleans Square in the early 60s, a concept for a "Thieves' Market" - eventually called the "Blue Bayou Market" - would be considered, a sort of indoor open air shopping complex set on boardwalks through a bayou at night. Visitors today can visit the real-life inspiration for this concept... at Jean Laffite National Park in Barataria, a narrow boardwalk through untouched bayous and rivers.

Notice that the first little tableau that can be seen once through the magic portal into the bayou is a small skiff floating beneath a cypress with a lantern sitting inside it; besides the pictorial value of the image it's a little hint at the sort of vessels Laffite's crew once sailed upriver to make their masters rich. Even in this distant, moonlit swamp... piracy is already afoot.

VIII. Pirates of the Caribbean at Disneyland

And so our boats cast off into the bayou. The name for the Blue Bayou comes from a short originally intended for *Fantasia*, in the version of that film that was expected to be continually revised with new material. Animation was more or less complete but the segment was never seen, eventually resurfacing in *Make Mine Music* with a new song by the Ken Darby Chorus. If you see that film, you will find that in visual design it's nearly identical to the physical installation at Disneyland.

It's a curious connection, a project from the fullest height of Walt Disney's creative life as a *filmmaker* which was scuttled and reborn two decades later as a pastoral opening section of the one ride which fully represents Walt Disney's creative life as a *theme park owner*. I wonder when exactly he visited Jean Laffite National Park and walked those boardwalks.

But there's another aspect to all of this that it's a little too easy to miss, and to catch it we should think back to Pirates Alley in (the real) New Orleans. That sign hangs there for a reason, even if it does not commemorate the location of real, meaning historical, pirates.

Now let's consider Platform 9 3/4 at King's Cross Station in (the real) London. Several million people a year visit this location, and there is now even a photo opportunity and shop to capitalize on this phenomenon. Harry Potter never lived, and Platform 9 3/4 doesn't exist, yet enough people have this memory that they come here anyway. And the thing about memories, unlike history, is that they don't need to be *actual* to be perceived. Author Dydia DeLyster terms these recollections of nonexistent people and places "social memories" and has explored how they have created situations where reality bends to the contours of fantasy to accommodate them, as on Platform 9 3/4 in London.

And that exact thing, that moment where a group recollection is made tangible, is what Disneyland did so well as to become the "brand name" in this sort of field. I've gone to such lengths in this book to surgically separate pirate myth from pirate fact because they're pretty much the same thing to us.

PART TWO: PIRATES IN WALT'S UTOPIA

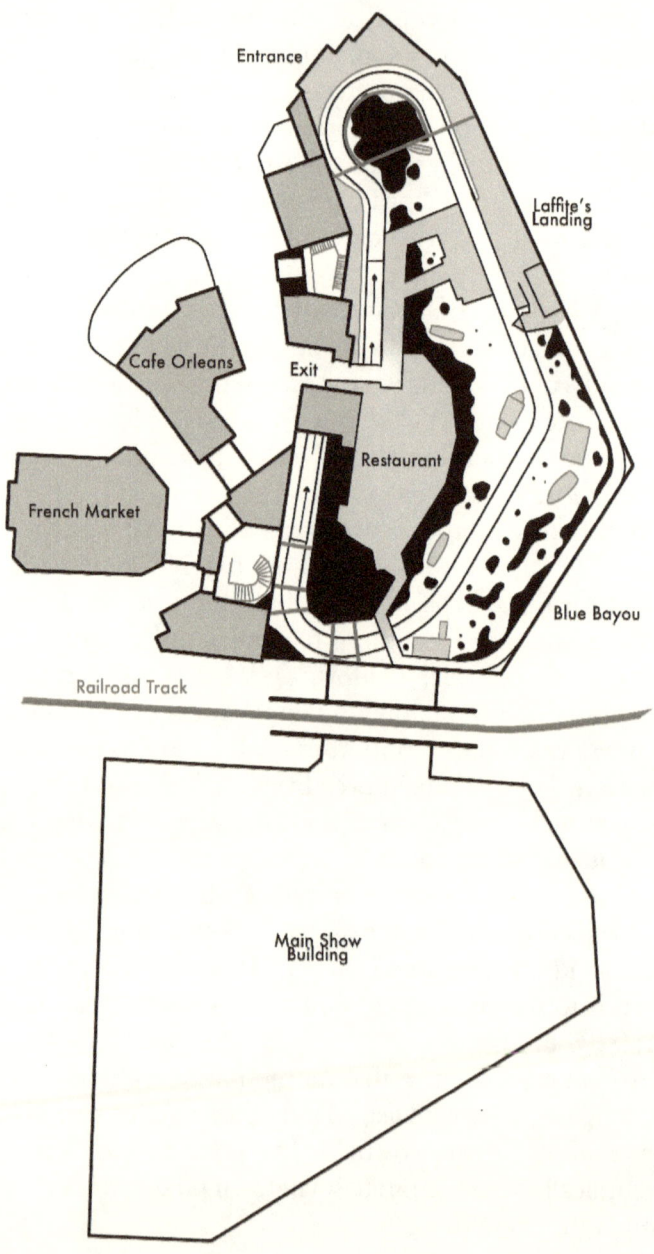

And this is perhaps why Pirates of the Caribbean is the *ne plus ultra* of Disneyland experiences, because it grows entirely out of these social memories - out of "the idea of pirates".

Perhaps the most famous thing about the Blue Bayou is that it houses a sit-down restaurant where diners can watch the boats cruise by on their way into the lower reaches of the ride. This may seem like a purely Disney invention, but in reality the Blue Bayou Restaurant has a lot more to do with Southern California than anything to do with New Orleans.

Los Angeles has always been a different place. In the first half of the 20th century it was the sort of boom town that fills those who live out where the bullfrogs croak with envy and rage; think of Silicon Valley for the 1920s. The motion picture industry made Los Angeles into a hometown known around the world, whether that be amusement piers in Long Beach (which stood in for Coney Island in thousands of movies) or places like the Chinese Theater and Schwab's Pharmacy. Informed or not, thousands poured into the city to "break in" to Hollywood, to move out to where the sun shines, or simply to escape.

All of this created a "new" city, planned on the modern (for 1920) principles of suburban houses and neighborhoods, displacing the cultural capital of established cities like New York and Philadelphia.

Angelenos were new citizens of a new kind of place, and they wanted their city to express the novelty of this newly-minted utopia. Such innovations as the ranch house, the outdoor grill, and Googie architecture spilled forth from Los Angeles, and themed experiences were among the illustrious.

Disneyland was invented in Los Angeles because there is nearly nowhere else on earth it could have been created. As Architect Charles Moore memorably put it, LA is a place where *"romance repeatedly seduces reality, and only new arrivals cry 'Rape!'"*

PART TWO: PIRATES IN WALT'S UTOPIA

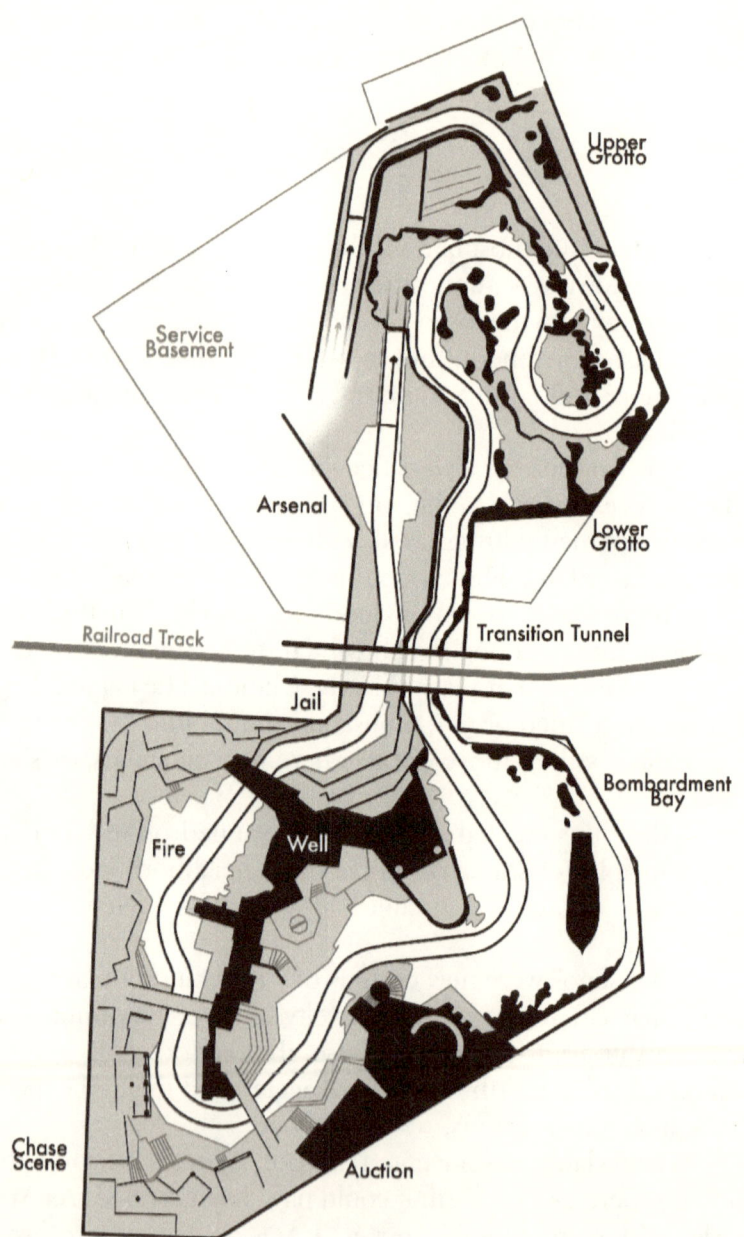

For a city of streets and freeways, buildings had to attract attention and convey their purpose from a car speeding by at 40 miles per hour; a hot dog stand that looks like a giant wiener and a donut shop where your car drives through the hole of the donut were logical extensions of business needs. This sense of play soon extended to all aspects of life; local bakery chain Van de Kamp's started building Dutch windmills atop their stores, and the Crossroads of the World shopping center smashed up a European village with an art deco boat to create one of the country's first outdoor malls.

The opening of the Ambassador Hotel's Cocoanut Grove nightclub in 1921 set the stage for further extravagances; it was simultaneously entirely artificial and the hottest, most exclusive nightclub in town. Done up in a "Moroccan" style with gilded lattice, gently hanging silk canopies, and an artificial moon and sky, it was a fever dream from the set of Hollywood blockbusters like *The Sheik* and *The Thief of Bagdad*. Tables were sheltered beneath real growing palm trees rescued from Oxnard Beach; stuffed monkeys with artificial glowing eyes cavorted in the treetops. Hollywood stars descended to dance to the band below a blue glowing sky illuminated by colored lightbulbs. If all of this sounds exactly like Disneyland, you're on the right track.

But the man who really fired the starting pistol for themed dining was Ernest Beaumont-Gantt, a hanger-on of the motion picture industry who had been leasing his south seas paraphernalia to productions as set dressing.

In 1934 he put all that stuff up on the walls of a small shop near Beverly Hills and called the place Don the Beachcomber; it was an instant sensation. The Don the Beachcomber location soon expanded, offering elaborately fantastical tropical drinks and cheap Chinese food whipped up into a confection. Don had a hose on the roof and he liked to turn it on to trick his customers into thinking it was raining; his ruse lives on today at the Enchanted Tiki Room.

Out of this cultural goulash of fantasy and romance arose Disneyland. Disneyland's innovation was to apply the Los Angeles mentality not to a nightclub, but to a whole outdoor amusement

The Cocoanut Grove Nightclub; Vintage Postcard

enterprise. It is no coincidence that the Enchanted Tiki Room was originally developed to be an actual restaurant until they bolted all of the dining chairs together and decided to open the thing to paid admission. Sitting alongside the Tiki Room was the Tahitian Terrace, an outdoor show with fire dancing and hula routines with a waterfall curtain below a huge artificial banyan tree. The Blue Bayou is the climax of this series of developments, a ploy to get Angelenos to make the drive down Interstate 5 to Anaheim and have a moonlight dinner at Disneyland. It's not just a Disneyland thing - it's a Los Angeles tradition.

Not far from Disneyland is The Cellar in Fullerton, an intimate bistro in a barrel-vaulted wine cellar. Uneven bricks jut from the walls, the plush booths are barely illuminated by the dim shaded lamps, and here and there rock walls (of the expanding-foam variety) spill forward, creating the impression of eating in some ancient grotto. Local tradition continues to assert that The Cellar was put together by "the designer of Pirates of the Caribbean", so strong and persuasive is the effect.

VIII. Pirates of the Caribbean at Disneyland

The actual man responsible is Gene White,[54] who appears to have been a local contract plasterer. But this is one of those oral traditions that speaks to a greater truth. Mr. White may not have been the designer of Pirates of the Caribbean or even an employee of Disney, but both The Blue Bayou and The Cellar hook into a larger tradition of Hollywood show and realized fantasy, a deep dip into a nocturnal world of dreams and dreaming that we are fortunate to still be able to visit.

After passing shrimp boats, a house boat, an alligator and numerous dancing fireflies, the boats pass the only scene of real substance in the Blue Bayou — a shanty on piers over the water. The flickering light of a lantern is visible through the windows, and from inside, we can faintly hear an unseen banjo player plucking away at "*Camptown Races*".[55] Marc Davis must have been very impressed at how well this "effect" worked, because he repeated it many times after. In October 1971, a very similar scene appeared alongside the Rivers of America at Magic Kingdom.

In 1972, the Rivers of America in Florida were drained to allow construction of the Tom Sawyer Island attraction, allowing Marc to go back and "plus" several scenes. One touch he added was a bit of animation to the shack scene along the river, an old man rocking in his chair waiting for a fish to tug on his fishing line. The live spiel written for the attraction christened this simple figure "Beacon Joe". By 1973 or 1974,[56] this "old man" figure was installed in the Blue Bayou at Disneyland.

You can tell that the "old man" in the bayou is a later addition, because if you look closely you can see that he's actually out of scale with the little house he sits next to. It's easy to miss because the figure is seated, but if he were to stand up, his head would be above the little shanty's roofline!

But Marc continued to incorporate the idea into scenes he designed; elsewhere along the Florida Rivers of America in 1971, he has river pirates drunkenly singing "Little Brown Jug" inside their cave hideout. In the queue for Pirates of the Caribbean in Florida, a lonely dungeon is accompanied by the sound of guitar playing, as if some unseen prisoner is whiling away his hours. Perhaps the most enchanting is also found in the queue for that attraction, near the boarding area. A cave lined with torches winds out of sight, and from inside can be heard the sounds of digging and pirates talking and laughing. If you stand in the boarding area and watch, nearly every person in line simply cannot resist leaning out as far as they can to peer around that blind corner in hopes of catching a sight of those imaginary buccaneers. It's a lesson in the dynamics of themed design accomplished with the simplest of means.

  The little boats press on into the darkness, passing now through a series of brick arches overhung with ivy. The explanation for these cannot be guessed at; perhaps they are the crumbling foundation of some large building? Perhaps this represents the outskirts of New Orleans? The architecture becomes confusing; the tunnel becomes darker yet we also come across another bayou shanty deep in the darkness.
  The layers of reality seem to peel away with each arch we float under, the sounds of the bayou fading away, as we strain to hear a voice in the dark up ahead... a very definite... whispering voice.

> *"It be too late to alter course mateys, and there be plundering pirates lurking in every cove, waiting to board..."*

  This is pure horror movie stuff, and on nights when Disneyland is quiet and you ride through Pirates of the Caribbean in your very own little boat, the effect is still, five decades later, pretty creepy. At last the boats turn the final corner and see, impossibly, a Jolly Roger come to life at the capstone of the final arch.[57]

VIII. PIRATES OF THE CARIBBEAN AT DISNEYLAND

This is one of the biggest innovations Marc Davis hit upon in the design of Pirates, a new idea that has spread like, well, an out-of-control fire. He didn't just use pirates and the iconography of piracy, but he actually *merges the pirates into their iconography*. So we have jolly rogers that come to life, skeletons who drink rum and steer ships, and parrots who wear teeny pirate hats and have sailor tattoos. The merging of icons prepares us for the less than serious tone of the piracy to be found ahead, but it also has become so ubiquitous in our culture that we no longer think twice when somebody has skeletal pirates firing cannons on their front lawns at Halloween, or toy stuffed birds sing sea shanties.

But the talking jolly roger is also the climax of a visual motif which has been building in the attraction since we entered. If we think back to the entrance foyer, the motif begins as we watch the little pirate boats float by in their improbably placed boat channel. Between the boats and the queue line is a brick-covered half wall; interspersed columns and decorative wrought iron lacework create arches through which we can observe the boats passing. The decorative scrollwork and hanging lanterns in their finery make these "belong" to the French Quarter house itself.

But past the boats, the little beach tableau that greeted us is further enframed beyond brick arches - sturdy ones that belong, visually at least, to the Blue Bayou. The arches collapse space and time, and as we look through them we can see something which should not be possible, where inside is out and a house is a beach.

Further along the queue line passes through its own arch, and this is the transition space as we are transported to Laffite's Landing, out onto the Bayou at night. This arrangement of manor house / boat channel / bayou makes absolutely no logical sense, although it makes fabulous poetic sense.

And as the boats wind deeper into the darkness, those enflaming arches return, transporting us inevitably even deeper into a dream. In those moments, the attraction pauses as time seems to stand still, poising us on the precipice of suspense as the darkness closes in around us.

If we entered expecting a rollicking pirate adventure in the Errol Flynn or Douglas Fairbanks mode, the attraction now reveals to us that we are actually in a ghost story, as the bottom falls out and we are sent down into the underworld.

ii. Descent Into Mystery

Our boat emerges into a luridly illuminated tunnel somewhere below ground though, as later events will demonstrate, it can't really be under New Orleans. The attraction now introduces the signature song "*Yo-Ho, Yo-Ho, A Pirate's Life For Me*", though if we expect to come across the pirates, we are deceived. The boat turns two corners and no pirates can be seen, and with a slip down another waterfall, even their voices vanish.

The cavern opens up on all sides to towering height around us as waterfalls pour in through the ceiling and we hear the first echoed warning:

"Dead men tell no tales..."

And finally turn a corner to encounter our very first pirates of the Caribbean - dead. Very, very dead.

Pirates builds up terrific suspense simply by hanging a sign out front: "Pirates in here!", then spending its sweet time getting to the pirates in question. We enter amidst paintings of historical pirates and a beach tableau of buried treasure, images that evoke, in Marc Davis' succinct phrase, "*The idea of piracy*". But then the ride slows to a crawl, we float amongst the mangroves and cypress. There's an old man rocking outside his cabin - is he a pirate? Underground we hear the voices of pirates, but they aren't there, and now we know why - the pirates are dead, all that's left is bones... and voices of condemnation.

That echoed phrase - "*dead men tell no tales*" - so famous, so influential, enters the pirate lexicon right here, where we turn the corner in our boats and hear Paul Frees intoning those words and see three skeletons gruesomely sprawled out on a beach. The phrase seems to have become colloquial in the 19th century, although never

Publicity slide. Jamie Maas Collection.

permanently linked to pirates until 1967. Emile Zola and E. W. Hornung wrote stories titled *Dead Men Tell No Tales*, although these are crime and adventure tales set in contemporary times.

How the phrase makes its way into the attraction is through Charles Ellms' *The Pirates Own Book*, and it's right there on the very first pages of that books' introduction. It is one of the first things Marc Davis jotted down in his notes while researching historical piracy.

Dead Man's Cove is Marc Davis dark humor at its best. The scene is grisly and scary, intentionally so, but softened just enough by a curious crab and nesting seagull to not seem in poor taste. The basic concept of men being executed to silence the hiding place of pirate treasure goes back to *The Gold Bug* and reached its apex in *Treasure Island*, where an entire expedition was extinguished by Captain Flint. Nowhere in Stevenson's book is the exact phrase "dead men tell no tales", though he does give us the immortal chant which is the basis of so much pirate iconography:

> *Fifteen men on a dead man's chest!*
> *Yo-ho-ho and a bottle of rum!*
> *Drink and the devil have done for the rest!*
> *Yo-ho-ho and a bottle of rum!*[59]

But Dead Man's Cove also firmly situates Pirates of the Caribbean not in the tradition of romantic pirates à la Byron or Fairbanks, but in the realm of the Gothic. In our times, pirates are just as distant and legendary as King Arthur, so it is appropriate that we first come across them in their modern state - as ghosts. All of that mood and drama built up upstairs in the bayou turned out to be an overture to an ocean-going mystery that will unfold as our little boats press on ever yet deeper into the darkness. That's why this scene is so effective as a transition point into the narrative events of the attraction; it's a little crime scene that allows us to reconstruct the events as we move past it. The shovels, the bodies; if we weren't already on the lookout and paying attention, Dead Man's Cove's great associative power nearly *insists* on our involvement.

And that's the brilliance of this scene and the cavern scenes to come. They situate the action of the ride inside a narrative device of a ghost story. Ghost stories are mysteries, violations of the natural order of things, demanding a resolution. By using the ghost story framework, the Gothic pirate tradition opens up a space for us to inhabit within the adventure, just as William Legrand and Wolfert Webber had. Like Captain Barbossa said, you'd best start believing in ghost stories - you're in one.

The cave rock formations in this area were, for 1967, state of the art, although they may strike modern viewers as quaint. At the water line and about ten feet up, the formations are concrete, resembling the ocean floor of the Submarine Voyage built by Fred Joerger in 1959.

Rolly Crump remembered: "*Fred was in charge of all the rockwork in Pirates, and for the ceiling of the rock tunnels he used paper! First he put rebar over the top of the ride, and placed it in a*

Publicity slide. Jamie Maas Collection.

wild kind of way. To this structure, he attached a special kind of insulation paper, normally used in houses, that has a thin metallic layer in it. When you crinkle it, the crinkle stays and resembles a rock surface. He attached the paper with devices called "hog rings". He then sprayed and flicked paint on the paper to give the color of rock."[60]

Notice the way in which the caverns open up. We enter near the ceiling, then drop down a ramp into the largest room we will see - the ceiling stays put, but we descend, twice. As we wind our way through the sequence, the ceiling of the caverns gradually get nearer and nearer to the boats, closing in on us as the tension builds. Blaine Gibson recalled: "*Claude Coats did a wonderful job in making this a suspense ride. He had this long grotto and then he squeezes the iris in just before you get to the boat. [...] I credit Claude for that, and it really sets you off for a start on that show that made it something very unique.*"[61]

The boat drifts on, winding between cascades and fantastical rock formations, past a skeleton piloting the wreck of a ship as a hurricane rages outside the mouth of the cavern.

This is the attraction's signature image, one that has burned itself onto the dream-scape of American culture. It's so common as to have become nearly a cliche, seen everywhere from miniature golf courses to fish tank decorations, but it began here. So powerful and recognizable is this moment that it served as the sole image on the teaser poster for the first *Pirates of the Caribbean* film.

As we travel along through the caverns, the skeletons progress from slumped piles of bones towards ever more lively actives like hoisting bottles and counting money;[62] the helmsman figure is a transition point. The power of the scene is in its ambiguity; does the helmsman turn the ship's wheel or does the wheel turn itself?[63] This is elemental stuff - the Hurricane Lagoon scene is a cultural cliche born fully grown; if you didn't know it originated here, you wouldn't.

Further along, the Captain's Quarters appears to our left, an absurd transposition of the pomp and finery of an eighteenth-century drawing room to a dripping, flooded cave. It's a marvelous juxtaposition, and one that speaks to the character of the long-deceased pirate captain and his pretensions of gentlemanliness. In a world stratified by class and social distinctions, piracy was one of the few ways to transcend a social station, as demonstrated by Captain Henry Morgan who died governor of Jamaica. Draped in cobwebs hanging as dense as lace, it's one of the most grandly surreal moments at Disneyland.

Across the way, two pirate skeletons drink from endlessly refilling bottles of rum amidst the clutter of an underground tavern; in the foreground, two pirate skeletons playing chess were added in 2006. The sound of pirates carousing with lady companions can be heard; a balcony at the rear of the scene is hung with dresses, implying a secret place for a rendezvous is just out of sight.[64]

Droll signs implore the pirates to "*Stow Yer Weapons*" and "*Thar Be No Place Like Home*". This is Marc Davis territory for sure; homey cross-stitch samplers that say unexpected things appear in his art constantly, and most famously in the Haunted Mansion's Tomb Sweet Tomb motto.[65]

Just as sure a marker of Marc Davis territory is a bar with a painted lady hung behind it; the one in Pirates was painted by Ed Kohn, who also executed the final changing portraits for the Haunted Mansion. These images appear again and again in Marc's work, and the motif reached a head in the Gay Nineties segment of America Sings, where nearly every character is hoisting a stein of beer and a quartet geese sing "The Bowery" before a painted nude of a goose.

In the 60s Marc painted his take on a bar-back nude for his favorite lunch spot, Alfonse's in Toluca Lake.[66] His piece shows four ladies who represent four different drinks: a martini, an old-fashioned, a Manhattan, and a highball. Interestingly, the lady who represents the old-fashioned is a spitting image of the Redhead in the auction scene. Persistent fan theory links the "Pirate Queen" portrait in the bar to the Redhead, and they even have a beauty mark on the same cheek - but I think it's just as likely that Marc had a "type" that he liked to draw!

Both the bar and the Captain's Quarters are basically just set-dressing, but what set-dressing! But these scenes are also about something else; they're a clue towards the pirate's *values*. The idea of a group of criminals trying to create a domestic space in a flooded cavern is droll already, but think for a moment about what the space they created tells about them. Everything we see is dedicated to weapons, drinking, women and gold. But the inadequacy of their efforts is telling; hanging up a crystal chandelier in a cave does not make it a mansion.

I think these scenes, as well as the Carousel of Progress, Haunted Mansion, Monsanto House of the Future and the Swiss Family Treehouse tap into a basic human desire to go into houses and see how others live, to understand others through their living spaces. The charm of the Swiss Family Treehouse is its ingenuity, but also the basic pleasure of peeking into a room and seeing a fancy bed. The Treehouse is a 50s suburban tract home built out of bamboo and ingenuity; they even have an icebox and all the comforts of home.

The Haunted Mansion expresses the values of its owners through its absurd opulence, now pleasurably given over to cobwebs and dust. The fact that these pleasures are layered inside of a fantastical narrative, where we encounter ghosts or survive in the wilderness, humanizes the adventure and encourages deeper audience involvement. Who hasn't wanted to walk down the "Corridor of Doors" in the Haunted Mansion, unlock each in succession, and peek into the hidden rooms beyond?

But up ahead now is the ultimate pleasure, the ultimate image we have been driving towards: the treasure vault. Piles of coins, plundered glittery things, and huge bolts of silk cascade from every crevice. Silk and cotton were the main object targeted for historical piracy. Although the Spanish peso, or "piece" of eight was the US dollar of its age - accepted everywhere - an English ship pulling into port in Jamaica loaded with foreign currency was almost certain to attract attention. Silk was valuable everywhere and could not be traced. For those interested, the only authenticated, itemized pirate treasure chest in history belonged to Captain Kidd, the very same chest he buried on Gardiners Island which created the whole myth to begin with. When the authorities retrieved the treasure, it was catalogued and verified by Kidd, and it contained medicine, nutmeg - and lots and lots of silk.[67]

Of course our attraction deals not in historical fact but ideas and images, so the pirate horde is predominantly gold - gold everywhere. There are candelabrums, axes, plates, a huge pile of gold bricks along the back wall, countless treasure chests, chandeliers, brass lamps, jewels, pearl necklaces... and in the center, a gigantic pile of gold coins, as tall as a person. At the apex is a skeleton with a handful of gold, frozen in a permanent display of greed and avarice.

The cavern sequence ends therefore on a perfect image, an *inevitable* image. I think it's telling that it took animators and illustrators to give to the world the image of pirate treasure it always longed for and had never seen; an impossible, overwhelming sight, the treasure horde to end them all. Washington Irving had a pirate treasure inside a pot sealed with wax; Edgar Allan Poe has a buried chest "subjected to some mineralizing process". Robert Louis Stevenson describes "great heaps of coin and quadrilaterals built of bars of gold", which comes nearer to the point, but it took Disney to finally get the job done and give us a treasure horde beyond all possible reason. It's satisfying in its inevitability; something unasked for delivered with aplomb. All subsequent treasure hordes cannot help but be a disappointment.

The scene is lit with glimmering, shifting light which is accomplished with an ingenuity that must be the mark of Yale Gracey.

Above the scene and out of sight are small boards, each with small pegs pounded into them in a grid. Hanging from each peg is a small reflective metal circle; pocket spotlights directed on the circles are scattered by a blowing fan. That's the sort of ingenious, low-cost solution that WED used to excel at.

After that all too brief glimpse of paradise, the boats press on into total darkness. George Brun's marvelous "Scare Me Music" fades out slowly, and two disembodied voices can be heard. The sole purpose of this tunnel is to move boats out of the original Show Building and below the railroad tracks into the main show. But the result is a break in the action and one of my favorite parts of the experience.

Originally the tunnel was dark; pitch black, essentially. The trip takes about a minute, over half of which was spent with no visual stimuli at all; it felt like a lifetime. All you could do is listen to the ghostly voices and wonder if the tunnel had an end:

> "No fear have ye of evil curses says you... *properly warned ye be says I!* Who knows when that evil curse will strike the greedy beholders of this bewitched treasure..."
>
> "Dead men tell no tales..."
>
> "Perhaps ye knows too much! You've seen the cursed treasure, you know where it be hidden! Now proceed at your own risk! These be the last friendly words ye hear - you may not survive to pass this way again!"
>
> "Dead men tell no tales..."

It's hard to put into words the effect of this, but for those who experienced it, it was indelible. After so much visual opulence and suspense, the pitch-black cave is an act break; the stage is cleared, and Act Three can finally begin. After so much preparation... the pirates are coming.

The Signature Image. Vintage Postcard, Author's Collection

Perhaps the most astonishing thing about this sequence, the most influential and evocative of the attraction, is that the ride designers didn't want it there at all. WED design honcho John Hench apparently was in favor of minimizing the trip through the new extra space below New Orleans Square and getting directly to the raid on the town - the reason they were building the ride in the first place. If you've spent years developing a pirate attraction, having Walt Disney suddenly instruct you to "add some caves and things" into the middle of the show must have seemed like a pointless exercise.

The sequence was slapped together in a big hurry; Claude Coats laid out the ride path around existing structural columns.[68] All of the skeleton gags used in the ride were drawn by Marc Davis in one big chunk in Spring 1966[69] months before the intended opening, speaking to their hasty installation. Indeed, it seems that there were originally plans to populate the caves not with skeletons, but yet more animatronics. Marty Sklar's 1965 continuity script featured a parrot who repeats dastardly plots in Captain's Quarters scene, and the treasure horde was said to be guarded by crocodiles![70]

Jason Surrell reports that one idea was to include a view of a "distant sea battle" beyond the mouth of the cave at the Hurricane Lagoon.[71] If that still isn't enough evidence, check out the souvenir Disneyland Fun Maps sold at the park. Well into the 1980s, the scene is called out not as "Haunted Cavern", "Dead Man's Cove" or some such term - they have it as "Pirate's Hideout"... the original abandoned concept.

Even after the skeleton concepts were approved by Walt, uncertainty lingered over the scenes - was it enough? After all, why were we wasting riders' time with all of these skeletons? How does it connect?

The task fell onto the shoulders of X Atencio, his very first writing assignment (!). "*The pirate ride had been pretty well worked out when I came to WED*", he later remembered.[72] His fix was that the gold was cursed and now you travel back in time to the Golden

Age of Piracy. It's easy to see how, at the time, one could feel that the skeletons were thrust upon a show that was already designed by circumstances beyond their control. In later years, Atencio expressed regret about the cursed gold conceit, but his idea would return as a plot device in one of the most successful adventure films ever made, *The Curse of the Black Pearl* - nothing to sneeze at. Francis Xavier Atencio's scripts for Pirates of the Caribbean and The Haunted Mansion are the best ever written for a theme park - they have a sparkle and intelligence that is part of the reason those two rides may well stand at the apex of the art.

Written, recorded, and not used were additional ghostly voices apparently drifting on the wind, one for each of the scenes in the caverns:

> *"Hear ye a dead man's tale of a dastardly deed. Brave sea-men, these... helped bury the gold they did, then silenced forever!"*
>
> *"Aye, gold and silver, satin and lace! Simple trinkets for the Captain's pleasure! Little mementos, you might say, reminders of his 'social contacts'..."*

This is delightfully purple vintage Atencio, but the scenes speak more eloquently by themselves and the ride team was right to cut these lines, saving the interplay of ghostly voices for the transition tunnel below the railroad tracks where they would have the greatest possible impact. As Claude Coats said, *"it gave us a chance, as we went under the railroad track, to do some good story development."*[73]

What of the surprisingly common story that the skeletons used in the attraction were once real? This was even addressed in Disney's official book on the attraction,[74] where Disney insists that the bones were removed and "given a proper burial".

The question is, why wouldn't WED just use plastic skeletons? The official story goes that the plastic ones at the time "weren't realistic enough", but it's not as if the skeletons on the ride can be examined closely... about the nearest you get to any of them is ten feet or so, not nearly close enough to make a difference. Also it seems to me that trying to get brittle human bones to do things like hoist rum bottles and steer pirate ships seems to be more trouble than it would be worth, so there has to be something else going on here.

Well, we could begin by investigating two industries that absolutely did use real skeletons in 1966: the medical profession and the film industry. According to Charles Wise speaking to the Los Angeles Times in 1988, "*For most of this century, India has been the only source of human bones for medical schools, for doctors and others all over the world. [...] Then two years ago India put an embargo on exportation of human remains. Natural human skeletons have been used for hundreds of years in teaching and studying anatomy in schools.*"

When you talk about using real skeletons in the film industry, the example which comes to mind for many is *Poltergeist*, a film which was supposedly "cursed" thanks to the use of genuine skeletons at the climax. As effects artist Craig Reardon points out, this practice in motion pictures is "*Extremely common. Common as rocks.*"[75]

The company that claimed to be the first to market plastic anatomical skeletons was Medical Plastics Laboratory of Gatesville, Texas, in 1949.

> "*Two local physicians, Oliver Wendall Lowrey and his brother Elworth E. Lowrey, ordered a human skeleton from a company in natural bones from India. [...] They were told there was such a heavy demand for human skeletons that they would have to wait eight months for delivery. That demand made such an impression on the two physicians they decided to launch a company manufacturing and selling realistic plastic skeletons. [At first] anatomists and doctors repelled the idea of using plastic skeletons. They wanted the real thing. But as time went on, the plastic skeletons gained more acceptance.*"[76]

The Los Angeles Times offers some 1988 price comparisons, and even then the prices for the plastic specimens are up to five times greater than an incomplete skeleton from India. These prices track pretty accurately with information Craig Reardon has given over the years about the skeletons in *Poltergeist*:

> "The skeletons I ordered in 1981 were featured in the catalog of a company that provides biological supplies. They came wired together for display in classrooms and included a metal stand and a vinyl cover. I ordered about 12 or 13 of them. [...] Alternatively, the company also offered plastic skeletons for the same purpose: classroom study. The drawback was that the plastic skeletons were really all replicas of one original sculpture or mold, whereas, the real skeletons were all different. This was pointed out in the catalog. Also, the plastic skeletons were actually more expensive, presumably because of the materials and labor required to produce one of them. For these reasons, purchasing the real skeletons was a no-brainer, and so I did."[77]

All of this makes for pretty convincing evidence that WED would have been incentivized in 1967 to use real skeletons, either purchasing them directly from one of these companies or perhaps acquiring a supply of them when hospitals or medical schools in the area were making the switch to plastic.

But that also can't be the complete story, because many of the skeletons in these scenes are holding poses, standing upright or holding electrified props. The two skeletons playing chess in the dungeon of the Florida queue are a sculpture by Adolfo Procopio, which was necessary to allow the skeletons to display the necessary "attitude posture" for the joke to read. I think the truth is that WED used a mix of real and fake bones to create the necessary figures, possibly patched together with sculpture where needed.

Jason Petros of the EarzUp Podcast, probably aided and abetted by a silent Cast Member source, has provided close-up photographs of two skulls in the Dead Man's Cove scene and another skeleton in the Jail scene that are reputed to be the real thing.[78] This author, for one, is convinced... sometimes there's a grain of truth in these old urban legends, after all. However, those planning on bolting out of the boat and running up to the bones to check for themselves should restrain the impulse; all of the attraction's skeletons were replaced during the extended COVID shutdown of 2020 - 2021.

Until 1967, the exact combination of caverns, skeletons, and pirates was not really *a thing* in pirate lore. Flint's Treasure is hidden in Ben Gunn's cave in *Treasure Island*, and the 1915 Harper Brothers version of that book illustrated by Louis Rhead contains an evocative illustration of Jim Hawkins packing the gold coins into bags with gold coins strewn across the sand. This would have been the current American edition that most of the ride's designers could have had access to as children.

Vintage Postcard

Perhaps just as fundamental is the myth of the Pirates of Lynn, Massachusetts. The story goes that a group of buccaneers set up a settlement in a remote glen north of Boston in a valley surrounded by ragged mountains; from the top of one of these, a commanding view of Boston Harbor was possible. Eventually the pirates were discovered and arrested, all except for one, whose fate is narrated by Charles Ellms in *The Pirates Own Book*:

> "Thomas Veal escaped to a rock in the woods, about two miles to the north, in which was a spacious cavern, where the pirates had previously deposited some of their plunder. There the fugitive fixed his residence, and practiced the trade of a shoemaker, occasionally coming down to the village to obtain articles of sustenance. He continued his residence till the great earthquake in 1658,[79] when the top of the rock was loosened, and crushed down into the mouth of the cavern, enclosing the unfortunate inmate in its unyielding prison. It has ever since been called the Pirate's Dungeon. A part of the cavern is still open, and is much visited by the curious. [...] The Pirates' Glen, which is some distance from this, is one of Nature's wildest and most picturesque spots, and the cellar of the pirate's hut remains to the present time, as does a clear space, which was evidently cultivated at some remote period."

Dungeon Rock, as it is better known today, was later purchased by Hiram Marble - a latter day Wolfert Webber who believed in the "golden dream" of untold riches. In 1852 he began excavating, a project which continued until his death in 1868 at a depth of 200 feet - all dug through solid rock![80] Marble kept at it because he believed himself in contact with the ghost of Thomas Veal, who guided him through Marble's spiritual medium. It's hard to say who Marble should have trusted less here, his medium or a long dead pirate![81]

Another potential source, not as far-flung as 17th century Boston, is just up the street in Buena Park. Bud Hurlbut's Calico Mine

Train opened at Knott's Berry Farm in 1960, and it was the Pirates of the Caribbean of its day, pushing the complexity of themed design forward. Several sequences in the Calico Mine Train prefigure Pirates, including an underground waterfall and huge cavern full of strange rock formations. Walt Disney had advised Hurlbut on the design of the Mine Train[82] and was an admirer of the experience.

Even more pointedly, Walt Disney brought Marc Davis over to WED Enterprises that same year and advised him to "go take a look" at ways to improve the Mine Train Thru Nature's Wonderland in October 1960.[83] Since Disneyland had debuted the attraction in June 1960, it's possible that the sophistication of the Calico Mine Train had spurred Walt Disney to seek out yet more improvements for Disneyland attractions.

And there's also the pure fact that caves work fabulously well in theme parks and always have. Early Old Mill rides crept through simulated caverns, and we shouldn't forget the lunar cave explored by riders in Frederic Thompson's "Trip to the Moon" dark ride, the namesake of Luna Park. Disneyland quickly added cavern exploration to its roster of attractions with Tom Sawyer Island in 1956 and Skull Rock in 1960. But for pure pleasure and impact, Pirates of the Caribbean tops them all. It's not the first cavern attraction... but it's the best.

It's a mark of the powerfully evocative nature of the cavern sequence that its unique combination of caves, piracy, skeletons and treasure has stayed in circulation in our culture for five decades. It's the highlight of the ride, the most often repeated "new idea" introduced by the attraction - and it's an accident borne of circumstance and inspiration.

But when your creative team includes John Hench, Claude Coats, Marc Davis, George Bruns, and Walt Disney, even the fumbling creations of improvisation can transcend time.

iii. The Raid Begins

The remarkable *scale* of Pirates of the Caribbean really comes into focus in the moments which launch the central action of the attraction. The boats turn a corner in the dark, and framed perfectly in the mouth of the cave ahead is an apparently full-size pirate ship, cannons blazing under the night sky. Even after witnessing so much impossibility since boarding our boats, this scene still strikes with the force of an epiphany.

Throughout his career, Walt Disney was willing again and again to spend a great amount of money to get something right - to do the concept justice. To bring riders to this point Walt dug a huge hole, filled it with structural steel, and still changed designs with construction underway. But when you see the vision in the context of the attraction, it's immediately understandable why he went through the trouble.

Here at Disneyland is where this scene - Bombardment Bay - was really done right. Magic Kingdom and Tokyo Disneyland have a similar reveal, but we first see the boat from too near for the scale trick to be really effective. At Disneyland, the long dark tunnel situates us so far away that it's possible to really and truly be fooled for a moment, for our brains to tell us we are indeed looking at a full-size ship. The impact of that moment is so profound that the remaining sixty seconds the prop is in view, our suspension of disbelief is total.

Notice how the ride vehicles round a bend, then head straight towards the bow of the ship, finally making a sharp turn to duck between the blasting fortifications and into the town. Later build-outs of the scene have the boats travel in a wide arch through the space - and actually have a larger room as a result - but the ship actually *feels* smaller.

In the model for the attraction WED had a huge number of figures aboard the ship, including crew members picturesquely perched in the rigging à la *The Black Pirate*. The scene originally showed pirates forcing a man to walk the plank, with sharks circling below. This really is a case where WED spent their money correctly. The scene is so impressive in its scale and conception that it hardly matters that there's really only half of an animatronic wagging a sword around on the boat and a few static heads that pop up over the rails. The cold misty fog hanging over the water and the blue light peeking up over the artificial horizon create a romantic, hallucinated

VIII. Pirates of the Caribbean at Disneyland

Vintage Postcard

impression of the open ocean stronger than the black void it would be in reality.

But even more to the point, the thundering cannons really amp up the action and make a better dramatic point that the attack on the seaport has begun. With thundering cannon the ride announces it is moving to another level.

So *why* are the pirates attacking the town, and did things like this really happen?

It's worth again stating our standing disclaimer the attraction is fiction and does not represent any actual point in history - this is mythology, not fact. Still, we can try to answer the question.

Today, we conceive of pirates as being totally independent of any political entity besides their own opportunistic desires, but this was almost never the actual case. During the golden age of seafaring whether you were a privateer or a buccaneer depended largely on whom you asked and when.

The Spanish had multiple places in the Caribbean where they transported goods to Europe; Porto Bello in what is now Panama, Campeche on the Yucatan Peninsula, and Havana in Cuba were the famous "treasure ports". If you want to peg a specific theoretical "place" where the attraction could be taking place, these are your best bets. All of these cities have abundant Spanish colonial-style structures in their oldest sections, and the remains of impressive fortifications at the mouth of their harbors.

These Spanish strongholds were therefore subject to raids and sackings by English pirates, largely operating out of Port Royal, Jamaica, a pirate haven conveniently overlooked by the English crown. Many of the squabbles and exchanges of treasure in the Caribbean involved captains acting under the auspices of Great Britain stealing treasure from Spanish ships and retreating to Port Royal, where the Governor of Jamaica could offer protection - essentially, hit and run tactics. All of this was occurring as a side theater to the Thirty Years' War in Europe, which had depleted Spanish fortifications and resources in the New World, leaving many fortresses and regiments poorly maintained and under-staffed. Once Portugal began threatening to secede from Spain, another front in the war in Europe opened. Spanish colonial resources depleted even further, and the opportunists swept in.

The inaugural sackings of fortified cities occurred under the command of Christopher Myngs, who attacked Santiago, Cuba, in 1662 and Campeche, in the Yucatan Peninsula, in 1663.[84] The primary method involved in these sackings was for the crew to land well away from the city and proceed over land, usually attacking by dawn's light. In this way the pirates were at the city nearly concurrently with their ships being spotted.

Among the boldest and most successful pirates in history is Henry Morgan, who carried out three of these over-land attacks culminating in his raid on Panama in January 1671.[85] These were traditional military-style attacks, requiring Morgan to capture and supply a defense point. He then marched over land with 500 pirates through a rainforest and successfully overwhelmed the Colonial forces.

The port city burned, although who struck the match is debatable; the English and Spanish, naturally, blamed each other. Most of the gold was successfully evacuated by the authorities, although Spain had to re-build Panama in another location.

But the buccaneer crew had struck a massive and humiliating blow against Spanish holdings in the New World, so much so that the English government removed Morgan from the Caribbean at the insistence of Spain.

Tellingly, Morgan does not appear in early editions of *The General History of Pirates* or the books derived directly from it, such as *The Pirates Own Book*. He returned to England, was knighted, and was granted governorship of Jamaica by Charles II - and was therefore excluded from Captain Johnson's gallery of criminals. Like I said, it depends on who you ask, and when. In our modern era being a pirate is a far greater honor than being governor of Jamaica.

But we need not be so prosaically historical here; just as likely a source is Twentieth Century Fox's *The Black Swan* from 1942. The film begins with a night-time raid on a Caribbean seaport which is torched; the atmosphere, the architecture, and even the lighting of the scene is startlingly similar to what is seen in Pirates of the Caribbean.

Sam McKim, Bill Martin, and Dick Irvine, all of whom worked on the attraction, were brought over from Fox to help design Disneyland, and the chances that one or more of them had known of or worked on that film is high.[86] I've looked in vain for a more direct link than this, but *The Black Swan* was the last really big film Fox undertook before the start of World War II and production never quite got back to its level of opulence. It would have been a natural model for any of these men to think back to when tasked with designing a pirate ride.

As the boats slip between the thundering battlements and into town, the fruits of this army of art directors who now call themselves "Imagineers" come into view.

The central town set is really an ingeniously designed piece, probably the thing that more than any of the attraction's crafty illusions really draws the experience together and makes it work. This brilliant work by Claude Coats is all jutting angles and architectural details, balconies and crumbling plaster. It's designed as a loop, with a few architectural pieces always on the horizon or just out of sight to create the impression that it's far larger than it really is. This is what Charles Moore means when he says that the attraction's *"idiom [..] falls somewhere between the creation of a setting and the telling of a story."* The trellised, ivy hung, colonial town and what happens to it *is* the story, action embodied as a tour of a location.

A lot of the texture of what you see on the attraction is in fact not dimensional but painted directly onto theatrical scenery flats. Lighting effects are painted right on the walls and supplemented by "hero" lights which punctate and illuminate their painted, carefully controlled effect. This work seems to have been designed by Clem Hall, an art director for Paramount and MGM, who had just joined WED. The work itself was done at the R.L. Grosh and Sons scenic shop in Hollywood.

According to *The Art of the Hollywood Backdrop*, all of these flats were overseen by James McCann and painted by twin artists Wilbur and Warren Ferrell. They were then crated up and delivered to Disneyland for installation. Wilbur and Warren, one left-handed and the other right, according to legend could begin at either end of a backdrop and meet perfectly in the center, and I like to imagine them doing this for the huge Blue Bayou backing upstairs.

Usually, areas closer to the boats will be done up more "in the round", with the furthest reaches being more impressionistically realized. Many areas with less detail are hidden by dimensional railings, windowsills, bamboo blinds, and hanging bolts of fabric. In theme park circles this is more or less a dead art form, because it was invented for Hollywood movies where things only needed to look good for the camera. Many attractions today have details, but details all around, or sometimes in places where you can't enjoy them. The upper areas of the town and the Burning City in Pirates are canvas stretched over wooden framing; you'd never know. The walls of the

Ballroom in the Haunted Mansion are a painted flat; nobody notices. It's this economy of knowing exactly how much to build and where to spend money that I really admire.

The first scene we come across is the Well scene, and there's a lot of detail here... perhaps too much. Most riders will never look all the way over to the right to see the ramp and entrance arch to the fort, or the entrance to the Mayor's house with the battering ram thru the front door. Way off to the left is a pirate with a peg leg and another with a wooden eye who do nothing but cackle menacingly every time Carlos gets dunked. Around the base of the well are three spouts which spill water every time he's lowered back into the water. We have about thirty seconds to process all of this.[87]

The old story is that when asked if there was too much detail in the ride or if they were producing more show animation than riders could possibly ever see, Walt Disney replied "*We get so much repeat business here that they'll have to come back again and again.*" In the days when riding Pirates of the Caribbean cost an E ticket - 75¢ or roughly $6 today - this was good business practice. Life Magazine reported that by September 1967, Pirates of the Caribbean was selling one million tickets a month.

The idea of dunking somebody in a well probably comes from Marc's early exploratory sketches for the attraction in 1960, where he had pirates dunking a rotund fellow in a large wash basin with a pulley. Everything the pirate crew does in the town is presented with a comic touch, but the attraction is also is pretty honest in presenting these events as what they are, which is atrocities. Walt-era Disneyland in general was pretty happy to ramp up the gruesome and troubling content, as he had been in his best films; as Karal Ann Marling put it, there would have been no need to invent an "architecture of reassurance" had the images represented in the park not been inherently unsettling.

So yes, there are cackling peg-legged pirates and Carlos' wife providing the worst possible moral support from the upper window of their house, but look elsewhere in these scenes and you'll see that Marc did bother to design, and Walt did bother to approve, figures that paint a fuller picture of what's going on. Off to the right of the well is a line of men tied up awaiting interrogation; they look terrified, and it isn't all that much of a joke. But the detail that I think about more and more the older I get was in the Auction scene. You had to look past a bunch of animatronic goats and chickens and goofy looking pirates to see it, but it was there. Amongst the women tied up in ropes was a young lady sobbing into a handkerchief; an older matronly lady behind her was comforting her by patting her on the back.

We mostly don't see the male colonial inhabitants in the ride, but we see a lot of the women: Carlos' wife defiantly throws open the shutters again and again, even after having been shot at. The Redhead, the fancy lady of the village, defiantly stands before the slavering buccaneers, primps, and shows them her leg. Other village women giggle as pirates pursue them; one gets to try to chase down a pirate of her own. There is a sense that the women are more than up to the task of dealing with these rowdy criminals.

It may be interesting to compare the gags Marc worked up for Pirates to those he did for another sixties show - the Ford Magic Skyway, with its caveman shenanigans involving the invention of the wheel.

Consistent in these gags is that the lady cavemen are the ones doing all the work - lifting heavy objects, hauling the family away in their brand-new wagon - always with a look of resentment. In these cases it's obvious that the joke isn't at the expense of the women, but at the attitudes of their crude society - after all, what else do you expect from *literal neanderthals*? This is another case where Marc's approach to crass behavior is to send it up, which I think is as close as we can get to an honest reading of the intention behind the humor in Pirates of the Caribbean.

And about that Auction scene, the most famous and iconic in the attraction. It's possible to read the original Redhead character as defiant; she stands there in her ruffles and lace, strikes a pose for the drunken sailors, and shows them her leg. Her outfit is a pure high Edwardian fantasy absurdly out of place in the early eighteenth-century Caribbean, but this, and the red color of her garments, marks her as special. Her red hair and red clothes imply she's a "madame of

Vintage Publicity Still, Author's Collection

the night". She knows rough men like these pirates and refuses to be humiliated while being treated like livestock. This isn't a reading I'm terribly enthusiastic about, but it's there for you if you want it.

The Redhead is enduringly popular and famous, probably the most popular and famous audio-animatronic who isn't a reproduction of a famous president, and the way you see her being written about doesn't tend to reduce her down to the status of a victim. There have been elaborate cosplay costumes built and worn by women of this character, something I don't think would have happened had their creators read her role in the show as being willingly complicit in her degradation. The Redhead stands out from the crowd because she refuses to be victimized in a terrible situation.

Vintage Publicity Still, Author's Collection

The Auction and Chase scenes represent sticking points for modern audiences. The Auction is the iconic highlight of the ride with the best animatronics and the best dialogue; it's also, honestly, more than a little sexist in concept. The Chase scene that follows is arguably the low point of the ride.

VIII. Pirates of the Caribbean at Disneyland

Every classic theme park attraction has a scene that doesn't work as well as its designers would have wished which has obligated future generations to keep going back in and messing with it. The Haunted Mansion has the Attic, and Pirates of the Caribbean has the Chase.[88]

I'm not going to waste your time here and try to defend the content because there's no point; humor based on victimizing women was going out of style in the 60s and now is pretty much unapproachable. What is fair to say is that the Auction and Chase scenes are based in comedy tropes, and as culture has shifted and the assumptions and worldviews of audiences have changed, the humor has suffered. Humor, after all, is very dependent on unspoken values and assumptions, which is why it's so hard to translate comedy and puns across cultures - and why the older generations are always baffled by the weird humor of the new ones.

And that's what I'd like to focus in on here: the comedy background behind all of this as a way to discuss why we see these jokes cropping up in this attraction.

If you go back to the foundational classic era American comedians like Charlie Chaplin, Buster Keaton, or Laurel and Hardy, what you will see is that these comedians worked more or less alone. To the extent that women appeared in these comedies they were almost always as romantic props; Buster Keaton had a habit of carrying around his leading ladies while unconscious like literal props. Laurel and Hardy's comedies often involve a battleaxe wife, but she's really only there to set up the jokes, as Stan Laurel stammers and shrugs or Oliver Hardy does one of his famous slow-burns. Charlie Chaplin's leading lady in 1936's *Modern Times* is the talented comedian Paulette Goddard, and even then she hardly gets to do anything funny.

But the fact is that by the late 20s this kind of comedy was already on its way out. In the late 20s the solo comedian act was evolving; female comics began to get bigger roles with more funny things for them to do. This resulted in the comedy style we call screwball, which reigned until the end of World War II.

Screwball comedies were essentially sitcoms. The basic idea was to build the entire story around a romance as opposed to, say, Buster Keaton trying to build a house. This meant that there were finally things for brilliant comedians like Carole Lombard, Claudette Colbert, Irene Dunne, or Ginger Rogers to do, as opposed to simply stand and wait for Harold Lloyd to do some crazy stunts and rescue them.

The most popular format turned out to be one where the female characters were the protagonists, bucking tradition and on their own way to find happiness while a gaggle of flummoxed male suitors watched on the sidelines. These games with gender roles and social expectations mean that screwball comedies have aged fabulously well for today's audiences, who still find much to appreciate in their quick wit and rambunctious silliness.

But the screwball cycle eventually ended, and heading into the 50s, the "battle of the sexes" concept stuck around, only with a much heavier emphasis on the "battle" part. GIs were returning, starting families, and marrying those ladies who had kept the economy running in their absence. Women were expected to pivot from building tanks and aircraft to returning to the domestic circle. This set off tensions in society that expressed themselves as comedy. Think of Jackie Gleason in *The Honeymooners*, constantly threatening to wallop his wife. Or Pepe le Pew smothering Penelope Pussycat in kisses.

And that sort of aggressive cartoon sexuality is exactly where you find Pirates of the Caribbean living; it's full of bawdy jokes about ladies and drooling, childlike men because that was the dominant mode of comedy at the time. Let's cycle back to the screwball comedies as a point of comparison. Revival screenings of gems like *The Philadelphia Story* and *His Girl Friday* are as common as crabgrass, but you've got to be a very dedicated cinephile to have gotten around to a mainstream 60s comedy films like *Cinderfeller, Under the Yum-Yum Tree* or *Quick! Before It Melts*. There's a reason why if you know somebody who watches old movies they

VIII. PIRATES OF THE CARIBBEAN AT DISNEYLAND

Courtesy Ted Linhart, Disneydocs.net

probably watch musicals, crime pictures, and horror movies. The social assumptions around those sorts of things have not changed, whereas what's funny has.

The past is a foreign country, they do things differently there, but asking audiences of any kind to forgive material on the basis of being from 1967 is asking people to engage with media on a level that most are not prepared to do. This really is an unfortunate case where trying to protect the good reputations of the attraction designers is a no-win game; denying that the material was hurtful only helps to perpetuate the erasure of victims which perpetuates why it was unacceptable to begin with. It's better here to admit that these sorts of jokes are a significant blemish on an excellent experience and move on.

The Chase scene in its original form was dominated by one central animatronic figure with ten cruder figures going around on turntables as a sort of "supporting cast". If you never saw this scene in its original form - which is going to be most of you reading this by now - I must point out that all of the ladies in this scene had open-mouthed expressions of amusement and giggling from both wenches and pirates could be heard; *this was not played seriously*. In the center of the scene was the "Pooped Pirate", who sat against a barrel with a high-heeled shoe and a lacy slip in one hand. Both shoe and the slip were straight out of 1966, for those of you still trying to claim that any of this was "historical".

Behind him, the lady companion he was in pursuit of kept peeking out of a barrel with a lit candle to see if he was gone yet. The Pooped Pirate's dialogue went like this:

> *"Heave to, maties - say, have ye set yer eyes on a bewitchin' maiden in yer travels? Oh, she be a lively lassie she were - It's sore I be to hoist me colors on the likes of that shy little wench! Favor -*

keep a weather eye open, maties - I be willing to share, I be!"

Marc's gag of the lady in the barrel remains pretty funny but overall this is pretty toe-curling stuff. A couple years ago I was assembling an audio reconstruction of the attraction and, even remembering the original version of the scene, I was surprised at my reaction of disgust upon hearing this again.

The "Pooped Pirate" here is based on Marc Davis' illustration of Henry Every for the version of the wax museum with the animated narrators. This is an interesting connection because Every was remembered for capturing a huge treasure and getting away with it, but just as much for forcing his attentions upon a Mughal princess. Most of the pirates in the attraction are pastiches of the popular image of pirates, but Marc put Blackbeard on the decks of the ship screaming bloody murder at his victims, and Captain Every as an exhausted old timer looking for a hook-up. Telling casting.

But setting aside the events presented in the scene, the Chase scene has another issue. Coming after so much pageantry and robotic spectacle, it just isn't all that impressive.

In later years Marc would bemoan the "bicycle action" of the figures in this scene. He wasn't being facetious; the animation here is literally based on a bicycle. Tires roll along the concrete show building floor while above them a figure is suspended by a rod. A turning crank mechanism animates the legs of these figures using the same principle that turns the pedals of a bicycle, so they actually appear to "run". The legs of the male pirates take strides, and the ladies have a cute butt shake animation. This is one of those cases where standing backstage and seeing the actual mechanism do its thing is vastly more impressive than seeing it from the boats.

The Chase scene has always ended with a topper gag that reverses the situation; here at Disneyland the final turntable had a fat lady pursuing a pirate. In 1973, Florida got a much better take, where instead of romantically pursuing a potential husband, the heavy lady was smacking him over the head with a broom. Tokyo got the same gag. Weirdly, multiple commentators in the years since have spoken of the Chase scene in Florida as if it once had the "fat lady lusting for a pirate" gag, which it never did. Disneyland still has this figure with her arms amorously extended just as they were sculpted in 1966; the solution in recent years, not wholly convincing, has been to place in her hands a rolling pin. I'll take the broom any day. Smack him, sister!

And yet, and yet. There were artful elements to the original Chase that have been lost. Upon entering the scene to the left was a small tableau of a table and chairs with tankards of beer resting upon it; the drinking has been interrupted by the arrival of ladies upon the scene. And if you still doubt the satiric intentions of this scene, let me point out that it was absolutely filled with chickens, and this was not accidental. Chickens are synonymous with stupidity, but also with sexual aggression, as in "getting cocky". Two chickens even chase each other in circles around the town water pump, driving the point home. Disney paid good money for all of those chickens, and they were there to provide commentary on the whole sorry scene.

Courtesy Ted Linhart, Disneydocs.net

All through the town portion of the ride are little bottles floating in the water, apparently having been emptied by buccaneers and tossed indifferently into the river. These are wine bottles, mostly the variety with the woven basket around their bodies, as any bottles transported across the briny deep in the sixteenth century would have been. But the fact that it's a wine bottle may be a surprising detail, as today the association between pirating and rum is so strong that it seems inconceivable that there would be any timbers shivered without a bottle of kill-devil lurking nearby.

Rum came about as a byproduct of the sugar trade, itself a sort of accident occasioned by the colonizing powers. By the time the Europeans realized that wheat and barley grew poorly on barren Caribbean islands but sugar grew amazingly well, they had "eliminated" so much of the local population that slaves from Africa had to be imported in vast numbers.

Sugar cane was pressed and boiled to cause its natural sugar to crystalize out; the resulting goop, a sort of industrial waste, was called molasses. Some of this was mixed into grain fed to livestock, or mixed in with eggshells, straw and horsehair and used as mortar.[89] Most of it was dumped into the ocean. But in not too much time, some began to wonder if running the stuff through a copper still could produce a tolerable alcohol, and rum was born.

By the early eighteenth century the Caribbean was awash in rum, as the investment in a still-house on the part of a plantation owner could defray the cost of cultivation of sugar cane. This almost certainly was largely unaged pure fire water, and probably not produced in the most sanitary conditions - author Wayne Curtis notes that during the initial ferment everything from rotting fruit, mustard, animal carcasses, and even the contents of a chamber pot[90] could be added to keep the yeast bubbling. The mash could then be distilled and kegged up for shipping.

The first large export market for rum was in the American colonies; the tropical heat and constant rocking of the merchant ships aged the fire water very quickly, and no doubt the colonists soon learned to age it even longer. Some even believed that the best rum was shipped first to England and let rest in the humid atmosphere of the London docks before being shipped back to the colonies. The most prized rum came from Jamaica, which produced rum with a distinct estery, funky flavor which adherents lovingly referred to as the "rum stink".[91] Indeed the Yankee colonies were so heavy with rumbullion that English attempts to tax sugar products met with such loud and organized resistance that the crown backed down - and devised laws to tax tea and paper documents instead. Thus, rum indirectly led to the American Revolution.

This means that pirates would certainly have known rum, which was something of a universal currency amongst sailors. But there's a gap in this story so large you could pilot a schooner through it. Piracy was an act of political sabotage largely directed by the English against the Spanish, and the Spanish colonies *weren't* the ones producing rum. Most rum came from Jamaica and Barbados - English holdings - and the Spanish colonies wouldn't start producing their own rum until much later.[92] This meant that any pirates raiding Spanish ports and looting Spanish ships would not be turning up bottles of rum but canary wines, madeira, port, sherry, and... maybe if they were very lucky... French brandy.

So what happened? Why do we now so inextricably link pirates and rum that Captain Morgan is the ambassador for the world's most popular rum brand? Well, it has to do with rum's image problem, one it has never quite shaken. It's right there in the name - rumbullion, an archaic term for an uproar,[93] and the American colonies' thirst for the stuff can't have helped.

American whiskies wouldn't start inching towards respectability for another century and a half, but the native drink of the Caribbean colonies has never quite shaken its party-time reputation. In other words, drinking rum in the eighteenth century was the modern equivalent of chugging a 4Loko or a Long Island Iced Tea. That's what accounts of Blackbeard were driving at when they characterized him as a rum-swilling maniac, and that's the image that stuck - pirates drank rum, that low, base, disgusting stuff they make out in the sticks. *The General History of Pirates* set the tone immediately:

> "...after they had got their vessel ready, in their usual debaucheries, they had taken a considerable quantity of rum and sugar, so that liquor was as plenty as water - and few there were, who denied themselves the immoderate use of it; nay, sobriety brought a man under a suspicion of being in a plot against the [crew], and in [that] sense, he was looked upon to be a villain that would not be drunk."[94]

This initial point, so vividly drawn in Johnson's fanciful text, passed into history as a tradition, a topos. But perhaps just as well, for without rum, we would have "yo-ho-ho and a bottle of madeira", which is not nearly so poetically satisfying.

And so we sail into the city aflame, the pirate band strikes up to the braying of a donkey, and the pirates degenerate into a swaying mass of inebriated vandals. The bare-footed pirate above the exit of the scene is holding a huge ceramic jug with flame shooting out the spout, a clever detail often overlooked. There's a pirate asleep in a pig stye and the fellow trying to escape with too many hats on his head; another favorite Davis gag. If Marc Davis isn't drawing people wearing silly hats then a sure topper is to put a sillier hat on top of a silly hat, because *what's funnier than hats on top of hats*? Nothing, that's what.[95]

Another buccaneer hangs off a lamp post with his torch, which would have been instantly recognizable to 60s audiences as a play on the cliche image of a drunk; notice there are no other lamp posts anywhere in the town.

Following the end of Prohibition through the 60s there was a great interest in "Gilded Age" drinking paraphernalia. Among the most common motifs was the old sawhorse of the drunk on the lamp-post, appearing on barware, ash trays, decanters, and lighted lamps. As we have already seen in the Tavern scene in the grotto, Marc loved his drunk gags, and had an impressive bar setup at home. The inclusion of this joke in Pirates is the 1960s equivalent of a "meme", an intentionally out of place gag that winks at the audience.

Really every figure in the Burning City scene is doing something funny, a calculated effort to blunt what is a pretty vividly realized crime scene. So how about it, are pirates bad guys? Well, I guess that depends on how you define a bad guy, doesn't it?

The Disney Studio product is so bizarrely different than the rest of its contemporaries that it can be hard to keep in mind that the Disney films were a product of Hollywood's Golden Age, which means they were subject to the same social conventions that shaped films as diverse as *Ben Hur* and *Casablanca*.

And the biggest concern that the Hollywood studios of that era had to face - besides schedules and budgets - was the Production Code. The Production Code existed to decide who a bad guy was.

Vintage Postcard

Hollywood, the films it produced, and the wide availability of those films had been viewed as suspicious from the very start. On Christmas Eve 1908, the Mayor of the City of New York ordered every single Nickelodeon closed on grounds that amounted to indecency and, as a minor side theater, inadequate fire exits. These sort of attacks never really slowed down, and by the start of World War I, most large cities had their own film censor boards, run as a side activity of the police or fire department. In retaliation against censorship the film companies attempted to invoke the First Amendment, but were overruled by the Supreme Court, which asserted that films were "a business, pure and simple".

These culture wars came to a head in the early 1920s, when the industry was rocked by a succession of scandals. The most visible was the Roscoe Arbuckle scandal, where the conservative press claimed (falsely) that the popular comedian had raped a young woman to death at a drunken party. There was also the murder of William Desmond Taylor, still unsolved, and the divorce and marriage of Mary Pickford and Douglas Fairbanks (divorce still being a scandalous affair in that age). All of these events led to an increasing public outcry for federal film censorship.

Hollywood struck back by hiring Will H. Hays, prominent conservative politician and a major player in the Warren G. Harding administration. Hays' job was to protect Hollywood product from censorship. But since so many states had different rules, this really involved navigating the numerous demands placed by censor boards in an effort to come to a consensus. In 1930 a formal set of rules was created; by 1934 Hays had appointed ultra-conservative Joseph I. Breen to ensure that the studios abided by this formal set of rules.

Because Disney produced animated cartoons - not musicals and crime pictures - the influence of the Code is rarely discussed in relationship to their productions. But The Code was such a pervasive influence on storytelling that it created norms which would have seemed so obvious to not even be worthy of mention. And in the case of criminal behavior, the Production Code is entirely clear: if you break the law, you've got to pay the price. This is why so many classic

Disney villains fall to their deaths: neat, clean, accidental... not-censorable.

Walt Disney and his animators had been working in, with, and under the Production Code their entire professional lives, as had every single movie they had ever seen. With a cultural influence that pervasive, it's impossible to imagine that it couldn't have had an effect on Pirates of the Caribbean, even if subconsciously. The attraction is a morality play and is entirely designed around the notion that pirates are villains. Think back to the production of *Treasure Island*, where Walt equated pirates with gangsters. As Marc Davis put it time and again, "*My primary concern is that none of this material was 'Disney.*"

Now, we can have a valid discussion about whether or not a group of terrorists looting and burning a town is really a good subject for entertainment - X Atencio expressed similar reservations to Walt Disney. But I reject entirely that Walt didn't know that his Rogue's Gallery was going to need a deft touch to maintain a delicate balance between a lightness of tone and the actual fact of what the pirates are doing.

But that tension has *nothing at all to do with Walt Disney and his staff*, that tension is the whole reason pirates remain stock characters in the English-speaking world; piracy is a flexible enough metaphor to withstand a good amount of bad behavior. From the very start with Johnson's *General History of Pirates* we see this dynamic playing out, with what Neil Renne terms a figure who

> "*Achieves complete personal self-gratification by means of an aggression that recasts the ideals of heroism into an ideology of self-assertion.*" [96]

If you try to pick apart that knot of contractions, to try to insist that pirates be one thing or the other, then you will kill what makes pirates special; you'll have not *The Pirates of Blood River* but *The Pirates Who Don't Do Anything*.[97] That cultural myth is why we remember Edward Teach - whose piracy career was relatively unsuccessful and short-lived - as Blackbeard, who is both a hero and a terror. Or Long John Silver, who is a scoundrel and a traitor and also a mentor and a father. Or the Pirates of the Caribbean, who do terrible things while they amuse and entertain us. You need both sides of that equation to have the correct invocation of the "*pirate myth*".

So I beg you: don't cut that knot. Those contradictions are why the whole thing works. It's the only thing keeping pirates moored into our reality.

It would be interesting to know who came up with the burning city finale. It seems to have been present in some form from the earliest incarnations of the show developed by Bruce Bushman[98] but of course Walt Disney, or John Hench, or really anybody could have suggested the idea. A fire is one of those bulletproof dramatic concepts for climatic action; it's used time and time again in Disney product from *Flowers and Trees* to *Dumbo*.

But really the big distinction is that Pirates of the Caribbean isn't a film; it has the immediacy of a lived - or perhaps more accurately *dreamed* - experience. The difference is memorialized in that oft-repeated story that the Anaheim fire department asked WED to install a special switch to turn off the fire illusion in case of actual fire.[99] This claim is really a brilliant bit of ad-pub - *the effect is so realistic, even fire fighters can't tell the difference!!*

But it's an absurd notion, because the effect doesn't look all that much like a real fire. There isn't even any smoke, something I'd bet you never considered until I just pointed it out. The obliviousness of the drunken, happy pirates only increases the surreal effect - any genuine human in that situation would soon be asphyxiating.

The scene works not because the flames are realistic but because the effect *looks* how a fire *feels* in your dreams, an impossible wall of flame engulfing everything. Bystanders watch on oblivious or helpless, like one of those slow-motion nightmares where you can't escape a threat.

It's a pure dream fire, summoned from the subconscious depths to tangible reality - a triumph of stage craft.

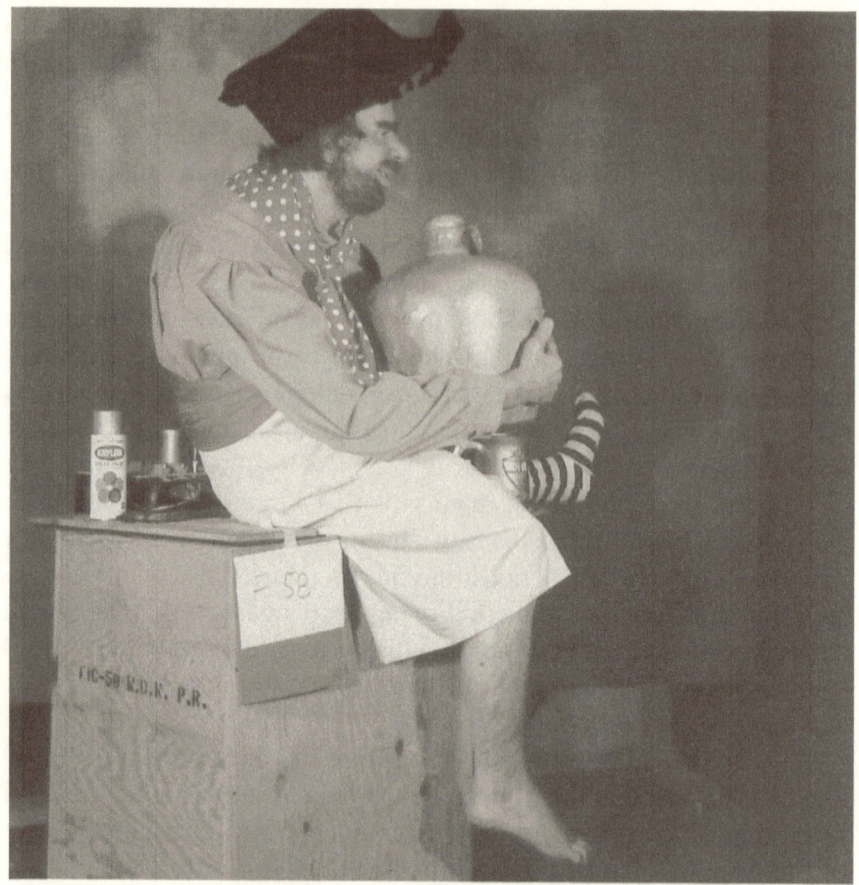

Courtesy Ted Linhart, Disneydocs.net

So, what was the first amusement enterprise? There had been devices and machines intended to amuse and entertain, but these were largely restricted to the upper classes. If you were of lesser means your chief public recreation was the theater. Some books on theme parks begin at medieval fairs, which doesn't seem right at all. So what makes a theme park, well, themed?

One possible answer to that is "fantastical illusion for an admission price", in which case the first truly "theme" experience could be The Panorama, created by painter Robert Barker.

Mr. Barker had hit on the idea to paint a scenic spot "in the round" by stringing together a sequence of flat canvas paintings so that they appeared seamless.[100] These indoor behemoths were illuminated with lanterns and accessed through observation platforms; patrons ascended a staircase and popped out in the center of the platform.

The result was immediate sensation and, just as it did following the debut of Disneyland, begat a deluge of imitators. But Robert Barker had done more than exhibit a colossal work of art; he had created one of the first simulations of reality available to paying visitors. The all-encompassing and optically correct simulation of an outdoor prospect in an indoor space opened a cognitive disconnect in the viewers, one which the human brain finds intensely pleasurable; you know what you're seeing cannot be true. As Eco put it, "*we not only enjoy a perfect imitation, we also enjoy the conviction that imitation has reached its apex and afterwards reality will always be inferior to it.*"

Double quick, iterations and improvements were foisted upon the Panorama. Soon, a panorama was made to rotate around the visitor. The Diorama followed thereafter, which didn't rotate the canvases but instead turned the entire audience in a darkened theater to face multiple painted scenes. Magic Lanterns added moving clouds and rainbows.

But the whole trouble with the Panorama and the Diorama is that these illusions required custom-built facilities to accommodate, which not every potential exhibitor could afford. The compromise this nascent industry landed on was not to hang the panorama, but to unwind it between rollers on a stage, making the whole production transportable. The act of rolling a picture through a frame meant that the entire prospect needs no longer be reproduced, and artists felt free to remove any views not of interest. This is very much like how theme parks would meticulously curate collections of architecture.

One common optical illusion which appeared in many panorama shows were fire and moonrise effects; illuminated rotating discs and hoisted oil lamps were deployed behind semi-translucent canvases, adding drama and optical illusions to the show. Sometimes, these shows began to resemble what could be called an amusement attraction. The most famous panorama lecturer of his day was Albert Smith, who recounted, apparently with much amusing humor, his adventures visiting far-flung ports of call. For his Alpine show *Albert Smith's Ascent of Mont Blanc*, Smith appeared on a stage which appeared to be the front of a Swiss Chalet, with a pond and water lilies separating him from the audience.[101]

But the most famous and influential multi-media showman of the era was John Nepomuk Maelzel. The climax of his show was always the same, a stage-filling illusion which drew on every aspect of stage magic and united them into a scene so awe inspiring that it marked those who saw it permanently: *The Conflagration of Moscow*.

This was a kind of diorama, with dimensional models in the foreground giving way to painted flats and then a variety of cloth backdrops — the set design of Pirates of the Caribbean uses the exact same diminishing scale tricks. The scene was the arrival of Napoleon's army in the city in 1812.

Maelzel rigged automated infantry to proceed across bridges in the foreground, with fire-pots and roman candles supplemented by boxes filled with falling pebbles to simulate musket fire. Carved channels filled with gunpowder produced weird colored light. As fire spread through the city, dozens of lanterns fitted with colored glass illuminated more and more of the scene, with the painted flats being pulled downwards by machines to appear to crumble in on themselves.

Historian Joseph Arrington prints an account from one woman:

> *"We quivered at the sight; saw men, women and children making their escape from the burning buildings, with packs of clothing on their backs. The scene was terrible, and so realistic that when we went to bed after returning from the spectacle, we hugged each other and rejoiced that our house was not on fire."*

This spectacle instantly produced imitations. One such knock-off show, performed by *"Miss Hall the American Enchantress"*, actually caused a court-house in Exeter, New Hampshire, to burn down for real in 1841.[102]

But if you reading this today and know the name John Nepomuk Maelzel at all, it's not for his fabulous burning city illusion, it's because he exhibited the famous chess-playing Turk automaton. Maelzel bought this from its inventor, Baron Wolfgang Ritten von Kempelen, and it wasn't a genuine automaton, but an elaborate hoax which kept intellectuals guessing for generations. But now we've gone back in time nearly 200 years only to end up where we started, with illusions of men ransacking a burning city.

Maelzel, Smith, and all of itinerant showmen who spun illuminated discs behind their moving panoramas are really part of a traditional area of human activity which reaches forward to Yale Gracey's indoor moon and wind-blown cellophane; the desire to capture baffling phenomena and place them on display. It's the same impulse which gave us not only dark rides but disaster films immemorial, where impossible things are harnessed and controlled.

We tend to think of theme parks as relatively modern phenomena, and indeed the entire term "theme park" has become something of a cultural synonym for the cheap and shallow. Disneyland may be a shrewd commercial reality, but if it wasn't always something *more*, then it wouldn't have lasted as long as it has.

Disneyland is an expression of a very real human need to play and pretend, to capture astonishment and awe in new and exciting ways.

iv. The Circle Closes

The pirate boats slip through a dark arch below the city in flames. There have been two small arched bridges dividing scenes in the ransacked city, but the attraction's arch imagery begins to return in force here, announcing that events are starting to cycle back to where we entered - to when the pirates were all dead.

Having widened out to encompass an open ocean, galleon with blazing cannon, and a city aflame, the world of the attraction again begins to tighten down on our little vessels as even the raucous music fades.

We find ourselves in some forgotten barrel-vaulted jail below the city. The roof of one of the three jail cells has already given way, spilling smoldering timbers down into the jail. The cell that is already buried was only home to a few skeletons, but the very much live and kicking pirates in the two remaining cells are looking to beat a hasty escape...

About those fallen timbers. As a painter, both in his fine art canvases and for the studio, Claude Coats was able to emphasize a sense of depth in his compositions, and as an attraction designer, he was continually able to bring out the best from very limited space by staging in depth. Uniquely in his attractions, Coats is willing to allow foreground elements to fall away into shadow to better frame and "sell" the depth illusions. This reached its gorgeous apotheosis in Horizons at EPCOT Center, but since that attraction is no more, think of the silhouetted tombstones in the graveyard jamboree of the Haunted Mansion, or the crumbling adobe walls at the start of the Grand Canyon Diorama which create the sensation of "stepping outside". So depth staging, especially silhouette foreground staging, combines with Coats playful sense of space and mastery of "reveal spaces" to create attractions which are as visually compelling now as they were when they were new.

Attractions mostly avoid these silhouette compositions today, but this example in the Jail Scene is really superb. The darkened timbers, illuminated only by glowing embers, hedge in and oppress the pirates in the jail cells beyond, giving dramatic urgency to their situation. A hanging chain adds dynamic visual interest, all topped with a lantern resting atop one of the fallen timbers to add a "motivated light" to the scene. The Jail would be repeated in later incarnations of the attraction, but never again given the masterful sense of depth composition here at Disneyland, and therefore never quite as effective at visualizing peril.

The Jail scene is another one of those prime, grade-A Marc Davis gags that looks easy but really requires an amazing amount of creative energy to pull off correctly. In this case it joins the Trapped

Safari scene on the Jungle Cruise and the stretching portraits in the Haunted Mansion as iconic examples of visual comedy done right, but this is also a case where context really improves the joke and makes it land. The pirate crew burning the city seem oblivious to the danger they're in, but here in the depths of the place are six pirates who know only too well what the consequences will be.

Contrasting their dire straits is the fact that a dog has the keys, so they cannot scream and wave their arms like anybody would be doing in reality because if they do the dog will run off. So these desperate men have to pretend to be very accommodating to the oblivious pup. The whole joke is probably the best contrast in the ride between the relatively grim material and the comedic tone its depicted in, a situation that's, as Billy Wilder once put it, *"hopeless... but not serious".*

But it also begins to cycle the attraction back around from its relatively raucous central action back into the morality play tone of the opening sections. The attraction is unambiguous about what reward is waiting for these men; even the ones who escape will die in the caverns of their absurd pirate haven, drinking rum that never stops pouring, counting gold they will never spend. There's a reason why the very first thing we see in the ride is a beach littered with the bones of pirates killed by their own crew. It's all a betrayal, an illusion. This is why you need the caverns at the start, why you need Dead Men Tell No Tales. It frames and sets expectations for the bad behavior enframed in the central section of the attraction, it's the necessary *editorial perspective.*

Turning a corner, the boats travel below the burning ruins of the city. The scene is crucial in that it is absolutely silent except for the sounds of the fire and the creaking of the city collapsing down upon the boats. There hasn't really been a truly quiet moment in the attraction since the Blue Bayou upstairs, where the croaking of frogs and chirping of crickets lulled us off into the ultimate dream. But the attraction pauses here and lets you linger for a moment simply on devastation; the timbers of the city will be crashing down into the sub-cellar very shortly. Every other version of the attraction whisks us off to the next scene after the fire, but here we pause for a moment. It's the first scene we've floated through in over five minutes that's totally desolate of human life. That absence is meaningful.

The truly superb Disney products have an incredible sense of varied paces and moods - the delicate interplay of joy and fear in *Snow White*, the great frieze of moving art in *Fantasia*, or even the pokey but perfectly judged adventure of *The Jungle Book*. Although it looks like absurd overkill on paper, Pirates of the Caribbean is one of the few rides to have a similar interplay of tones and feelings. The ride experience is not only captivating as it unfolds, but it provides constant, unhurried opportunities to reflect on its scale, its delicate moods, how truly beyond anything else it is. In this sense, in the willingness to go On Beyond Zebra, and in the willingness to take its time doing it, that we can sense the impression of Walt Disney at his best.

The "burning timbers" scene is also significant in that it is almost always broken, which is another reason it very probably wasn't repeated in any other version of the ride. The whole wooden structure above the boats is supposed to rock and sway. That's why there's a tiny chair and table up there - when the scene is in motion, it really looks as if they're about to come crashing down onto your head.

A bit further along are two big fat timbers that meet in a kind of "Y" shape above the boats; they're hinged and supposed to swing to and fro ominously. There are a few prop bottles on the timber that actually seem to roll back and forth while it's swaying. The whole scene is a kind of successor to the "spinning rock canyon" in the Mine Train thru Nature's Wonderland ride.

But it's also a moment where the audience is supposed to realize they're in danger. It's an interesting question if the pirates in the attraction are aware of our presence. The dead ones are for sure - the talking jolly roger speaks to us directly in the manner of the Ghost Host in the Haunted Mansion, and the ominous echoing voices in the caverns are warning *us* in particular. The "Pooped Pirate" also speaks directly to us, but otherwise the buccaneers seem entirely oblivious to our presence, making the central action contained in the port town even more like a movie, or a dream.

At last we come to the final scene, the arsenal. As originally built, the color coding of the attraction was quite explicit: the dim blue twilight of the bayou has been slowly shifting towards the flickering blood red of the arsenal over the course of the 15-minute experience. Everything in this room is coded to convey a sense of escalating danger, from the colors to the dozens of red barrels placed everywhere labeled "Explosivo". A giant cannon is pointed directly at the boats off to the right as they enter, subliminally increasing the sense of threat. A group of three barrels hang from a winch over the boats, threatening to knock us on our heads. Wooden boards hang precariously above the vessel, seeming almost close enough to touch, increasing the claustrophobia. To the left and right, drunken pirates are engaged in a shootout. Danger has finally closed in around us.

The attraction has mostly kept the pirate figures well away from us till now, but these guys at the end are right up in our faces, almost uncomfortably close. Even with the protective layer of the theme park environment, having a drunken pirate pointing a gun directly at your face is pretty alarming, like the cowboy who shoots at the camera in *The Great Train Robbery*. With bullets ricocheting off the walls, the guns being waved in our faces, and the flames licking the barrels, it's the climactic scene in the attraction - the sense of danger we were promised by the attraction marquee. When the scene was shown in television animated ricocheting bullets - complete with the sounds of passengers screaming - really played up the peril angle, perhaps better than the attraction does.

The boats often back up here and in the "burning timbers" scene, and I have to imagine the placement of the two biggest peril scenes in the attraction at the point where boats will be waiting to ride back to the top floor has to be intentional. The Arsenal scene originally was intended to be a dialogue scene, with the pirates barking such things as "*I be doing it with me eyes closed!*" and "*Somebody's rockin' the ruddy boat...*" as the pirates shoot back and forth at each other. This was changed to a simple reprise of the theme song, and I have to wonder if this change is what also prompted the placement of the theme song in the "upper grotto" after the first drop.

It's an interesting question if Disney really ever intended to have some effect of a massive explosion behind you on your way up the waterfall. This was depicted in the 1967 television special, and according to Imagineer Tom Morris, in a 1965 story meeting Walt suggested that the explosion "launch" the boats back to the surface. I think if any of these ideas got far beyond the ideation phase it would be obvious today; the return channel's just too darn wide and open for any real chance of effects lights to carry the notion of an explosion. It's perhaps just as well but it's a real example of how Walt Disney had trained his staff to try and exploit every angle for show value.

As they have since 1966, the boats calmly scoot up the waterfall and out of danger. This is an interesting inversion of standard attraction design - think of how many rides you've been on in your life that begin by hoisting the ride vehicles up a hill. Pirates of the Caribbean ends how most rides begin, all because Walt Disney did the opposite of most attractions and dug his building into the ground. This opens up a nest of associative possibilities, possibilities exploited by the trip up the waterfall at the end of the attraction.

Next door, the Haunted Mansion is literally buried underground, but we don't have the strong sense of inhabiting a subterranean world that we get at Pirates. Some of this has to do with the fact that the subterranean part of pirates is *literally designed to look underground*, but our sense of orientation is flattered by being able to sense that we are literally beneath the areas we traversed on foot as we entered. We have no strong sense of where we could be besides somewhere below. Thus, literalizing our return to the surface adds a pleasing circularity to the experience that's difficult to describe.

One remarkable thing about Pirates is that's its somehow still enthralling even when nothing is happening. As we slowly ratchet our way upwards to the surface, the sense of dream logic is only compounded by the sense of returning to a place we already know but which is in no way any less fantastic. As the boats ascend, the pleasing blue of the bayou comes back into view, framed through one last enframing arch, the door home. George Brun's moody, peaceful Pirates Overture can be heard again, as the boats crest one final hill and splash down in the bayou. The boats return to Lafitte's Landing - we stop to look up at the sign, everyone does - and we disembark, strolling along the trellised exit.

Taken by the Author, January 2022

Part of the power of Pirates of the Caribbean is that it is basically a ghost story, one sprung on us as a surprise. We enter expecting adventure, but instead we find ourselves in a doomed time loop, as the cannons fire endlessly, the town burns endlessly. The pirates of the Caribbean are just like their picked bones we encounter as we enter - pinned down in place for all time. Most theme park attractions place us in the midst of extraordinary events that we simply stumble upon - we just happen to be in New York City while the Statue of Liberty is stolen, we just happen to be saved by Indiana Jones. Aren't we lucky! By presenting its narrative as a time slip, we can return again and again to the events of Pirates of the Caribbean, preserved under some supernatural glass dome, with no such accommodation.

So we step back out into the California sunlight inside a pocket version of New Orleans. How do we feel?

Author Griel Marcus birthed his own Disneyesque myth when he coined the phrase "The Old, Weird America". He describes the impact of the experience on riders, leaving them "*utterly, fabulously confused, half-humiliated, half-filled with wonder.*"

Charles Moore, who cleverly described all of Los Angeles as a "series of rides" with Disneyland as its true downtown, was a bit churlish, but only because he prefers the Haunted Mansion (for which we can forgive him). "*It's astonishing how this pin-brained apotheosis of sloth and stupidity can be so fascinating.*" I think he was referring to the pirates as stupid, but I'm not sure.

Umberto Eco, as usual, is enthusiastic about the artifice, coasting on clouds of dense, gorgeous words:

> "The pirates moved, danced, slept, popped their eyes, sniggered, drank - really. You realize that they are robots, but you remain dumbfounded by their verisimilitude. [...] The pirates and ghosts sum up all of Disneyland, at least from the point of view of our trip, because they transform the whole [park] into an immense robot, the final realization of the dreams of the eighteenth-century mechanics who gave life to the Writer of Neuchatel and the Chess-playing Turk."

A more common review, which can be heard by simply standing at the exit at any time: "Can we go again?"

I can only speak for myself, but upon experiencing this attraction for the first time, I was gobsmacked. I grew up with the version in Florida, which is a very good ride, but this version was deeper, wider, denser - the difference between a swimming pool and an ocean. Each time I've returned the spell has repeated itself, but for me it was exactly the right experience at exactly the right time in my life, and the horizon it has unfolded for me is still ongoing.

What did the WED design staff think about it? My overall impression is that they were a little confused - they thought they were building a rollicking adventure and ended up with a fatalistic morality play.

Only with the passing of time did the special achievement become apparent: "*Those mystery caverns at the start worked very well*" Marc Davis later admitted to The E Ticket. Marty Sklar put a pin on it in his autobiography: "*Ultimately,* [Pirates] *would become the most valuable single property ever created in the theme park business.*"[103]

How about Walt Disney?

It's curious that a creative talent who according to his daughter couldn't even attend a funeral would turn at the end of his life to two attractions with such a morbid bent - Pirates of the Caribbean and the Haunted Mansion. He didn't get very far into the Mansion, but Pirates was all his - as X Atencio confirmed, "*He had seen the show pretty much complete, the only thing missing was having him at the opening day.*"[104]

Depositing these two rather dark attractions inside an area themed to New Orleans - an American city better associated with culture and festivity - is one of those Walt Disney creative decisions that seems inexplicable on the face of it. But the contrast is brilliant, as sharply etched as the southern sun falling across a shaded portico. The New Orleans area is inviting, soothing, comfortable. Moore described it:

> "*This setting is not a reconstruction but an impressionist interpretation of a piece of the American past. The considerable conviction of the New Orleans-inspired detailing in these intimate spaces creates a sensuously romantic, swashbuckling, yet gentle scene.*"[105]

Pirates of the Caribbean and the Haunted Mansion hold down the north and south side of this area; taken together, New Orleans Square at Disneyland is arguably the best and most important piece of themed design ever attempted. There are numerous parallels and connections between the two attractions because they were created by the same creative team in sequence. But they don't seem redundant; each seems to be a necessary flip side to the other. Pirates of the Caribbean is an amusing but creepy parable that crime doesn't pay; the Haunted Mansion is a creepy but amusing adventure where death isn't all that bad. Both of these literal underworlds are bizarrely contained in an area of so much life, creativity, and energy.

Those connections go deep. Back when New Orleans Square was just two separate deskfuls of ideas spearheaded by Bruce Bushman and Ken Anderson, Anderson planted the idea that the "Ghost House" was haunted by a sea captain and his murdered bride. The idea likely suggested itself by the nearby docking area for the Columbia Sailing Ship, a forthcoming addition to Disneyland when both men were working on their proposals in the late 1950s.

The Columbia still docks in front of the Haunted Mansion, which still contains one very dead bride, and the sailing ship is used at night as a pirate ship in Fantasmic, just as it was on the press day for Pirates of the Caribbean. And speaking of, they're auctioning brides inside the attraction. And that painted pirate lady behind the bar in the caverns, she looks an awful lot like the portrait of a Grecian woman who transforms into Medusa in the Haunted Mansion...

We can play these games all day, but the point is, they go back to the inception of both attractions. But these subconscious, subliminal linkages are more than just a parlor game for Disneyland obsessives. At Magic Kingdom in Florida, where Haunted Mansion and Pirates of the Caribbean are on opposite sides of the park, most visitors still intuit a connection between them, because to be a fan of one is to be a fan of the other. But here at Disneyland, where they sit side by side, their true nature can be perceived. They're like a great A side and a great B side, all sharing either side of the same material - pirates, ghosts, and ghost pirates.

Taken by the Author, January 2022

I think it may be useful to see Pirates as essentially three distinct rides, each of which interweaves and informs the others, much like one of Irving's multi-narrator novels. The legend of the Pirates of the Caribbean exists everywhere and nowhere at once, hanging over the bayou, the caverns, and the town - locations stretched across time and geography - the same way the legends of Kidd, Teach and Lafitte create interchangeable pirates who never were. This surely contributes to the sensations of lucid dreaming, that the pieces of the story don't quite add up.

So what Walt gave us was an attraction which pieces together little scraps of what we "already know" about pirates, cultural memories that they bury treasure and drink rum, effectively dispensing with the need for any exposition whatever. It weaves out of these cultural memories a new powerful mythology, steeped in fatalism and circular in structure.

It all feels *so right* it's almost like we've known it before - like we've always known it. What could have seemed disjointed comes off as thrilling; each new turn of the plot seems infused with some baleful significance which can only be guessed at.

Pirates of the Caribbean is an American myth. It's built of second-hand stuff, but as author Simon Callow pointed out, the idea is nothing beside execution; the real creator is the person who can liberate the idea's potential.

Walt Disney's attraction did this for piracy, and in the process supplanted all previous pirate myths that came before it. To be a pirate was to be from Disneyland.

Decades later, X Atencio was at the beach and saw some boys playing pirate; they were singing " *Yo Ho, Yo Ho, A Pirate's Life For Me*" as if it were a real sea shanty. For those boys and millions since, the attraction has become **the brand name** in timber-shivering. Every return to its subterranean netherworld is like going home again.

Part Three
EXOTIC PORTS of CALL

IX. PIRATES OF THE CARIBBEAN AT WALT DISNEY WORLD

"Can management produce Disney product after Disney? That's the sixty-four-dollar question."
- Walt Disney, Fortune Magazine, May 1966

"Man the tiller and hold on tight - thar be squalls ahead!"
- Talking Skull, Pirates of the Caribbean Florida

i. The Pirates Are Coming! The Budget Cuts Are Here!

Walt was dead, to begin with.

That's where the trouble really started. Walt Disney Productions was entirely centered around pleasing one guy: Walt Disney. He had trained his creative team to tailor all of their decisions and suggestions around this immutable fact, this immobile pillar around which everything turned. This arrangement flattered the ego of Walt Disney, but it did nothing to help them when Walt Disney ceased to be on December 15, 1966.

Compounding the problem, Walt Disney's creative strategy was to let his artists run wild then pick their best ideas. The canny ones would learn over their careers to aim to produce work that would appeal specifically to Walt, but in the end the entire creative pipeline was based around a narrowing funnel of concepts with Walt Disney as the faucet at the end of the pipe.

As Randy Bright remembered, "*Walt left an organization that wasn't used to making decisions. It was used to saying, 'Well, [Walt] will tell us if it's right or not.*"[1] This meant that there was no particular reason to foster a community spirit; once Walt turned his back on the studio's animation pipeline in the early sixties the group degenerated into factionalism and in-fighting.

Indeed, the entire leadership structure of the studio was bifurcated. Walt hired people he saw promise in and put them to work upon (often ill-defined) tasks; Roy Disney hired financial guys he trusted to check in and make sure the artistic types weren't going to take over the asylum. This created sometimes bizarre situations. There was one four-year period where Walt and Roy refused to speak to each other over a contract dispute, communicating through a limited array of people who straddled the lines between the opposing camps.

The whole point of Walt setting up WED Enterprises separate from the studio is that it gave him a place to go to hang out with his kind of people, the creative types, without having to deal with Roy, the animation union, or motion picture people. "*When Walt died, Roy had been in the WED building only once, to my knowledge, and Card (Walker) and Donn (Tatum) not at all.*"[2] recalled Marty Sklar. Walt Disney was the duct tape holding everything together and his presence disguised deep seated problems.

With Walt now gone, Roy Disney stepped in to see his brother's final few projects through to reality - the projects currently underway at Disneyland (Pirates of the Caribbean, the new Tomorrowland, and the Haunted Mansion), the college of the arts up in Valencia, and the huge new resort complex down in Florida. To give Roy all of the credit he is due, this was one of the single most courageous acts in the history of American business. Disney in 1966 was just a rinky-dink studio with a small group of old timers making cartoons on their own schedule, a few soundstages, and one park down the highway in Anaheim. Four thousand employees, total.

There was a great temptation here to cut losses and cancel some or all of these projects, but Roy did not. Walt Disney World saw Disney and WED jumping feet first into political negotiations with the state of Florida, city planning, zoning regulations, environmental control, infrastructure like power and drainage... on top of operating two hotels and an entirely new theme park. It was an insane venture, a leap out into the stratosphere - and it paid off voluminously. It also changed the company forever in ways nobody could have predicted.

Roy insisted on doing the Florida project right, completing the initial build-out of Walt Disney World to the highest standard possible. He rode every ride, just as Walt would have done, to verify its excellence - even the carousel. The construction dragged on and on, ballooning to $400 million and almost depleting the company's cash reserves. Roy soldiered on. He let the creative staff express their perfectionism. Disney made the construction crews tear down the canopy over the carousel and start over because it was two inches off spec.[3] Walt Disney World opened in October 1971, it was considered successful by Thanksgiving, and Roy Disney died a few days before Christmas.

Unlike Walt, Roy had picked a successor... but it didn't entirely work out that way.

Who ended up running the company was a conglomerate of individuals headed by Donn Tatum, a sharp former television executive who had risen to a place on the Board of Directors through the 1960s. Donn was a Roy guy, although he was one of the few who could move between both spheres with ease. Waiting in the wings was Card Walker, a publicist who was firmly in the Walt camp. With Walt and Roy gone, the last person left in an executive role to insulate the creative types at WED from the Board of Directors and stockholders was Richard Irvine, the former 20th Century Fox art director who was in charge of WED.

Despite these corporate upheavals, cultural change down on "Cannibal Island" arrived only slowly. Following the development and opening of the Haunted Mansion at Disneyland, Marc Davis began to seriously attack the question of what to do with all of the company's new land out in Florida. From his earliest days at WED, he had been encouraged by Walt to go out to Disneyland and see what worked with the public and what could be improved. Lessons learned in the Enchanted Tiki Room were amplified and improved in Country Bear Jamboree. Lessons learned at the Carousel of Progress resulted in The Hall of Presidents. Marc began to consider what an improved version of Pirates of the Caribbean would have looked like.

"*My feeling kind of was, 'Why take Pirates to Florida?' when they've been promoting pirates for several hundred years down there.*

PART THREE: EXOTIC PORTS OF CALL

Souvenir Slide, Author's Collection

And everything is kind of pirate named, so I thought it would be kind of great to take the West to the East."[4] Westerns remained a viable genre through the late 60s; the stretch from 1965 to 1970 saw *Bonanza, Gunsmoke*, or some combination of the two in the top-rated television programs. The same era gave us memorable westerns such as *Cat Ballou, True Grit, The Professionals*, and *Hang 'Em High*, not to mention a glut of classic westerns earlier in the decade.

Marc's concept was appropriately grandiose, housed in three giant buildings bisected by the Walt Disney World Railroad, all covered in artificial rocks to resemble Monument Valley. Across the top of the butte, a runaway mine train, a log flume, and hiking trails carried passengers through an updated version of the Nature's Wonderland attraction from Disneyland. Some versions of the show building have a restaurant in the boarding area, carried over from the

Blue Bayou. But all of this was in service of the show inside, the Western River Expedition.

Western River Expedition took the dramatic beats of Pirates of the Caribbean and reworked them into a musical western. Instead of the stylized but still tactile world of Pirates, Western River was to be a boldly unrealistic satire of the genre, with color styling by Mary Blair. And every single character in the attraction was intended to be singing an attraction theme which would progress from cowpoke ballad to a double time rag to a sparsely pounded rhythm on First Nations drums. Marc wrote in a 1968 outline: "*Spoken dialogue will be minimal. This attraction is basically a musical, treated in a theatrical manner. It takes place in the American Southwest and we will attempt to visualize the setting with exciting shapes and color.*"

Guests would embark on boats through a canyon at sunset, then enter a cave where stalagmites resemble Western animals and the dripping sound of water introduces the theme music. Outside the cave under an indigo sky, the song is picked up by lone cowpokes around a campfire, mooed by cattle, and howled by coyotes.

Around the bend, a group of masked bandits have held up the stagecoach - their horses wear masks, too. Their song is played in ominous mariachi style by their resident *guitarró*. The bandits indicate in song that they will meet up with the boats again.

The boats head into a Western town, where the whole place is rollicking on a Saturday night - saloon girls sing in a chorus line, a medicine show is in town and one cowboy has gotten his horse up onto the roof of the saloon. Marc recalls: "*I wanted to do things with colored lights against these cliffs so that you had a feeling that maybe the sun was kind of setting... I wanted to do things in a way that you wouldn't expect with this material.*"[5]

Around the bend, bandits have knocked over the Assay Office and are in a shootout with the sheriff, a dainty Calamity Jane type. One man has joined the fight at the door of the Barber Shop, still covered in shave cream.[6] The boats travel through the shootout; at the end of the street the Mortician stands ready in his doorway in anticipation.

The boats pass out onto the plains where the native peoples now play the drums of a rain dance; the rain is pouring down only where the circle dances. The storm increases in intensity as water begins to pour down the sides of a canyon; the boats begin to chug up a waterfall. At the top of the falls, riders find themselves in a forest set afire by lightning strikes, the trees creaking and threatening to crash down onto the boats. Dead ahead are the bandits and their masked horses, ready to demand your money or your life. The boats slip down a waterfall to escape, splashing down back into the canyon at sunset.

The Western River Expedition went through numerous design incarnations between 1968 and 1971. Cut was the interior restaurant, the exterior flume and train ride (the latter would shortly return), and an introductory sequence where the boats pass through a huge diorama alongside the Walt Disney World Railroad where bears cavort in a forest.

This "full strength" version was current as of 1969 and the initial promotional frenzy for Walt Disney World, meaning it was featured in many early promotional images for the resort, leading to decades of rumors of insane cost overruns. In reality WED was indecisive and already cutting the thing down; the 1970 model for Walt Disney World shown at the Preview Center included the huge show building but without the runaway train or log flume.

By December 1971 the attraction had gotten down to fighting weight, the purest distillation of its best ideas. The diorama of the American West had become the opening "night on the prairie" sequence and much of the fat from the attraction had been pared away. As part of initial construction for Magic Kingdom the land was cleared and a conduit tube for the DACs system[7] was run to the attraction site. Marc Davis was hopeful... the WED model shop even began sculpting coyotes and buffalo for the opening sequence. But it was not to be.

Western River Expedition had been cut from the opening lineup for the Magic Kingdom - alongside the costly Space Mountain roller coaster complex, which was pretty much all of Tomorrowland. The costs on Walt Disney World had ballooned from $100 million to $400 million, and in order for Magic Kingdom to be a successful full day experience, large-ticket attractions had to be sidelined. The most elaborate attraction, The Haunted Mansion, had its development costs split between Disneyland and Walt Disney World, with the attraction versions manufactured in sequence. Much of WED's efforts went into three new theater shows, since it was thought that visitor demographics would skew older and folks would want a place to get out of the heat.

Country Bear Jamboree and the Hall of Presidents would be substantial hits, but the most complex, The Mickey Mouse Revue, never quite attracted the audiences it could have. Pirates was nowhere to be found. At this time Disney made its best revenue by selling ticket books, with attractions labeled A through E, bound together and sold for costs ranging from $3.95 to $5.95. The latter number is nearly equivalent to $40 today, and the park would need to have a full array of each kind of ticketed ride. As Operations chief Dick Nunis put it, "*To add that one attraction we would have had to eliminate five more.*"[8]

There were other issues at Walt Disney World besides construction costs, however.

The new park had opened with just too little of just about everything. Marty Sklar recalled to The E Ticket:

> "*We really didn't have a breather because we had to meet some surprising demands from the public. Buzz Price had originally projected six million people for Walt Disney World's first year. By the time we were really building the Florida site in 1969, Disneyland was already getting eight million a year. We tried to increase the capacity to handle eight million, and we felt a constant pressure during the Florida development. [...] But soon we were doing over ten million the first year alone.*"[9]

Roy Disney stated in the company's 1970 annual report that "*This increased scope has necessitated the addition of several rides and the expansion of others, which, in turn, has given rise to some substantial additional costs.*"

WED had carried over the open-air queues found at Disneyland without taking into account Florida's punishing sun and rain; a roof structure had to quickly be built over the Mad Tea Party. Popular attractions got whole enclosed shaded queue extensions: 20,000 Leagues Under the Sea, The Haunted Mansion, The Jungle Cruise, and the Hall of Presidents. Even worse, the demographics were skewing far younger than Disney had expected, and all of these teenagers and young adults were asking for a thrill ride.

Just as problematic was feeding people. Several restaurants that had been delayed in the rush to open were quickly brought online. There was nothing in Tomorrowland but a big orange wall; a hole was cut into the side of it and pizzas were sold through the new window. A small stretch of Fantasyland facades was pressed into service as a new food service window. A small building behind the antiques shop in Liberty Square sold cold sandwiches. Orlando journalist Edward Prizer documented the chaos on the ground:

> "Even more urgent than the opening of new attractions has been the problem of attending to two of the basic requirements for the park's operation: transportation and feeding. With an average day's crowd, it's been possible to move guests smoothly from the main entrance to the theme park aboard the present monorails, trams, and steamships. But just let a swarm of extra people descend on the place and soon there are long lines waiting to get across to the scene of the action. I've had to wait as long as an hour, myself. Then, once you're in the park, it has on occasion been a real challenge to get into a restaurant or up to a food counter for some grub to assuage a rampant appetite. All the smiling in the world doesn't pacify a crowd of hungry guests."[10]

Restaurants weren't the only thing missing. Guest after guest said the same thing: that they wanted to see that Pirates of the Caribbean ride which they had seen on television.

By December 1971, Western River Expedition had reached its final, streamlined form. Disney could begin building it on its reserved plot of land in Frontierland at the end of the street at any time. It's very likely that Roy Disney may have approved it to move forward, had he not died. But now the new leadership team of Donn and Card faced a choice: move forward on Western River, or give the people what they had asked for.

The December 71 version of Western River was in many respects very comparable to the version of Pirates they ended up building. It was housed in a similarly sized building; it would have been about the same length and had roughly the same number of figures. Intriguingly, a December 10th 1971 memo regarding expenditures at Walt Disney World speaks of forthcoming features including the Plaza Swan Boats, Space Mountain, and even a sports complex and a "Willie the Whale" marine life complex. But next to Frontierland Train Station, where the Western River ride was to be built, it simply reads: "Hold on Area Development".[11]

Western River was expected to be built on a cul-de-sac at the end of the street in Frontierland, situated off by itself on the edge of town. In terms of realistic places that Pirates of the Caribbean could be situated in Magic Kingdom, only an unoccupied stretch of land beside the Jungle Cruise made any sense. This land was not studied and prepared for an attraction, and to build it, Disney was going to have to move the railroad.

But it presented new opportunities too, because this area was on the obverse side of the existing Pecos Bill Cafe restaurant, meaning an additional food location could be built there without the need to build a new kitchen.[12] Instead of building one attraction off on its own at the edge of Frontierland, this vacant land could be capitalized on to offer restaurants and shops alongside a similarly budgeted thrill attraction and additional pedestrian space.

It was a puzzling series of decisions, especially given that Disney had already invested significant amounts of money in Western River, including drawing up the construction sheets. Maybe Card Walker lost his nerve, maybe Marty Sklar had his thumb on the scale.

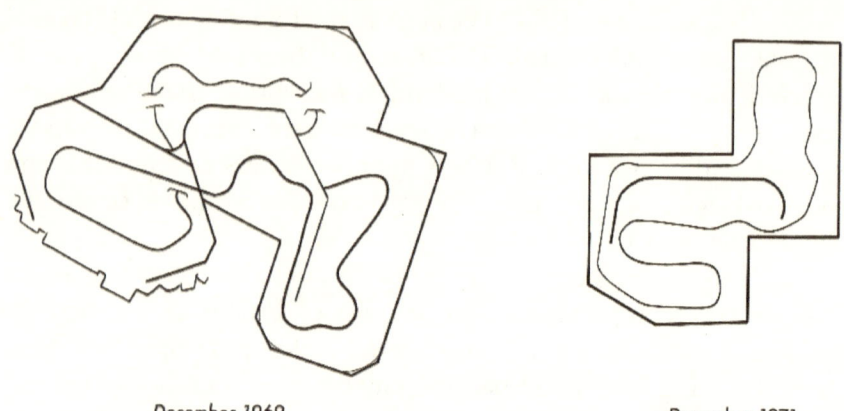

December 1969   December 1971

Sklar later remarked, "*The sketches that Marc did are really quite wonderful. But I wonder if that thing had been built, if we could have afforded both the time and the money.*"[13] Card Walker decided to go for Pirates in April 1972,[14] Marc Davis was assigned to work on new scenes for this compact version, and the window of opportunity for Western River Expedition closed. Tony Baxter recalls:

> "*Very quickly, WED knew they had a problem and moved forward with ways to get a pirate ride down in Florida as soon as possible. [...] John Hench had always felt that the caves were unnecessary due to the fact that the basement area they occupied at Disneyland was a leftover space planned for the Wax Museum. This sped up the construction effort and reduced the cost considerably.*"

Charlie Ridgway spoke to the Tampa Tribune and referred to the Pirates of the Caribbean construction being underway by Fall.[15] The paper noted, "*Many of the visitors have asked why it is missing at Disney World*", a constant refrain from Disney through this whole period. The cost for the attraction and surrounding area was $10 million.[17] Interestingly, Ridgway did mention the "Western River Ride" as a forthcoming attraction, a sentiment echoed by publicist

Truman Myers a few months later. But by December 1972, Western River was out and Dick Nunis was speaking more regularly of a "Thunder Mountain Railway" alongside such familiar forthcoming attractions as Space Mountain and the PeopleMover.

Interestingly, Disney did heavily feature Western River Expedition in the post-show area of The Walt Disney Story in May 1973, suggesting that at least somebody still thought it was a good enough idea to promote it to the first generation of park goers. In display cases alongside a segment of the legendary attraction model, the ride was introduced by "Hoot Gibson", an animatronic owl whose design dates back to Marc's work on *Bambi* and *So Dear To My Heart*. He introduced himself as "the star" of the upcoming attraction and lectured on the programming of audio animatronics - there is no concept art anywhere showing such an owl figure as part of the attraction, making the whole thing even weirder. It's very likely that Hoot Gibson aside, Western River was unofficially buried by this time.

The publicity for Pirates churned along all through 1973. Buttons were distributed to Cast Members across the resort: "*The Pirates Are Coming!*".[17]

By October and November 1973, Disney was trooping reporters through the construction zone. The Orlando Sentinel marveled as Wathel Rogers demonstrated the programming of animatronic figures. "*We determine their actions - their major changes of position. The computer is programmed to take care of the small in-between motions that make an act or gesture lifelike.*"[18] This was indeed a big leap forward for Wathel, who remembered using second-hand 78 records to program the California show six years earlier.

Wathel posed for a publicity shot with two prisoner figures and Marc's pirate parrot. As generations of later visitors would be, the Sentinel was most taken by the bird: "*Moving through it all is Pegleg Parrot, a swashbuckling creature with his beak into everything - including a farewell admonishment to "watch out for the moving gangplank".*

Orlandoland Magazine editor Edward L. Prizer got the dream tour - a walkthrough with Yale Gracey and Fred Joerger, deep into construction. Prizer describes Gracey as having "*the liquid blue eyes of a dreamer and that fleeting pixie expression I've come to recognize amongst the creative people who worked around Walt Disney.*" For Yale's part, he said: "*Walt Disney invented the title of "Illusioneer" for me. I had a white robe that I'd put on when he brought people in to see me.*"[19]

Joerger was focused on bringing the show in on time: "*Our biggest problem is unlearning men what they've done their whole lives. The plasterers and stone masons are used to getting everything perfectly square and even. We have to teach them to make things look rough and out of line.*" Prizer interrupts: "*A plasterer grinned down from a scaffold where he was applying cement to a cornice. 'Be sure to take a hammer and hit that a few times" Mr. Joerger called to him.*"

Disney got the show open in time to deal with the Christmas crowds on December 15, 1973. This was just weeks after the Oil Embargo hit, causing nationwide gas shortages. In those days, most visitors arrived at Disney World by car, posing a very real problem. Disney set up a hotline so motorists could find the nearest gas station with a supply of petrol. Immediately, almost anything not already underway was cancelled - Disney very seriously was ready to pull the plug on Space Mountain, but construction had already gone vertical. Imagineering staff was cut from 480 to 150.[20]

The end of Western River may have been a loss for the art of themed design, but it was the correct decision for the better good of the park to move ahead with Pirates. Westerns began declining in popularity as an everyday genre, replaced with other action-adventure concepts like science fiction and superheroes. Members of the Ogala Lakota forcibly occupied Wounded Knee South Dakota in 1973, creating new awareness of the unjust treatment of Native Americans and making it even more difficult to treat them comically in a new attraction.[21]

Just as significant was the retirement of Richard Irvine as head of WED Enterprises in 1973. Responsibility now passed on to Marty Sklar and John Hench, and they were aligned with Card Walker in

IX. Pirates of the Caribbean at Walt Disney World 175

aggressively pursuing the development of EPCOT - not as a city of the future, but as a permanent, prestigious Worlds' Fair for the computer age. After America Sings, Marc found it harder and harder to get management interested in his ideas. He took to posting his artwork on display in the halls of WED with notes attached: "See Marc for more details!". They never came.

Frustrated, Marc Davis formally retired from WED in 1977. His talent in the field has never been equaled.

Vintage Promotional Photo, Courtesy Orlando Public Library

I don't think it's unfair to say that Pirates of the Caribbean in Florida represents the attraction that WED thought they were building in the mid-60s.

Let's run down the major alterations: an atmosphere of high adventure is established from the start, without the strange left turns into mystery. It has a streamlined action in which the setting does not fluctuate wildly as it does in California. There is no time travel conceit - WED places you in a setting evocative of the action of the ride, as you survive a night raid on a Caribbean seaport.

The action is linear, the setting unified between the attraction and its surrounding area, there are no contradictions or ambiguities. It's also the weakest version of the ride that exists.

Which is *not* to say that Pirates in Florida is a *bad* ride, it's one of the best in the park. But in every other park that has a Pirates of the Caribbean, that attraction is the "brand name" for the most elaborate attraction in the park: the show stopper. At Magic Kingdom in Florida, Haunted Mansion and Pirates are almost inverse cases. The Mansion in Florida was revised and allowed to grow into an ideal form of itself, whereas Pirates was revised and shrunk.

Of course, millions have grown up with Florida Pirates and they like it just fine, and the second incarnation of the attraction is extremely innovative, even if its innovations don't really result in a better experience. When WED brought Pirates East, they experimented and discovered that - surprise! - what made Pirates tick was not what they had expected at all. The error would not be repeated, leaving Florida Pirates a dead limb on the family tree, a mutant abnormality.

But there are good ideas in it... even if they don't fully gel... and one of the best is the area surrounding the attraction, Caribbean Plaza. It's a bit too easy to bag on Caribbean Plaza, especially compared to New Orleans Square. It was among the first WED projects to really be under strict time and money restrictions, and as with Bear Country at Disneyland, they definitely got what they paid for. One big issue is that of pure size. The forced perspective scale of Magic Kingdom gradually shrinks the further away from Main Street you get. This was an intentional strategy; Western River Expedition was expected to be rendered as a huge Monument Valley-style butte at the far end of the park, so the scale of Frontierland was pulled lower and lower the nearer to its footprint the architecture rambled.[22] Built just on the opposite side of the smallest scale area in the park, Caribbean Plaza doesn't have much space or height to work with, and certain extremely downscale and markedly unconvincing upper-level windows and porticos on the side nearest Frontierland make this area look even more toy-like than most of the park.

Approaching Caribbean Plaza from Adventureland, there are certain grace notes. The area is introduced with a visual rhyme. Adventureland's central structure is the Balinese pagoda of the Enchanted Tiki Room, a symbol of a world ruled by mysterious pagan gods. Just past this, our view slips away and another tower comes into view: a Caribbean Clock Tower, attached to a hulking fortification. Here as in the rest of Magic Kingdom, the clock represents order, stability: clocks appear on the Main Street Station, City Hall, Cinderella Castle... heck, even the Hall of Presidents. Clocks are for authority figures... squares.

Throughout Adventureland the foliage spills forth from all sides, encroaching onto the pedestrian path and here and there held back only by fences made of split logs - temporary, haphazard stuff. As we head towards Caribbean Plaza formal planters begin to appear. The random rocks and textured "green ground" pavement transitions to orderly cobblestone. Everything about Caribbean Plaza speaks to a colonizing power plunked down into the middle of the jungle bringing their economic and military authority. The Spanish colonial settlement has tamed the jungle, or at least believe they have. But the pirates are coming...

WED embraced Spanish Revival architecture for Caribbean Plaza. This style was extremely vogue-ish in the 1920s and a lot of Los Angeles was built in it; the keynote was whitewashed stucco, red tile roofs, and shaded porticos with dark wood beam ceilings. It was differentiated from the earlier Mission Revival by embellishing all with brightly painted tiles, splashing fountains, and lots of lots of dark wrought iron accent pieces. The result looked nothing like actual Spanish Colonial architecture but an awful lot like Hollywood soundstage recreations of "Old Mexico" or "Cuba"; one practically expects Wallace Beery to stroll by wearing a sombrero. All of this means that if you grew up in Los Angeles, which is nearly all Imagineers, it feels an awful lot like WED simply raided the hardware store to put Caribbean Plaza together.

But I think this is a case where WED knew what they were doing. A lot of Magic Kingdom was re-thought to work better for an East Coast audience; Disney expected most of their visitors to come from New York State and the Upper Midwest.[23] This is the whole reason why Main Street was re-conceptualized from a Midwest small town into a booming East Coast resort city, and why Liberty Square presents scenes from Philadelphia and New England. These were fantasy locations that they expected their audience to recognize. The Revival style creates for this audience an atmosphere of romance quite removed from any of their day-to-day experience.

The rear of the Caribbean Plaza is anchored by the Castillo del Morro, which marks the entrance to the attraction. There's actually three real life Castillos del Morro; one in San Juan Puerto Rico, one in Havana, and the other in Santiago de Cuba. All three of these were built to repel 16th century raiding parties, meaning they were veterans of the actual pirate wars. All three share features which were evocatively smushed together by Disney, although the example in Santiago - the *Castillo de San Pedro de la Roca* - looks the nearest to what they built. Disney, of course, did not have access to Cuba in the 1970s, so a lot of the colors and textures of the Castillo in Caribbean Plaza were drawn from the example in Puerto Rico.

Another nice detail lost to time is that the cannons lining the roof of the Castillo actually used to let loose with volleys of cannon fire. A patch of broken plaster hides a speaker, and plumes of mist used to shoot from each cannon as they went off. This was sometimes loud enough to be heard from Main Street. Besides drawing guests deeper into Adventureland to find the attraction, this helped liven up Caribbean Plaza considerably. The cannons ceased firing in 2006 with the introduction of Captain Jack Sparrow's Pirate Tutorial; this show was intended to run for one summer only but was finally ended after a dozen years of performances in 2018.

The cannon fire was more than just an attention grabber, however; it helped establish that the Castillo del Morro is under attack, which of course is the key and only plot point of the entire Florida version of the attraction. Without the energy and clear, unambiguous story point, the show inside can too easily come off as just a bunch of disconnected events.

All of this builds to a whole that, well, probably is less than the sum of its parts but still very interesting - especially if you really take time to absorb its details.

Caribbean Plaza creates a spatial relationship with the attraction it houses that would never be attempted again; it really does feel as if you're in a space continuous with the one seen in the attraction inside, as if you could simply walk back around the rear of the fortress that the town would be "back there", and you could go inside Carlos the Mayor's house and raid his pantry. It's this sort of internal logic that really gives a lot of Magic Kingdom and Disneyland its punch, the feeling that this place somehow has a history that existed before you arrived and will continue to exist after you leave; that it's more than just a big set to amuse you.

And with the bright Florida sun beating down on its plastered walls Caribbean Plaza creates pockets of darkness in its shaded porticos and breezeways which continually open into sun-splashed courtyards and side corridors. Caribbean Plaza uses the sunlight in Florida in ways that the rest of Magic Kingdom really doesn't.
Those pockets of darkness foreshadow the onset of the artificial night, as if the pirates are already gathering in the shadows, ready to steal out and nab you at a moment's notice...

With all of this effort, then, it is amusing that Pirates of the Caribbean still bears the mark of the questionable decision to build it at all. Despite all efforts over the course of five decades, a lot of visitors seemingly just can't figure out how to make their way back to the ride. Lines for the attraction don't really start building until the early afternoon, and of the major attractions in Magic Kingdom, it is usually the first to lose its line. Until recent years and the addition of the Little Mermaid ride in Fantasyland, it was the only ride at Magic Kingdom where you had to walk into an apparent dead end to access it.

To help visitors find it, the ride opened in December 1973 with an entrance sign near the clock tower and large brass bollards out front printed with text explaining the nature of the attraction inside. These were similar to the signs outside of Disneyland's version, the key word on them being "thrilling adventure cruise". Disney took a similar tact in promoting the new ride to attendees at Grad Nite '74 and in all other publications, emphasizing the waterfall feature. Today, we are almost disappointed when a boat ride doesn't go over a waterfall,[24] but in the 1970s before the wide proliferation of Arrow's log flume, this was a key selling point. It's amusing and curious to consider that for most audiences in 1967 and 1973, a boat ride with a drop was a thrilling new concept comparable to the technical wow of today's super-blockbuster attractions.[25]

Within a few years, jolly rogers riddled with cannon fire had appeared on the clock tower and flying from the fortress, trying to drive home that yes indeed the pirate ride was inside this big building. Signs were added to the large arch at the West side of the Plaza, as well as painted on a wall near the Jungle Cruise, pointing the way to the ride.

But seemingly none of this was enough, because at some point in 1975, WED took stronger measures. In early 1972, noticing that guests weren't aware of the show inside the Enchanted Tiki Room in Florida, Operations director Bill Sullivan[26] made a suggestion to place a talking bird out at the front entrance, similar to what was initially tried at Disneyland in 1963. That obviously worked, because they did the exact same thing at Pirates of the Caribbean.

Marc Davis had designed a pirate parrot for the attraction's unload area, with a tiny hat, bandana, sporting a shaved chest and anchor tattoo. This parrot's entire job was to stand in an alcove above a door warning riders about the "heaving gangplank dead ahead" - the Goodyear Speedramp that was employed to take them back up to the Magic Kingdom's pedestrian area. Supposedly the parrot would cause a bottleneck, so he was brought outside to the attraction entrance to help drive home that, yes, there is a ride inside this building. Marc's concept art revision is dated August 1975, giving us a probable timeframe in which the move was made.[27]

IX. Pirates of the Caribbean at Walt Disney World

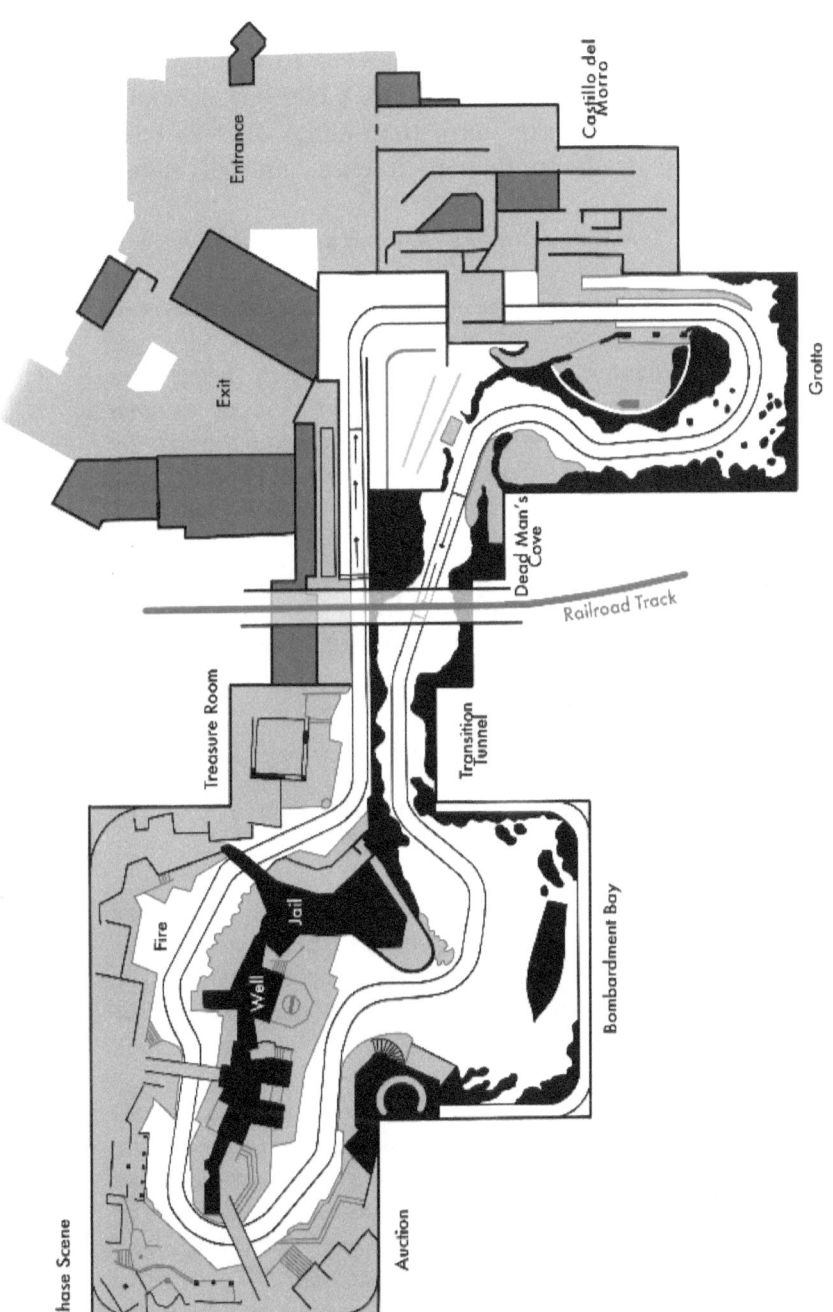

In this new location, "Pegleg Parrot" was classic Disney magic. I don't like using that term, but that's exactly what this was. Most of us who grew up with Pirates on the East Coast have fonder and stronger memories of the "barker bird" than we do the ride behind him. He would dance around, puffing up his chest, and call out to the walkway:

"Gold and doubloons! Gold and doubloons!"

"Heave to, maties! Ye come seekin' adventure and salty old pirates, eh? [whistle] Salty old pirates! Salty old pirates! This be the place! This be the place! [chirping] Chart a course through the arches, matey! It be a short march through the old fortress, past the dungeons to Pirate's Cove! Pirate's Cove! Pirate's Cove! Thar be longboats waitin' to take ye aboard!"

"All hands on deck! Ahoy ye swabbies! Stand by to repel boarders! Repel boarders! Repel boarders!" [whistles]

[Dances to 'Yo Ho' Music]

"Yo ho! Yo ho! A parrot's life for me! Parrot's life for me! Parrot's life for me!"

"Avast there, ye lubbers! This be the place! If ye be seekin' adventure and salty old pirates! [whistle] Salty old pirates! Salty old pirates! We pillage and plunder, rifle and loot! Yo-ho, me hearties, yo-ho!"

"Heave-to, maties! There be longboats waiting down by Pirates' Cove! Waiting to take ye to the Spanish Main! Right this way! Through the arches and down past the dungeons in the old fortress! [whistles] We sail with the tide! Sail with the tide! [chirps] Don't miss the boat, maties!"

IX. PIRATES OF THE CARIBBEAN AT WALT DISNEY WORLD

Photo by Mike Lee, 1995

Besides re-introducing some of X Atencio's more piquant dialogue lines back into the attraction, the Barker Bird often had a small crowd simply watching him go through his paces. Most of these people would then go ahead right into the attraction, just as he said. So let's join the crowd pressing through those arches into the air-cooled darkness of an artificial Caribbean fortress in an artificial Caribbean night and see what WED's $10 million bought them back in 1973.

ii. Down Past the Dungeons

This chapter has been about cuts, confusion, and compromise. But like they say, May flowers grow from April showers and here, friends, is the place where Florida Pirates can stand up on her own two feet and say in a loud, clear voice: "Damn right, I am somebody!" Because here is where circumstances forced WED to invent the themed queue.

There were other themed queues before, yes, but what you and I mean when we say themed queue - an experience which prefaces the larger attraction by establishing setting, mood, or narrative information - starts right here. The only previous example that comes close is the boarding area for Claude Coats' Adventure Thru Inner Space, which was one room packed full of narrative information, rather than a full walkthrough experience. Here, Pirates innovates one of the key storytelling devices of modern themed design, prefiguring such lush pre-boarding experiences as Indiana Jones Adventure and Harry Potter and the Forbidden Journey. The ride waiting for us at the end of this dark fortress may be no match for her California sister, but the pleasure and artistry of the walk to the boat helps round out and reinforce the attraction's strengths.

Passing through the arches at the attraction entrance reveals a bright, sunny plaza. The dominant colors are warm ochres and dark umbers, comforting colors that play well with tropical foliage and blue Florida skies. Real sunlight splashes in from the left and right while above, skylights forever illuminated make the entrance look inviting.

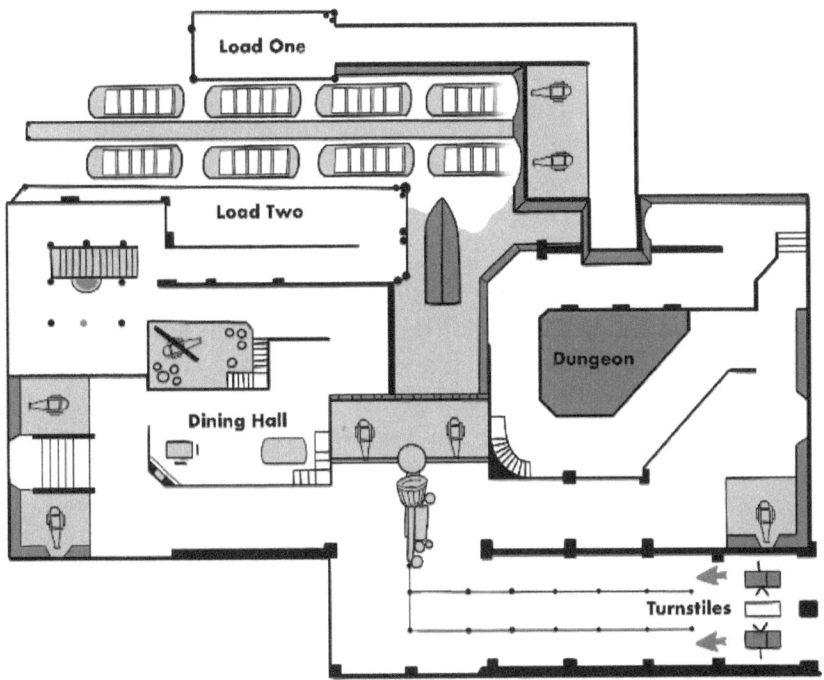

More than anyplace else in Caribbean Plaza the dominant visual motive here is symmetry - a wide, bright, open plaza with columns as regular as clockwork. At the back, two huge wooden doors set into the side of the fortress are open wide, with a dozen lanterns shining in the darkness beyond. The plaza is reassuring, but it draws us towards a destination which is anything but. The bright yellows give way to moody grays, browns and reds - danger colors. Say goodbye to the orderly non-reality of the Spanish Main for once you cross that threshold, everything starts to go sideways - the pirates attack!

It's hard to say how good this queue is was a result of planning and how much was a product of pure inspired luck. But even if it was alchemical magic instead of pure design brilliance, the queue for Florida's Pirates remains a highlight for experiential design even five decades later. The slow retreat from the bright courtyard into the darkened fortress interior creates a simulated sunset, the same feeling of plunging into an underworld which the Grotto sequence of the original attraction creates so well. Rather than opting for George Brun's romantic "Pirates Overture", WED chose to play the more menacing "Pirates Arcade" music here, setting an appropriate keynote of potential danger. The walls tighten in on us, and even the air conditioning - unremarkable elsewhere in the park - enhances the feeling of being someplace cold, wet, and ancient.

The queue as originally built was divided into two sides. Each side presented a different show and different succession of rooms; veer left, and you would travel through the functional part of the fortress where the soldiers lived and went about their routines. The key show scene here is a dining hall complete with table, chairs, and a huge barrel of wine; veer right and your path would lead you through the dungeons of the fort.

This dungeon path was the original "main load" side of the queue, and for good reason, because it was in its original form a fabulously effective experience. Both sides of the queue head up the same barrel-vaulted main entrance and split at a tiny indoor courtyard; but whereas the "garrison" side of the queue continues level, the dungeon side immediately sent guests around a blind corner and down a ramp, creating the sensation of heading underground. In reality no such thing happened; you walked up a ramp, turned a corner, then walked down another ramp and ended up back at ground level, but the impression of a subterranean descent was very effective.

With its undulating elevations, confusing side-staircases (as Cast Members we had to place trash cans in front of these to prevent people from walking up them), and blind corners, the dungeon was a harrowing journey to take alone - almost a haunted house. With rough stone textured walls and scarce light from flickering lanterns, the queue is stocked with cannons and rifles - creating a sense of impending violence. Every corner is a blind corner, but the layout is very compact, creating an uncanny sensation of going in circles - like one of those dreams where you're running in place, trying to escape from some threat. Speakers are placed perfectly at a central elevated platform to create the impression, bouncing off the faux stone corridors, that the pirates could be around any corner, as if you could come upon them at any moment.

I sadly cannot give due credit to whomever put together this terrific entrance experience. In his walkthrough with Ed Prizer, Fred Joerger credits Collin Campbell with designing it. I have no reason to doubt Fred, and Campbell's contribution should be better known, but it also may not be the whole story. In this period Collin Campbell was more of a straightforward illustrator, although he was just branching out into art direction with the magnificent Florida Tom Sawyer Island. So much of the East Coast Pirates and Caribbean Plaza around it is thuddingly literal and simplified, but here suddenly - as if delivered down from the mount - *somebody* has discovered that you can intertwine spaces around each other to create interesting effects.

I suspect that Campbell may have devised the concept and scenery and somebody else actually laid out this masterpiece of labyrinthian passages. Regardless, this is a major milestone in the lexicon of themed design, and is rightly revered even by those who don't much like the ride behind it.

A small detail that contributes to the sense of danger but which usually goes unnoticed is that nearly every light and lantern seen inside the fort is orange or red. It's not that Disney is under some impression that the official light bulb of piracy is orange - this is actually an interesting point of historical accuracy.

Glass panes are one of those things that simply blend into the background for most of us in modern life, although they once were a precious commodity.[28] For Caribbean Plaza, WED turned to commercially available pebble and seed glass. The yellow and amber glass colors used throughout the area is intended to denote the less refined clear glass of the period.

Once inside the Castillo, you may notice that every single light or lantern in the ride has had its glass panes painted on the interior side with a translucent, wavy pattern. When I was young I assumed this was simply to make everything look grungy; this is only partially true.

188 PART THREE: EXOTIC PORTS OF CALL

Taken by the author, October 2003

In the seventeenth century glass was expensive, and a lantern was such an item of widespread utility that most lanterns were not going to use glass. Many lanterns until the late 19th century actually used animal horn. This stuff was sawed open and boiled, whereupon it could be worked into a variety of shapes. The resulting pane was thin, with an opaque yellow color and rippled appearance very much like what is seen in the ride. So in Pirates we see WED taking modern glass paned lanterns and treating them to resemble the common lanterns of the era, which is an impressive touch even if you're not sure what you're supposed to be looking at!

In the days when Walt Disney World was a quieter place than it is now, it was possible to wander into Pirates of the Caribbean after nightfall and be totally alone in the queue. For those of us who grew up with the long, lonely march through all that stonework and past the dungeons, it was a pleasant, even essential component of the ride experience. But a good number of tourists, never having set foot in the place before, would panic.

More than once while working the attraction I would welcome guests to the ride, only to have them return several minutes later telling me that the ride was closed. I would guide them the rest of the way, through all those blind corners where they had stopped in their tracks, assuming they had reached a dead end.

There's a small room that connects the two sides of the queue; it's not even tall enough to stand up in; maybe four feet tall. But you can look clear through it and see people walking through the queue on the other side; many tourists would assume they're on the wrong side of the line and duck through that tiny room to join them.

Near the end of the line the corridors open up and the environment takes on a less sinister, more romantic note. On the dungeons side, guests could peer down into a sunken jail to see Marc Davis' classic "eternal checkmate" visual gag, with two skeletons hunched over a chess board. On the opposite side of the queue, the line passes through an outdoor courtyard with a trickling fountain; a forced perspective pergola above is hung thick with silk wisteria. Heard in this area is a short acoustic track of Spanish-style guitar playing which adds a hauntingly wistful note to the scene, as if a lonely but unseen soldier is whiling away his hours, unaware of the siege about to take place.

And at last we arrive at Pirate's Cove, where the sound of seabirds and ocean surf predominates. Ships are being built here, with the tools of workmen still scattered around. Our ride vehicles emerge into the cove, returning to the load area suspiciously empty of guests! The suspense of the queue-line gives away to a hushed sense of encroaching danger as we load onto our tiny boats to escape the coming attack.

Through arches opening out onto a moonlight bay, we can see the lights of a pirate shop anchored offshore. This is the same ship we will soon meet face to face on the attraction. There's no music, simply natural sounds. We watch clouds drift across the moon as the "distant" flickering lanterns of the ship play across the water. It's a little masterpiece of illusion that we pass by far too quickly. Then our boats scoot out of the sheltered cove and drift into a cavern... it's off to meet the pirates.

iii. The Abridgment Too Far

If readers compare the maps for Disneyland's attraction in Chapter 9 and the Walt Disney World version provided here, something very crucial to the overall impact of the attraction will become apparent: the Walt Disney World version was laid out with little regard for "show value". The upper level is a single, wide, lazy turn towards the downramp, and the remaining space after the fire scene is a single left hand turn to get boats back to unload. It's all laid out for efficiency, not effect.

It seems evident that Marc Davis actually was given this completed layout and had to design his new scenes around the space; I haven't found anything to contradict a date of April 1972 for the attraction's approval, and all of his art dates from May and June. This was not the way WED did things in those days and the attraction very obviously suffered for it.

As a single example among many, consider for a moment the red powder kegs stacked throughout the queue, labeled "Explosivo". In every other version of the attraction, these are a major plot point as a storehouse of them is blown sky high by the fire and destroys the drunken pirates. In Florida they're simply... something you see in line. If they returned at the climax we could be speaking of "Chekov's Powder Keg" or some such thing, but the whole dramatic irony of the pirates being destroyed by the fire they started doesn't really figure into Florida. All of this contributes to the sense that the Florida ride is less dramatically satisfying than her sisters elsewhere.

The attraction kicks off with a large cavern. This scene was originally brightly illuminated in amber and introduced a vocal version of "Yo-Ho"; many riders would clap along to the song.[29] Turning a corner past a modest waterfall, the tunnel begins to narrow and darken, and this continues all the way through the scene until there is seemingly almost no room for the boats. At Disneyland, the caverns are mysterious and macabre, but not really scary. In Florida, they're actually trying to be menacing: with the repeated warnings of "Dead Men Tell No Tales", the lowered ceiling and the loud storm sounds, the effect of having stumbled into an actual dangerous situation is impressive.

Those scary scenes consisted of a smaller version of Dead Man's Cove shoved up into a corner. Lost in the move East is the impressive arching motion as the boats travel around the scene at Disneyland, first revealing the beach then approaching each skeleton in turn. Instead the scene is just shoved up into a corner; you see it then move on. Around the corner, boats pass a new version of Hurricane Lagoon. The skeleton is staged closer to the boats, and actually stands upon a wrecked piece of decking which slopes down into the boat channel, a nice embellishment. But the skeleton oddly faces away from the boats, and we approach from the side, meaning riders have no real opportunity to enjoy approaching the figure and watching him turn his wheel, as we do in California and Tokyo. On the other hand, with the new staging the skeleton seems to be trying to pilot his wreck in the direction our boats are traveling, increasing the sense of "danger ahead!"

Across from our ghost pilot, a talking skull and crossbones was set into the cave wall off to the left and slightly above the bow of the boats. No hat, crossed swords, or curtain backdrop as at Disneyland, just a dimensional skull and bones. He did apparently at one point have an eyeball in his visible socket, a nice touch. In my time he was illuminated via blacklight and glowed a soft green.

Courtesy of Dave Ensign

I've always wondered if the placement of this figure, off to the side and alongside an emergency exit, was a sign of having been added at a later point; if he was there from the start, why not stage him directly above the drop, as was done at Disneyland? Regardless, unlike X Atencio's hushed, literate introductory incantation at Disneyland, our talking skull here simply spouted prosaic safety announcements: "*Avast thar lubbers! Thar be rough waters ahead! Sit close together and keep yer ruddy hands inboard! Dead men tell no tales! ARR!*"[30]

IX. Pirates of the Caribbean at Walt Disney World

Once over the waterfall and at the bottom of the ramp, guests floated through a pitch-dark cave listening to a truncated version of the "transition tunnel" narration at Disneyland:

> *"No fear have ye of evil curses, says you? Ah, properly warned ye be, says I!"*
> *"Dead men tell no tales..."*
> *"Now proceed at yer own risk. These be the last friendly words ye hear! You may not survive to pass this way again..."*
> *"Dead men tell no tales..."*

This made almost no sense and indeed is the only reference in the attraction to a "curse". All references to "cursed treasure" have sensibly been clipped and although the supernatural voices and animate skeletons upstairs are definitely sufficient proof that pirate ghosts are afoot, it seems to be a bizarre miscalculation to bring up the idea of a curse at all. Ghost pirates definitely are part of cultural memory, but cursed treasure isn't necessarily and needs further elaboration.

Once downstairs and into the raid on the town scene, most of the really high-value alterations to the attraction become apparent. Certain design eccentricities about the Disneyland show have been revised. The layout of the scenes in the town were originally designed to squish together into the basement dug for the walk-through version of the attraction in 1963, which means certain scenes abut each other in odd ways. All of this was ironed out and improved in 1973, making the "meat" of Florida's ride a bit better designed and paced.

The biggest improvement is to the Well scene; at Disneyland, the scene sort of faces away from the boats and the boats turn towards the Auction before it feels like they truly ever get close to the action. This is interesting, and it makes the Well scene feel like it has a huge cast, but much of the detail of it is lost. Florida has the boats approach the scene, run alongside it, then turn to start approaching the Auction, making many of the clever details possible to enjoy. Marc Davis or somebody has placed a large, handsome two-towered building between the Well and the Auction, which holds up the roof of the building but also adds a nice beat between the scenes where our attention can gradually shift to the Auction up ahead.

That new tower was not wholly motivated by aesthetics. The new shape of the show building dictated the moving of the attraction's spur track[31] to a spot between the Chase and Fire scenes. The change makes possible a very nice dramatic beat before the fiery climax, where the raucous noise of the raid recedes and we may notice a moonlight illuminated tree and Yale Gracey's cloud projections cutting across the sky. The effect is contemplative. Disneyland's Pirates is full of such moments where we may reflect upon how impressive the experience is, but Florida's version is all go all the time... except for here, and it's nice to have it.

Marc designed a new figure for this quiet space between scenes: Old Bill, who sits alone down a quiet alley and tries to feed rum to stray cats. Old Bill was brought back to Disneyland in 1974 or 1975, alongside Beacon Joe, whose twin relocated from the Rivers of America to the Blue Bayou.

Bill is nice to have at Disneyland, but the scene is more memorable in Florida, due to the sense of having come to some quiet corner of the Caribbean village. Next to Old Bill is a facade of a house, with a shaded portico, hanging flowers, and an inviting looking chair. It's one of those few moments where you feel like maybe you could open that door, find a nice bed inside, and lay down; like you could very possibly *live* down this charming side street forever under attack by pirates.

But let's not go too far in lading out the compliments; the new track layout also spoils the forced perspective of Bombardment Bay and the Burning City, which are significant losses. Coats' original flume layouts pointed the boats straight at the pirate ship as well as the rear wall of the Burning City, with its forced perspective hill in flames. This makes both scenes in Disneyland look huge, life size. In Florida the boats approach both at a shallow angle, making them look less dreamlike and impressive and more like what they are, which is very detailed sets.

Losing the subtle realignment where the boats turn a corner in darkness and see the pirate ship perfectly framed in the mouth of a cave means losing one of the great moments in themed design; in Florida, the ship comes across as an interesting sight which you happen to perambulate past on a pleasant stroll.[32] This is despite the fact that the Bombardment Bay scene in Florida is significantly larger than it is at Disneyland; it's larger but it looks smaller. So it goes.

The ride at least was given a unique ending that combines the Jail scene and a new Treasury raid, but like the new arrangement of scenes in the caverns at the start of the ride the lack of space is a real problem.

The Florida Jail scene has been cut by 30% and left open on one side. Originally, the boats simply turned past the Jail and proceeded thru the new climax - again, the effect is less of being in an actual place than of passing by some clever scenery, like shop windows. In fact, given the way that so much of the reconfigured Florida ride feels like you pass by blocks of scenery on the left and on the right, that shop window analogy may be getting close to the heart of the problem; you rarely feel like you're truly *immersed* in a location.

Our new climax was the object of most of Marc's efforts on the Florida show. Pirates have discovered the town's treasure vault and, having tied up the guards, celebrate by rolling about in treasure and firing their pistols into the air in celebration. There was a lot to look at here; a pirate captain with a bottle sits drunkenly on two sailors, another pirate has removed his boots and thrust his bare feet into a chest of pearls, a third has wedged his butt into a barrel and is stuck. Over the whole scene, a small parrot sings a version of the theme song recorded just for the East Coast ride: "A Parrot's Life For Me".

But the open space between these two scenes meant that the Jail scene dialogue was sometimes drowned out by pistol shots, and really the problem here went deeper than acoustics. In Disneyland the Jail is dark, cobweb draped, and quiet; it really is credible that in all the excitement these guys down below the city could be forgotten. The staging lends dramatic credibility to the situation. That dramatic credibility is what makes the scene funny; it isn't funny if they aren't actually in trouble. The lack of division between the Jail and Treasury scenes in Florida just made both groups of pirates look foolish. If the jail pirates are really in such dire straits, why aren't the crew just ten feet away trying to help them?

Interestingly, the basic concept of the treasury scene is not a total fantasy; the store-houses of treasure seem to have been real. The whole point of piracy operations in the Caribbean was to intercept and steal valuable goods from Spanish holdings; Spain, for their part, weren't about to make it easy on the bandits. Panama, Campeche, and Havana were the key stops on the chain which brought the wealth out of South America to Europe; each city was heavily fortified.

The *General History* elaborates:

> "It was about two years before that the Spanish Galleons, or Plate Fleet, had been cast away (sunk) in the Gulf of Florida; and several Vessels from the Havana were at work, with diving Engines, to fish up the silver that was on board the Galleons. The Spaniards had recovered some millions of Pieces of Eight, and had carried it all to the Havana. They had at present about 350,000 Pieces of Eight in silver, then upon the Spot, and were daily taking up more. [...] The money before spoken of, was left on shore, deposited in a Store-House, under the Government of two Commissaries, and a Guard of about 60 Soldiers."[33]

The Treasury scene at least ended the attraction on a visual high note. Beyond enframing arches, two soldiers could be seen tied back-to-back to a chair. The chair was up on a table, which looks silly and is about the right amount of levity for the scene to work. Inside the Treasury bales of cloth, gold plates, heaping bowls of pearls, and gold statues could be seen. In 1973 WED seems to have gone to some trouble to create custom little doubloons and gold bars for the attraction; in later years, mass manufactured Mardi Gras coins were used.

In terms of details, this tableau was among the most lavish in the attraction. If you entered the Jail scene and turned around to look behind you, totally hidden away in a corner were hundreds of muskets and cannonball at the ready to defend the fortification. On the wall behind the pirates were announcements for the soldiers stationed in the garrison, with seals and signatures from the Governor. Treasure was everywhere, draped across the figures - and yet still the effect was less impressive than it is at Disneyland; there really is *something* about that pile of coins out West that cannot be beat. It is satisfying in ways that are hard to explain.

Finally, the trip back up the waterfall was removed. This was one of the few things Marc Davis would approve of about this version of the ride, always saying he hated going "*chug chug chug up the hill wondering what the hell you're going to do next*". To each their own, but to this writer to slow return to the Bayou, the undoing of the spell by traveling out of the subterranean depths, is a big part of the appeal of the ride.

Actually, splitting off the riders from the boats for the return to the surface has nothing at all to do with aesthetics and everything to do with logistics. An empty boat is a known quantity, because you designed the boat yourself; it'll always weigh the same amount. In order for an unknown number and weight of riders to safely ascend to the surface up the waterfall, the arrangement requires a chain lift, elevated surfaces for the boat's road wheels to ride along, guide rails to keep the boat aligned, and a rollback system. Magic Kingdom has no such thing; a big ol' conveyer belt scoops up the boats, shoots them up a very steep ramp, and spits them out upstairs. Because the boats are supposed to be uninhabited, they squeeze through some very tight clearances to get there. As Cast Members we liked to ride the boats from Unload to Load, which required one to lay flat on the bench and endure a pretty harrowing uphill climb.

Taken by the author, March 2005

We can debate the show value of the Upramp, but from an operational perspective, the downstairs unload is a big improvement. Disney was not oblivious to these issues in 1973 and I'd bet feedback from Disneyland Operations had a lot to do with this.

Also, WED began splitting their load areas away from their unload areas starting with the Adventure Thru Inner Space in 1967 for similar reasons - it's easier to direct crowds using a separated exit to avoid congestion. Given that Pirates of the Caribbean and the Haunted Mansion opening at Disneyland was the one-two punch that finally pushed Disneyland over ten million visitors a year, it's sensible that they would want their huge ride to spit out far away from the congestion of its entrance.

Pirates in Florida is the very first attraction in history to exit through a gift shop - even if it was less of a shop in 1973 and more of a themed space, with flower carts and sombreros. You had to head indoors to the "House of Treasure", complete with its own quiet rear courtyard, to buy your toy rifles and plastic eyepatches.

And so here's the thing. We can look at all of these changes and additions on paper and see what they were thinking. An elaborate fortress facade, a revolutionary queueing system, a simplified setting, a more direct tone. On paper, it should be as good as the version in California... but it is not.

Don't get me wrong, Pirates of the Caribbean in Florida is a fabulous attraction that makes new fans from around the world every day. It's a key attraction in the history of Walt Disney World, showing WED responding to the demands of their new audience and inventing things that are still part of the toolkit of designers today. It saw advances in technology; the original two-sided load area used a basic computerized logic relay to send boats into[1] the attraction - a similar system would be used in Space Mountain to safely run many trains on the same track.

It was an enormous effort that few who worked on seem to have been all that happy with, as Blaine Gibson said years later, "*I don't think the one at Walt Disney World has nearly the same impact.*"[34] Speaking as somebody who grew up with the version in Florida, it's tough to go back to once I knew what I was missing. As my friend Michael Crawford said, the version in California is not better because it's *longer*, it's better because it's better.

There is an idea floating around out there — I'm not going to dignify it by calling it an urban legend; so let's call it a "*narrative*". There is a "*narrative*" floating around out there that The Haunted Mansion turned out the way it did because of a disagreement in the design stage between Marc Davis and Claude Coats; that Marc Davis wanted the ride to be funny and Claude wanted it to be scary. The resulting blend, so the story goes, was the compromise result. If you've read nearly any account of the development of the Haunted Mansion, you've heard this story. It has become traditional, almost axiomatic within Disney circles.[35]

Model of Caribbean Plaza, Author's Collection

This narrative is complete nonsense, and it's easy to disprove, because actually Marc Davis designed *everything* in the Mansion - funny, scary, or somewhere in the middle. He did so in collaboration with Claude Coats, who was the show producer and sensitively chose the best ideas that everyone contributed and helped blend them into a brilliant whole.

Yet that story persists, and stories that persist do so for good reason. This narrative dramatizes the situation WED Enterprises found themselves in 1967 - adrift without their leader, forced to make it up as they went. But one reason I've never liked this story is because it seems to ignore the fact that even had there been disagreements, *these guys still made the Haunted Mansion, one of the greatest dimensional media experiences of all time.* The mere fact that the Mansion is as good as it is proves that Walt's instincts were right, that his team could be trusted, that they could - they did - produce good work after he was gone.

No, if you want a story where WED flailed towards a compromise, it's here - Pirates of the Caribbean in Florida. It's here that they prioritized expedience over design, prioritized opening on time over doing the job right, and ended up with an inferior product.

You don't miss the absence of Walt Disney in the Haunted Mansion - but you sure do here. Walt would have insisted that they come up with something newer and better. Walt would have insisted that they spend more money to do it right. Walt may have even moved forward on Western River Expedition, or come up with something even wilder.

But Walt was dead. And so we have Pirates in Florida, a strange creature that is literally less than the sum of its parts. It's a long way indeed from the seminal attraction that Walt Disney started building, tore down, then started building *again* to get it right.

X. THE PIRATES SACK ASIA AND EUROPE

i. Pirates of the Caribbean at Tokyo Disneyland

> "I didn't understand what the whole thing was trying to say. What impressed me was that the fireflies were computerized... You know, we used to have Japanese pirates around the Inland Sea, but we are more familiar with those mountain bandits who raided and stripped travelers naked. I would have understood [Pirates of the Caribbean] if they had those bandits in the show."
> - Elderly Japanese visitor, speaking to author Masako Notoji in 1988

Japan and Disney go way back.

If you are of a certain age, you probably had a grandmother or aunt who had a collection of cute ceramic animals placed around her house. These were cheap, widely available in department stores, and most of them were made in Japan after the War.

The most common was a certain design of wide-eyed deer, who cavorted across bureaus and curio cabinets across the country. The design of these deer was almost certainly "inspired" by Bambi, which was released in Japan in 1951.[36] Thirteen years later the cycle would reverse as these midcentury deer inspired the look of Rankin-Bass' Rudolph, the Red-Nosed Reindeer... animated in Japan under the direction of Tadahito Mochinaga.

Sitting in the theater in 1951 soaking up his first Disney movies was a young cartoonist named Osamu Tezuka, who claimed to have seen Bambi 80 times during its theatrical run. He would produce a manga adaption of the film the same year, obtaining an official Disney license through Daiei Studio, Bambi's Japanese distributor.

Tezuka would go on to become "The Walt Disney of Japan", revolutionizing Japanese comics and inventing the first homegrown cartoon, *Astro Boy*. Tezuka's literally Bambi-eyed protagonists became the template for a new style of Japanese art and culture, all influenced by Disney designs and storytelling.

And then there was Kunizo Matsuo, who flew to see Disneyland in 1955 and instantly wanted a version to open in Japan. Matsuo apparently negotiated a deal with Walt Disney to license Disney characters for a "Nara Disneyland" in Japan, but the licensing deal fell through. Nara "Dreamland" opened in 1961, built entirely by local contractors and artists but based heavily on its original model in Anaheim.

None of this activity escaped Walt Disney's eye. In 1961 Claude Coats, Al Dempster, and Jack Cutting were sent by Disney to Japan ostensibly on business, but Walt knew very well that the group would be unable to resist touring Nara Dreamland and reporting back to him.[37] The report from the group must not have been very glowing, because no more was heard of this upon their return. Still, Nara Dreamland survived until 2006, only to be reborn after its closure as an urban legend, a creepy abandoned knockoff of a real Disney theme park in Japan. This legacy is unfortunate and unfair to an early attempt to export the Disneyland concept overseas, one begun with the apparent cooperation of Walt Disney himself. But once Walt was gone, Japan came knocking once again.

And so it's apparent that almost instantly, Japan wanted a Disneyland of its own. Why is this? It may be wiser to simply let the question linger. But I can contextualize.

Disney was one of the first truly successful cultural imports to post-occupation Japan. Japanese public television launched in 1951, and the early airwaves were filled with dubbed American television shows like *Lassie*, *I Love Lucy*, and, yes, *Walt Disney's Disneyland*. Television playwright Mika Meguro commented: "*Our generation probably received the biggest Disney influence because of the popular TV show. We later became parents when Tokyo Disneyland was opened. So naturally, we wanted to take our children.*"[38]

And then there was the Japanese bubble economy. Despite having been bombed and defeated by the United States, Japanese took to the luxury goods and Western lifestyle of their new representative democracy like ducks to water and, much to the horror of American onlookers, had the world's fastest growing economy by the 1970s. A certain degree of innate tech geekery, a booming manufacturing sector, and an aggressively competitive work culture all combined to give Japanese households huge amounts of discretionary money to dump into cameras, and audio equipment, and anything else that money could buy that denoted a modern sense of status. In other words, a Japanese confluence of elements combined to make success and prestige synonymous with Americanism... and there is nothing more American than Disneyland. It was a birthright.

The Oriental Land Company was formed by a railway company as an effort to reclaim a marshy set of islands off the coast of the Chiba prefecture, west of Tokyo. This motive force was Keisei Electric Railway, a private train line connecting Tokyo to Narita. Keisei's relationship to the Chiba recreational development was therefore very comparable to the American trolley lines which began mass construction of amusement parks in the 1890s to incentivize utilization of their transit solutions.

The Tokyo Bay reclamation project complete, awaiting the construction of... something. Tokyo Disneyland and You, Author's Collection

By 1970, most of the property was dry and the company was developing plans for what they called the "the best recreational facility in Asia". In 1974, the Chiba prefectural government had signed off on a proposal themed around "Wonderful People and Their World", with an auditorium, a mall, hotels, and a "themed play land".[39]

Concurrent with all of this, following the success of Walt Disney World, Disney was gearing up to look seriously at the prospect of an international park. A team inside the company headed by WED's Frank Stanek was preparing studies of various locations for a possible "International Disneyland". Stanek recalled:

> "Once Walt Disney World became a success everybody and their brother wanted a Disney World project in their back yard. Lots of people came out of the wood work... At the end of 1972 I got a call from Mike Vagnall and he said; we want you to do a study - Walt Disney World has been such a success, we want to think about doing it internationally. We want to know where we should do this project next: in Europe or in Japan. So we worked on this for four, five months studying both these areas. I compiled all of this information - plus my own reading - and I wrote an executive summary at the end. I said: "If we're going to do a project internationally both Europe and Japan could support the project but Japan offered the highest potential of success."[40]

As a result, Oriental Land Company found Disney in a newly receptive mood when they approached the company a few months later. Disney executives travelled to Japan in December 1974 to hear the proposal and tour the location, and the companies had signed a basic agreement by 1975. WED got to work on developing what they then called an "Oriental Disneyland", with a menu of existing popular attractions based on proven successes in Anaheim and Orlando. For an international touch, Claude Coats began developing concepts for a Main Street replacement called World Bazaar based on the then-current futuristic mall look of World Showcase at Walt Disney World.

It's been common amongst Western Disney fans to describe Disney's relationship with Oriental Land Company as reluctant or at least suspicious. This position is overblown, but it does seem to reflect Card Walker's reticence to get involved in the project, a position Marty Sklar attributes in his autobiography to Card's experiences in the Pacific Theater of World War II.[41]

Now to be fair to Card, he was incredibly reticent to spend money on *anything* **not** called EPCOT Center regardless of merit. Still, Disney had an incredible number of irons on the fire in 1975 - their Annual Report alone enumerates a Bicentennial celebration, an EPCOT Theme Center, a World Showcase which had not yet merged into EPCOT, an International Shopping Village, a ski resort in Northern California near Lake Tahoe, and now the first overseas Disney park.

It's not all that surprising that they would view this deal, somewhat opportunistically, as a quick cash infusion to keep their outdoor entertainment ambitions turning smoothly. And thanks to Walker's reticence to open the wallet, that's pretty much the deal they struck, taking no stake in the success or failure of Tokyo Disneyland outside of a modest yearly stipend. Disney provided their design services the way Sears may sell you a refrigerator.

Looking at photos and layout of the park, it seems to be a bizarre hodgepodge of elements. Castle from Florida? Sure. Toontown from California? Yes. Weird not-a-Main-Street with a roof on it? Why not. On paper, it looks like a greatest hits mixtape tossed together without especial care. But looks can be deceiving.

Almost nothing is an exact copy. Buildings which present as "historical" in Magic Kingdom have been given simplified textures and bright primary color schemes. The bottom 15 feet of Cinderella Castle are simply chopped off, removing the heavy base and making the castle visually read as smaller and cuter. Tomorrowland buildings have been shrunk to more reasonably human scale. This makes the already toy-like theme park structures read as ever yet more imaginary.[42]

All of this results in a park that *looks* like Magic Kingdom but *feels* like Disneyland. Magic Kingdom has larger buildings than Disneyland but it also has a bad habit of pushing the pedestrian space right up against them, meaning you spend a lot of time looking at things like the underside of awnings. This contributes to the feeling that Magic Kingdom is sometimes a bit like an eight-year-old wearing Dad's suit and tie. Tokyo Disneyland provides more open space around everything, which allows you to step back from those same Magic Kingdom buildings and take in in a way you can't in Florida. The fantastical colors and scale really work and transform the whole area. Elsewhere, the park can draw down to a more intimate scale in places like Adventureland, modulating the experience and providing a needed contrast to all of that open concrete.

If you've been to Tokyo Disneyland, you know what I mean when I say that it's remarkable that it feels as intimate as it is. There's an area in Westernland that feels wide enough to land a 747, or perhaps host a drag car race with school busses. The park mostly takes Magic Kingdom's average of 20-foot-wide path as the narrowest possible roadway, and spreads out to Epcot-level promenade sizes when it feels appropriate. But when the park is full, that extra space really makes a difference, and dedicated theme park trekkers may find that their time-honed crowd avoidance tactics simply aren't all that necessary here.

All of this is culturally appropriate for Tokyo, a city of baffling sprawl and density. Yes, Cinderella Castle is big to the average Midwesterner, but it's got nothing on even a moderately sized Tokyo skyscraper. Tokyo Disneyland works for its predominantly local audience in the same way that Disneyland in California does, as a break from the crush and the concrete of the metropolis around it.

If the whole park is a credible middle ground between Disneyland and Magic Kingdom, then that's also an apt description of what WED delivered with Pirates of the Caribbean. Based on the basic show in California, but integrating some of the refinements of Florida, the attraction strikes a deft balance. This means Tokyo enjoys the New Orleans facade and bayou but Magic Kingdom town and exit area. Deciding to include the Blue Bayou meant copying New Orleans

Aerial Photo, October 1982. The Japanese construction crews were so efficient that the park was ready to open in January, the only Disney theme park in history completed under schedule. Imaginews November 5 1982, Author's Collection.

Square, but not necessarily all of it. The area is chopped in half, terminating abruptly at what would be the Court of Angels. There is no Pirate Alley in Japan! All of this places Pirates somewhere between the categories of attraction-supporting neighborhood and subsection of World Bazaar, which it sits next to. Instead of the American angle taken at Disneyland, this mini-mini-New Orleans comes off as more tropical than anything, leading off to a theater nestled amongst stands of bamboo and island flowers. "French Caribbean" blends into "Victorian American" effortlessly, removing the New Orleans details from their historic context and instead reading as simply exotic.

Once inside the attraction lobby, the "olde Caribbean" vibe continues. Where Disneyland has aged plaster walls, Tokyo presents tropical green paneling and salmon colors. Framed pieces of Marc Davis art create a domestic feeling quite different than the spare interior of the Disneyland original. Around the corner, in a seldom-used side room, nautical charts and portraits of an unnamed sea captain create a strong "governor's mansion" feeling. The brick arches and tableau past it have been minimized, with the beach scene having just a few shells, boat, seagull, and Jolly Roger. Since the boats return upstairs empty, there's no need to entertain riders with anything else.

The bayou beyond has been faithfully realized. The Blue Bayou at Disneyland is lovely, but it's also, you know, pretty much just a backdrop. The Tokyo version attempts to create a little more depth. The shrimp boats are realized a bit closer to full-sized, as is the "old man shack", which emphasizes these structures and pulls attention away from the background. I personally think California's is more haunting and romantic, but some bayou is better than no bayou.

Generally speaking, Tokyo Disneyland attempts to realize Pirates of the Caribbean with more detail and more texture. Brilliant as it may be, there's areas of the original Pirates that feel exactly like the relic of the 1960s it is. By the early 80s WED was operating scenically at a very high level, and the Japanese Pirates reflects this with a much more sophisticated visual treatment. Theatrical expediences in California like the plain black tube the boats shoot down on their way underground are gone, replaced with transitional scenic areas.

The naive tar paper caverns from California and Florida are now fully sculpted à la Big Thunder Mountain. The Caribbean village is fully realized in the round - very few painted theatrical flats to be seen. The "stone walls" in the Jail and Arsenal Shootout are rendered in California in a very basic freehand "cartoon castle" style. These same rock walls in Tokyo are detailed and pockmarked, looking like they were mined out of volcanic rocks. If this doesn't contribute much to the impact of the attraction it does at least make it feel a great deal more modern and textural.

These sets were built at the legendary Toho studios, home of Godzilla. Toho seems to have provided many of their contract talent to help on Tokyo Disneyland, including producer Teichiro Hori and multiple actors who voiced the park's various characters. The idea that actors from Godzilla and Akira Kurosawa movies populate Tokyo Disneyland's various attractions is a fascinating one.[43]

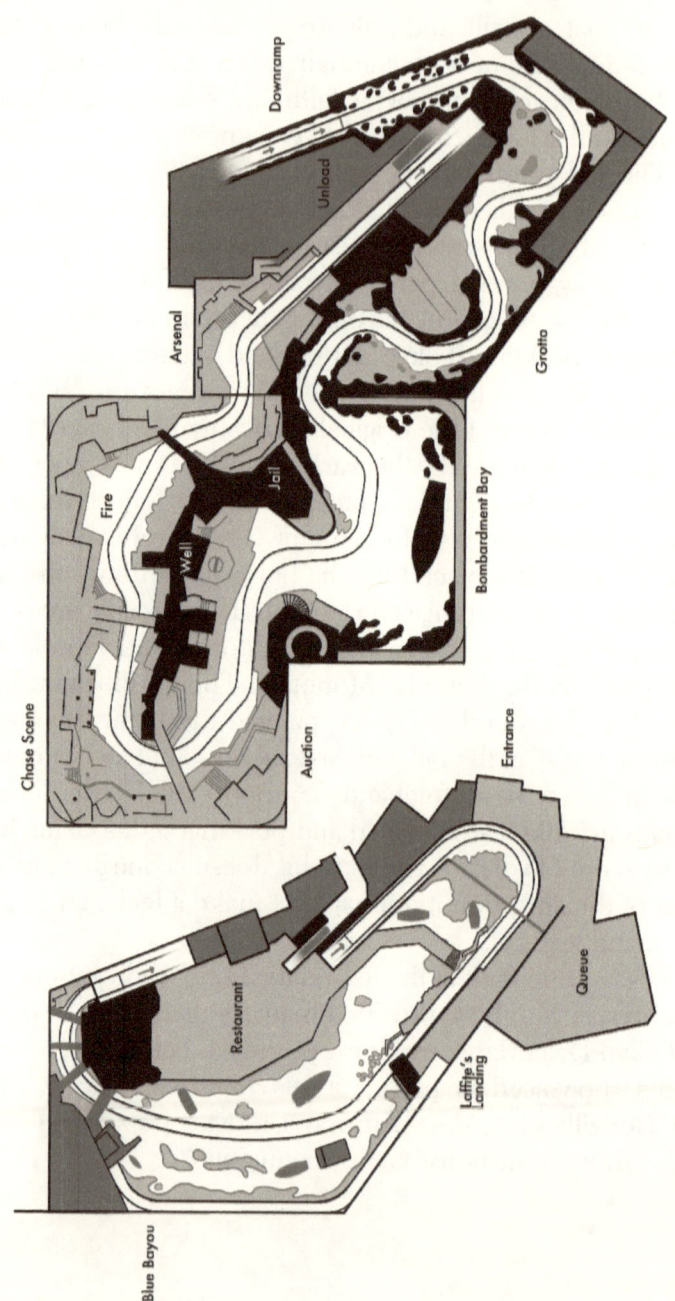

Due to the underwhelming show value of the Walt Disney World Railroad, the decision was made to run an elevated train around just the Jungle Cruise and Rivers of America, making the train experience into more of a ride. This means that Disney could choose to build the two halves of the Pirates show building as one large structure for the first and only time,⁴⁴ and the results are interesting. Because the caverns and arsenal are below the bayou but the attraction has only one downramp, space in these sections is constricted. The ride makes very good use of this, with gushing waterfalls inside the caverns that make riders feel as if they may be drowned below a tight ceiling and pirates firing guns overhanging the ride boats in the climax. Those majestic soaring caverns at Disneyland are missed, but the overall effect is less claustrophobic than it is in Florida.

As part of the construction effort as well as to make good on their promise to Oriental Land Company to provide an "authentic overseas experience", WED sent several of their top Walt guys over to Tokyo to oversee the project. Fred Joerger in particular really did not want to go, but the globe-trotting Marc Davis and Nihonphile Claude Coats took to Tokyo like a duck to water. Marc was a very tough boss when it came to how his ideas were to be staged within the attraction - he was so unhappy with how the Graveyard scene at the Disneyland Haunted Mansion turned out that he would go over to the show installation of the Florida version and request change after change. Disney was relying on the same perfectionism of the old pros to deliver a true Disney-quality show in Tokyo.⁴⁵

Look especially at the Hurricane Lagoon, the scene Marc had drawn two times before. The version in Tokyo exactly matches his concept art going back to 1967, with the skeleton almost doubled over in the force of the gale. With its grinning skull fixed on the boats instead of ahead into the storm, the effect is genuinely creepy in the way that none of the other versions of Hurricane Lagoon can begin to approach.

The Arsenal scene at the end is likewise improved. "*Use red and amber filters to get an "explosive" look to it. It should have a look of going into hell!*" Marc wrote on his concept art. Hell is a stretch, but the scene is better laid out and feels just as dangerous as it does in California. The low ceiling sets the tone. Iron bars on all sides contribute to a feeling of entrapment. Behind every barred arch are stacks and stacks of our red "Explosivo" barrels. This creates the feeling that the only way forward is through the dangerous shootout.

Taken by the Author, April 2023

Taken by the Author, April 2023

The bullet ricocheting effects really work here, including a very neat one where a bullet grazes the top of a pile of spilled powder, seeming almost to ignite it. I think if a criticism can be leveraged against the arsenal scene at Disneyland it's that it's almost too lighthearted, and this version definitely dials up the pressure on the riders.

It's a little too easy to damn the Tokyo ride with faint praise, working as we are in this book forward from the Disneyland original. Were I some pint-size world traveler as a child who knew only the versions in Florida and Tokyo and only came to the California one later, I would view the original as not being that much better than what Japan got. The ride absolutely manages to split that hair that Florida failed to, delivering a tighter take on the brilliant original that also has enough improvements to stand on her own. Given that WED managed to work that trick only once it's a bigger deal that it seems.

Today, Tokyo Disneyland seems to belong as persuasively to Japan as it does to America. If the park was originally pitched as the nearest thing to a holiday in the US, the modern theme parkist looking for points of connection to the home territory is going to be mostly bemused and distracted. Even more so than Disneyland Paris the park feels divorced from historical context, presenting purely and simply as a vivid, clever fantasy. It's also simply in amazing condition, maintained as it is by the most meticulous race of people on earth.

All of this creates a bizarre feeling of lucid dreaming. Going to Tokyo Disneyland is a lot like hallucinating; the trip there is so long you inevitably crash in exhaustion upon arrival and awaken at a place that's very much like someplace you've already been but everything is colorful and bizarrely different. Absolutely every attraction not only looks like it was built yesterday, but has been kept in a form very close to its original state. Pirates still chase wenches, ghouls still leap out of trunks and scream, cabins still burn. Jack Wagner still announces park hours, 1970s park music still plays, and it's cleaner and better run than any other Disney-branded park in the world.

You travel halfway around the world only to come home again. Whatever era of Disney you grew up loving, your childhood is patiently waiting for you in Tokyo Disneyland, the Kingdom of Dreams and Magic.

ii. *Pirates of the Caribbean at Disneyland Paris*

In the end, Tokyo Disneyland changed the company forever.

Costs on EPCOT Center - the park everybody pinned their hopes on - spiraled out of control and the park opened during the Reagan Recession. In contrast, Tokyo Disneyland opened during Japan's legendary economic miracle, and probably could not have failed. EPCOT Center proved to be a one-off, but Tokyo Disneyland became the most profitable Disney theme park on earth. Everyone was sent scrambling in an effort to quickly repeat the miracle.

How quickly? Tokyo Disneyland opened in April; by August it had already broken the single day attendance record set by

Disneyland in 1969. In the first year alone, Tokyo Disneyland's attendance was already close to matching Disneyland's 9.9 million.[46]

Disney wasted no time. In November 1983, embattled CEO Ron Miller was talking up the possibility of a Disneyland in Europe, especially in France or Spain. The $600 million dollar venture was announced in March 1984, but Ron Miller would not be on hand to oversee it. Instead, a series of hostile takeover attempts and corporate maneuvering on the part of Roy E. Disney led Miller to be removed as CEO and Paramount executive Michael Eisner elevated to his role. Mouseketeers everywhere recoiled in horror. Was Disney... going Hollywood??

The location for the "Europe Disneyland" continued to be debated. Barcelona, Spain, had better weather but new boss Eisner contended that the location had bad rail lines, mediocre highway infrastructure and not even a reliable phone hookup.[47] In December 1985, Eisner signed a letter of intent with the French government to build a theme park in Marne-la-Vallee, a Parisian suburb then mostly known for boldly depressing apartment complexes. The French government agreed to contribute $6 million francs to help the resort complex come about. Eisner told the Associated Press that next to the United States, France *"is the most enthusiastic of all countries towards Disney, its merchandise, its culture."*[48]

That statement would send eyebrows flying through the roof today, never mind in 1985. It seems Eisner was absolutely smitten with the prestige of locating Disney outside of Paris. The French were not. Upon arriving at the Paris Stock Exchange for the initial public stock offering, Eisner and chairman Frank Wells were pelted with food by protesters. It was the opening salvo of a contentious shotgun marriage. To get built the park would endure union strikes, outright deception from the French construction crews, and even the bombing of a power line in an apparent act of sabotage on opening day.[49]

So it's worth considering exactly what Disney had in its stable of properties in 1985. Walt Disney Productions had been trying to come up with modern blockbusters since 1975 when they embarked on *Island at the Top of the World*. This and subsequent efforts like

The Black Hole, *TRON*, and *Something Wicked This Way Comes* had all fallen flat at the box office.

The company was slowly expanding out into producing more serious dramas, and titles like *Night Crossing*, *Tex*, and *Never Cry Wolf* are well-regarded little movies. Under Ron Miller's auspices, Disney had begun finding promising young filmmakers and letting them make their movies their way. This same benevolent, film-first attitude gave Disney *Splash*, a monster hit that finally began to put the studio into the black - but it was too little too late to save Miller's job.

Things were hardly better on the animation side. Each film released since *The Jungle Book* in 1967 had been less and less successful. So much of the production of *Robin Hood* was spent arguing and second-guessing that the film was simply not going to be ready on time, and a chopped down ending and new song sequence using recycled animation had to be dropped into the film at the 11th hour. Things got so bad that Don Bluth, an animation director on *The Rescuers* and *Pete's Dragon*, walked off the lot and took nine other animators with him to produce his own films. The commercial and critical pit for Disney was *The Black Cauldron*, a costly venture which was soundly trounced at the box office by *The Care Bears Movie*.

All of which is to say that Disney's most valuable assets in 1985 were its theme park attractions; nothing else came close. In fact it's possible to cynically argue that EPCOT Center was nothing more than a hodgepodge of the styles of Disney's only successful business segments in the early 80s - educational films and amusement centers.

Had the European theme park come along even a few years later it could have drawn on the success of films like *The Little Mermaid* and *Aladdin* - zeitgeist defining works that were still in the future. When Disneyland Paris was being planned and built, the most valuable assets in the company's portfolio were things like Fantasyland and Pirates of the Caribbean, and the park that was built reflects this fact.

Simultaneously, market conditions in the United States had put Disney in a position where their product was - at least until Universal Studios got ambitious - relatively unchallenged. Early attempts to copy the success of Disneyland had slowly subsided through the 60s as park operators discovered why it took a movie studio to pull off a Disneyland in the first place. Leaps and strides made in roller coaster technology in the 70s and 80s pushed nearly all regional parks in the direction of de-emphasizing theme and re-emphasizing thrills, and as this happened Disneyland and Walt Disney World began to tear away from the amusement industry as a whole and increasingly resemble national institutions, a market reality which has persisted to the present day. When theming nerds like this author wax poetically about the stretch from 1965 to 1995 when Disney built ambitious new concepts like Space Mountain and World Showcase, we tend to forget that all of this happened at a time when Disney had nothing reliable except theme parks to sell. Of course they could take time for a boldly experimental things like If You Had Wings - they controlled the market.

But things were different in Europe, and when project lead Tony Baxter took a tour of European attractions, he knew that Disney's usual style of park would have to evolve. Baxter recalled; "*We are going into one of the most culturally developed and sophisticated cities in the world. I'd like the challenge of shaping this place against all of* [Paris'] *art and architecture, instead of the arid asphalt of Anaheim or the swampland of Orlando. I'd like the challenge of amazing people.*"[50]

All of which is to say that Disneyland Paris was a perfect maelstrom of ambition and market realities that we will never see again, and every inch of the park oozes this fact.

Disneyland and Magic Kingdom comport themselves with the national identities of Americans; this is why the entrance plaque speaks of historical relevance and areas on the west side of the park tend to be rooted in some conception of historical accuracy, however dramatized. This conviction of being, say, a reasonably accurate simulation of New Orleans is a lot of what gives Disneyland its curious power; its sense of being simultaneously an amusement center and national monument.

The question of whether or not Europeans would connect with all of this is a good one, and a large reason why Disneyland Paris' design went heavy on Fantasy - and not the toy-like naive charm of Tokyo Disneyland. Every area of Disneyland Paris is a Fantasyland; fairy tale connections are emphasized, and everything from colors to textures are pushed to stylized extremes. A sign that at Disneyland or Magic Kingdom would be small and rough-hewn is now 15 feet across and uses the most intricate typeface possible. All of this rich detail in such a small space gives Disneyland Paris the patina of one of those terribly detailed engravings in old books; one wonders how anybody had the time to sit down and create all of this.

Of the key areas represented at Disneyland, the one most in need of a conceptual reboot for Europe was Adventureland. The original Adventureland at Disneyland was rooted very much in the tropes and beats of old adventure movies, with a tropical bazaar redolent in the nicotine haze of 40s Humphrey Bogart pictures; a two-fisted man's world of pulp fiction. Adventureland at Magic Kingdom instead went in a feminine direction and emphasized mysterious exoticism; with shaded balconies and richly decorated architecture which brings to mind the romance evoked by names like Macao, Old Singapore, or Shangri-La.

Additionally, the Jungle Cruise was cut from the Parisian attraction roster for a variety of reasons. Given that this single attraction is responsible for most of the landscape and layout of Adventurelands past, it was clear that the Parisian Adventureland was going to be something very different. But what? What was the European equivalent of those dusty old tropes, fever dreams of a world not yet connected via international travel?

The design team landed on *The Thousand and One Nights*. The entrance to the area is a Moorish castle with rich tile-work and fantastical turrets; sand dunes at the entrance create an uncanny feeling of arriving at the kingdom across some vast desert. Beyond, a courtyard with heavy North African design cues gives way to a dense "jungle".

Much of the south side of Adventureland has a heavy African influence, probably considered a more appropriate exotic location for Europeans than the Polynesian fantasies present at Magic Kingdom and Disneyland. But turn north and cross a bamboo bridge into Adventure Isle, and the full scope of this Adventureland unfolds before you.

Disney has always been fabulously effective at creating persuasive environments. Yet it's not entirely accurate to say that the theme park spaces they create are free of restrictions. They're not exactly playgrounds, but they're a bit less formal and structured than traditional theater. As Eco put it, "[Disneyland] *visitors must agree to behave like robots* [...] *if the visitor pays this price, he can have not only "the real thing" but the abundance of the reconstructed truth.*"[51] But still, too much restriction can be just as stressful as not enough, and it's easy for theme parks to tip over into the "too much" category.

So there's a real need for "in between" areas that feel more unscripted, to unwind or simply disconnect. Disneyland's Tom Sawyer Island provided such a place and ritualized the disconnection by requiring riders to arrive via raft. But that raft does limit who is willing to take the journey across the water, and so Paris' take on Tom Sawyer Island allows adventurers to come and go as they please via bridges to the mainland.

Adventure Isle may be the best thing in a park filled with brilliant things. The south side of the island has a castaway theme, and is home to the Swiss Family Treehouse. Benches and water fountains are constructed of bamboo and salvage. Explorers may proceed to the east side of the island, where the wreck of the Swallow may still be observed, bisected by a floating barrel bridge.

Moving north through sensuously entwining caverns, the landscape tilts to the dramatic, as tropical caves and grottoes dominate the island. This is where Captain Hook has moored his ship beside Skull Rock, a tableau brilliantly placed so that it is visible from Fantasyland and Peter Pan's Flight. Behind that are a series of baffling caverns in which skeletons and lost pirate gold is stashed. These are designed so that it feels as if you should be able to get to the treasure, which you can see easily, but can never find your way there. Significantly, the widest path on the island winds you between the pirate ship, behind skull rock, and deposits you on the doorstep of

Taken by the Author, April 2015

Pirates of the Caribbean. If none of this can put you in the mood for a spin through the attraction, theme parks may not be for you.

At Disneyland, the entrance to Pirates of the Caribbean is a couple of doors. At Walt Disney World, it is a whimsical colonial fortress with a coordinating public street. In Paris, Pirates of the Caribbean is an entire subsection of the park, one large enough to house all of Main Street. I can't think of another theme park anywhere which devotes so much real estate to contextualizing a single attraction. It is housed in a colonial fort, but if you're thinking of the cute toy-like building at Magic Kingdom, you're mistaken. "The Castillo" of Pirates of the Caribbean is a hulking ruin which appears to have sat decaying in the Caribbean sunlight for centuries. The area in front of the attraction is an intricate network of Spanish colonial terraces; these border a beach littered with shipwrecks. If you proceed south from the attraction and into the pirate caverns on Adventure Isle, you can peek through holes in the rock and find skeletons of pirates who seem to have lost their way and died. If you walk all the way past the gift shop exit and all the way past the restaurant you can find a lighthouse all the way out on the edge of the jungle. All of this lavish detail is in the service of wordless place-making that cuts across cultures and across generations. All you have to do is look at it to understand it.[52]

The pure scale of the fortress is hard to impress upon those who have not been there. From a distance it looks big; when you are standing beneath it looking up it feels like some huge creature bearing down upon you. This is because the building that this Pirates is housed in is absolutely massive, dwarfing even modern extravaganzas like Escape From Gringotts and Rise of the Resistance. It contains, on various levels nesting together, a restaurant, adjoining river ride, an indoor queue, the entire Disneyland "Caribbean town" section, haunted caverns nestled *below* the queue, two downramps, two huge pirate ships, and a new elevated mezzanine level that bisects the building. For good measure, the train runs through the center of the thing.

Not content to stop at rebuilding the crown jewel in the Disneyland diadem on massive scale, the Parisian Pirates got a drastic rethink. If the Pirates at Tokyo represented the original design team taking one last shot at faithfully executing their old boss Walt's most ambitious attraction, then the version in Paris is an epic tribute by the first generation that grew up riding, and loving, this classic. It enshrines Pirates of the Caribbean as a masterpiece even as it blows it up to epic scale.

Ducking inside the massive looming fortress, riders pass through a series of rooms representing the lower depths of the Castillo. As we press onward we slowly ascend upward, passing a room where the floor appears to have exploded, falling into the caverns below. Alerting us to this is a skeleton clinging to a chandelier in the center of the room, frozen looking downward into the hole. If we position ourselves correctly we can see through this hole into a ride scene below. A little further along we pass a forgotten dungeon where the remains of some prisoners are still chained to the wall.

Proceeding further into the inhabited areas of the Castillo, signs of an immense battle are everywhere. Iron doors have been forced off their hinges and holes have been blown in the wall; racks of swords and guns have been tipped over. At one point we can peek through a barred window into a small room where a skeleton at a desk

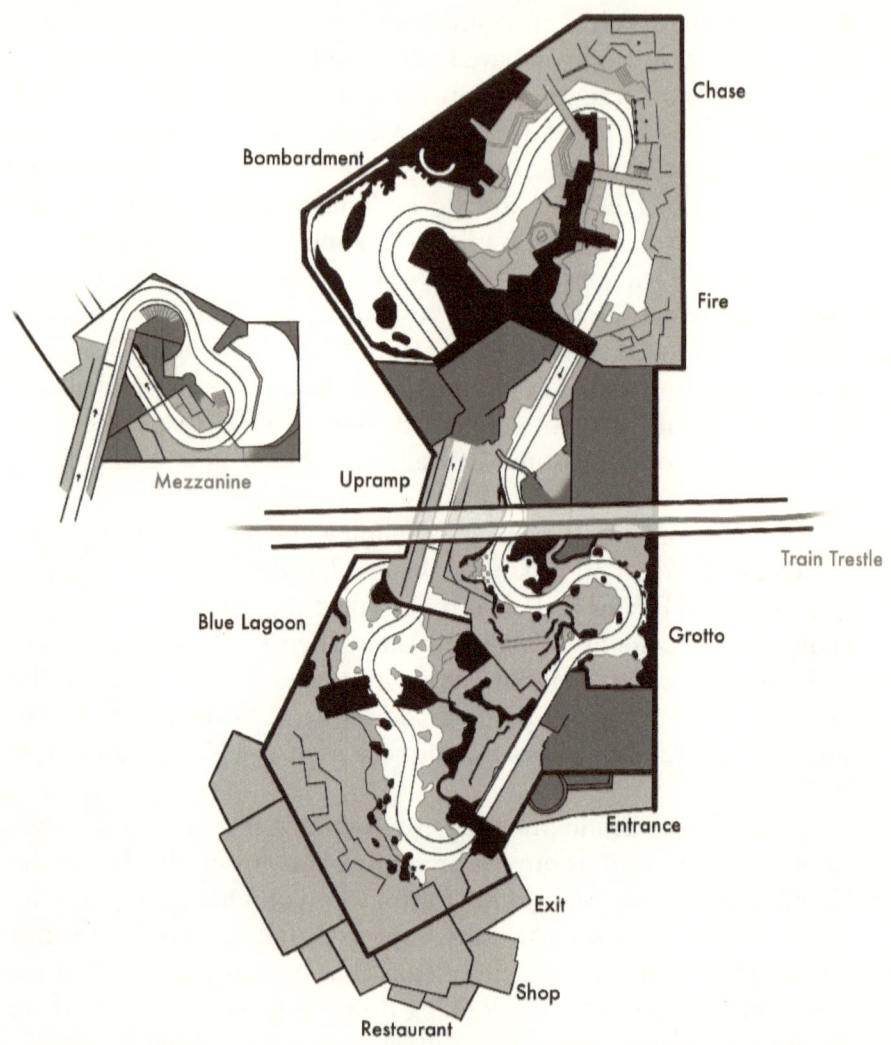

has a sword run through its back. This queue walk fills the same narrative role as Dead Man's Cove does in the Disneyland original: it plunges us into the scene of a crime and asks us to sort out what has happened here. It is the warning, the "dead men tell no tales" that alerts us not to proceed.

But then the mood lightens as we pop out on the battlements of the fortress and look down upon a Caribbean port at night. Torches blaze under the night sky as the line winds its way through a tropical jungle; the figurehead and bow sprit of a ship pokes through the foliage above our heads. This is a detail designed to linger mysteriously in our minds. We are sorted into our boats and shove off past the Blue Lagoon restaurant, a sort of castaway version of the Blue Bayou.[53]

One great thing about the Paris version of Pirates is that the attraction is laid out in logical and full-size relationship to itself. I spoke about how in Florida it's nice to feel that the exterior and pedestrian space in front of the attraction feels as if it's connected to the village we visit on-ride out back; Paris takes all of this to its furthest extreme. The queue line actually does sit on top of the skeleton caverns, and if we pay close attention to details we can see exactly where they connect. The mezzanine level atop the fort really does directly connect onto the town on-ride in logical ways.

But maybe the best example of this occurs as we round the corner in the Blue Lagoon and see the wreck of an ancient schooner, almost full size, blown in half and resting placidly on the shore. This is the vessel that we glimpsed the figurehead of before we boarded our boats, that detail that seemed so bizarre and incongruous when we first spotted it... and soon we will find out how it got that way. All of this really helps contribute to the sense of satisfaction and completeness that we experience here, as we investigate the scene of a crime, gather yet more evidence of the pirates who raided this fort, then are swept back in time to the night of that fateful island raid. All of it laid out in clear and logical order without the need for narration.

Also, if the Blue Bayou is a fabulous illusion, it's still mostly a painted backdrop, and that backdrop isn't really hidden all that much. Disney revisited the Blue Bayou twice in the early 80s, the copy in Tokyo and for the Mexico pavilion at EPCOT Center, a sort of curious cousin of Pirates of the Caribbean. Both times they increased the depth and detail of the illusion, with more trees and more forced perspective. But if I can speak for myself, having grown up on the Plaza de los Amigos at EPCOT Center, Disney jungles are far more enchanting than Disney bayous, and the jungle-thick of the Blue

Lagoon is Disney's best fake jungle ever. The gushing waterfalls, the bridge that connects the restaurant's lobby to its eating area, the torch and closed turret door, and the dancing fireflies, it all gladdens this author's heart. My only complaint is that it's all over far too quickly.

Yes, the speed of the boats. As an American, one of the most salient points that makes Disneyland Paris feel ever more clearly like "crazy world Magic Kingdom" is that all of its ride vehicles were built by European manufacturers and "feel different". In some cases, as in the Storybook Land Canal Boats, it's a huge improvement. Then there's the doombuggies in Phantom Manor, which are unfortunate at best (in *Boundless Realm* I belabor this point for almost a full page, for you gluttons for punishment). The boats developed by Intamin for Pirates and Small World fall right in the middle, neither better nor worse, but different. If the 1967 Arrow ride system floated along at a pace best described as contemplative, then Vekoma boats scoot along with efficiency. I feel this does slightly harm It's a Small World, which becomes a blur of color, but here at Pirates the increased speed really does help key into an action-adventure tone. It also means that a ride that could have topped 15 minutes is over in 8. The largest Pirates of the Caribbean in size (Paris) is almost as exactly as long in duration as the smallest Pirates of the Caribbean (Florida).

Passing through the wreck of the ship, we spot a playful octopus and crab who have discovered a treasure chest, a premonition of the attraction's penultimate scene. Then the mood darkens as we pass the mouth of the lagoon, see the open ocean beyond, and pass a Jolly Roger washed up on the shore of the inlet. The boats head back into the fort, where a change has taken place.

The fortress no longer appears to be derelict upon our return; blazing torches and an upbeat rendition of "Yo Ho" seem to speak to human habitation. Moreover, a massive piece of machinery, run on weights and counterweights, has spring to life, hauling boats up a long ramp. As we ascend, the sounds of distant cannon fire can be heard. The pirates are attacking.

One fascinating aspect of this "cargo lift" scene is that WDI chose to bring over the "rat eyes" from the Upramp at Disneyland, the intriguing last thing we see at the end of that iconic ride. I don't know if this was done simply as a tribute to a small touch that stays with everyone who has ridden the original, but their meaning in Paris seems to be wildly different. To begin with there's maybe seven of them in Disneyland but it feels like Paris has at least fifty; they blink from all sides all the way up the lift hill. More intriguingly the "rat eyes" return at the end of the ride, just before we disembark. This seems to link them to the curse that befalls the Pirates of the Caribbean, some strange manifestation of fate tightening its noose around the criminals.

Upon arriving atop the fortress, we can now peer down from the battlement and into the Bombardment Bay scene. But the boats quickly dart away through low passages and flooded arches, creating a real sense of attempting to escape the battle. All around the sounds of musket fire and clattering swords create a tense atmosphere, and shadows of the soldiers of the garrison can be spotted reloading muskets and charging back into the fight. Two cats are trapped on floating boxes, seeming to parody our dire situation. Pirates are climbing over the wall of the fort, and one swings over our heads on a rope.

Finally we come across the jail with its prisoners trying to escape. The ceiling timbers actually start to split and break above the boats as they slip through a hole in the wall, down a drop, and splash down alongside the blazing cannon in Bombardment Bay.

This opening sequence really is the attraction operating at a high level. Even the attraction's biggest boosters would probably never describe Pirates of the Caribbean as "tense", but the opening minutes of the Paris ride really are unforgettable. The peaceful tone and epic scale of the Blue Lagoon and shipwreck start to tighten down into ever smaller interior spaces. There's no music, simply the sound of a raging battle. This stretch of the ride featured an early and incredibly effective use of mixed media, with silhouetted *laserdisc projections!* giving the impression of a fleetingly glimpsed pitched battle. Our first glimpse of an audio-animatronic figure was only a partial view, followed by the pirate swinging above our head on a rope, a gag which still takes first time riders by surprise. And if the drop down into Bombardment Bay abbreviates and blunts its hallucinatory majesty, it's at least an exciting climax to the ride's first real thrill. The opening four minutes of this attraction are the most successful transformation of a legacy attraction at Disneyland Paris, and still pack a punch.

At this point the attraction picks up the Disneyland original relatively faithfully. The Well and Auction scenes are repeated, and the Chase scene has been truncated to simply one pirate chasing one wench and one wench chasing one pirate. New in the scene is a pair of dueling pirates who sword fight for the honor of a lady. For the development of Disneyland Paris, Imagineers were careful to draw as many connections to Hollywood movies as possible for their French audience, figuring Europeans were more familiar with our movies than our mythology. This is an interesting case where there is an injection of a romantic pirate into a Gothic pirate work. One could almost expect the sword fighting pirate to be Errol Flynn.

Following the fire scene, boats slip into an underground arsenal and plunge down a waterfall as the entire room blows apart around it, finally making good on the deleted ending of the Disneyland attraction. The placement of this second drop seems to reference the baffling placement of a second drop in the Disneyland television special *From The Pirates of the Caribbean To The World of Tomorrow*. Disney liked to boast that this explosion involved the activation of "72 special effects", which sounds more impressive before you count a special effect as, you know, a single flashing light.[54] When I saw this in 2015 it was basically a camera flash, although a 2017 refurbishment restored things such as water splashes, smoke, and so on.

The echoes of ignited powder kegs seem to fade to the peal of thunder as the boats drift into the caverns below the fortress to discover what happened to the Pirates of the Caribbean.

The first room here is a beauty, with waterfalls on all sides, a half sunken boat with seagull, and a compact version of the Hurricane Lagoon. That scene never had the impact here it has in the other versions, probably because riders are still all a-twitter at having been dumped down a waterfall.

The relocated caverns sequence does change the meaning of them. At Disneyland they act as the initiation of the mystery; here they're a simple and even obvious "crime doesn't pay" epilogue. They're also shorter than they are in any other version; barely a 90 second postscript compared to the near four-minute introductory section at Disneyland. I will not go so far to say this makes it *worse*, simply that the placement and the length, after so much spectacle, does temper its impact. The caverns sequence in Paris is the decompression space where the spell is winding up and we have time to digest what we have seen. In the plus category this does mean that the attraction ends on the image of the unreal treasure cache, perfectly summarizing the pointless greed of the pirates: gold gold everywhere and not a bit to spend. This brings us full circle to the octopus and crab cavorting with the discovered treasure chest in the hold of the sunken ship, the plundered wealth that transformed the world into an inferno.

There is a lot to like about this version of Pirates of the Caribbean. It's faithful to the Disneyland original and takes care to replicate even the minor details which make that attraction so entrancing, but it also isn't so indebted to that original model to be afraid to innovate. The designers throughout keep in mind the salient characteristics of the attraction but also want to create the best, most logical, most consistent and clear version possible. It is probably the geekiest version of Pirates of the Caribbean, which is not necessarily a bad thing. But is it the best?

Well... I personally say no, but I admit it's possibly a close second behind the original. It transforms the material into an action-adventure without sacrificing the haunted, moralistic bent. And it does so in a way that's consistently spectacular, innovative and crowd pleasing.

Disneyland Paris: From Sketch to Reality

Disneyland Paris suffered a fate worse than it deserved. Disney was very naive in attempting to open this park. Eisner's greatest successes up to that point had been basically impulsive gestures and, buoyed by one of the most remarkable business turnarounds in modern history, Eisner sincerely seemed to believe that Disneyland Paris could not fail.

Disney used models developed at Walt Disney World and Tokyo Disneyland to predict the behavior of Europeans, assumptions which did not hold. Europeans may take longer vacations, but they spend less to make up the difference and tended to want to do the park on the cheap. Not helping anybody was Gary Wilson, whom Eisner had poached from Marriott, insisting on building an absurd 5,000 hotel rooms plus a campground.[55]

Eisner spent lavishly, not just inside the park where it counted, but *everywhere*. He insisted on an entertainment complex on the front doorstep of the park, initially designed in a budget conscious Cape Cod style. Eisner instead commissioned Frank Gehry to create an abstract representation of the ruins of a power plant. In one legendary

X. The Pirates Sack Asia and Europe

instance, Eisner nudged a single building on the model of the park a few inches to the left. The nudge cost the company $1.5 million.[56] Nobody could tell Eisner no. Presented with evidence by Larry Murphy that the mounting costs had crippled the park's ability to service its own debt, Eisner exploded: "*I don't understand this. The pro formas said we could spend this.*" "*That's because people told you what you wanted to hear,*" responded Murphy.[57]

And oh yes, the debt. Wilson had engineered a byzantine ownership agreement which protected Disney to the greatest extent possible. The problem is that when money is spent, *somebody* needs to go into debt, and in this case the resort itself was somebody. A plan to sell off the five hotels past the Disney Village never materialized, in part because attendance was so low. The resort opened with 3 billion in debt that it simply could not hope to recoup.

It's an open question how much Eisner blamed Imagineering for the failure, but the fact is that from 1992 onwards the division would be working with reduced expectations and reduced budgets. Eisner prized himself as a creative at heart and never publicly spurned the group, but the subsequent history of the Walt Disney Company demonstrated that something inside Michael Eisner had shifted. As Jeffrey Katzenberg later said, "*It was his Waterloo.*"

But in the end, gloomy financial predictions and rough starts be damned, Disneyland Paris remains a rich and intoxicating experience. Tony Baxter set out to amaze people, and amaze people this park continues to do.

In a larger sense the opening of Disneyland Paris was the final step in the journey that began so long ago when Walt Disney began secretly buying land in Florida. Disney had come a long way from being a studio devoted to the interests of one weirdo to a now massively multinational corporation.

The epic crossing of the globe was now complete. Like the British Empire, the sun never sets on a Disney castle.

XI. PIRATES 'R' GOOD ENOUGH

When does a classic become a classic? Ten years? Fifteen years?

Everyone who rides Pirates of the Caribbean loves it, but by the early 1980s it was becoming apparent that the ride was something more than the simply amusing adventure it may appear to be on the surface. The lines for the ride actually *grew*, not shrank, requiring a pedestrian bridge be built over the constant flood of humanity trying to get in to see the show. Tributes to the attraction's enduring popularity began to appear in print. In the 70s, such accounts simply referred to the attraction as a "favorite among guests"; by the 80s, writers were getting more verbose.

Ned Powers in the *Star-Phoenix* logged an article[1] supposedly about the popularity of Disneyland but which over half of is simply a description of the attraction. After calling the ride "unique and dazzling", the animatronics "magical and unbelievable", and the details "magnificent", he sums up his report by stating "*It's the kind of attraction where people rub their eyes in disbelief the first time through. If you have the time, the Pirates of the Caribbean deserves a second or even third look.*" His article ends with news that Fantasyland also exists.

Appropriate for a writer from a theme park town, Rob Morse in the Orlando Sentinel[2] wrote one of the best essays on the attraction from this era. "*It's time to celebrate the Disney imagineers' most amazing feat, the greatest amusement-park ride of all time: Pirates of the Caribbean. Hollywood producers should be riding it over and over to figure out how the Disney organization turned rape, torture and all that other juicy stuff into palatable middle-American entertainment. The Rev. Jerry Falwell could board the little boat, take the 15-minute ride and never realize that the whole thing is about human degradation.*

[...] All of this is not to say that Pirates of the Caribbean should be banned, or even condemned. It's an incomparably entertaining ride, and probably a lot less harmful to children than the average cereal commercial."

Los Angeles Times writer Robert Gore had some fun in 1980[3] following a group of Chinese sailors to Disneyland, supposedly the very first to visit from Mainland China since the Communist takeover. Apparently toeing the Red party line, the sailors declared their favorite ride to be "the world of children", but even they couldn't resist the robotic criminals: "*It was underground. It was a dark society and we don't like such kind of persons.*" Silly, that's the whole point.

Perhaps even closer to home was Israeli activist Natan Sharansky, who spent years in prison in the Soviet Union, and went to Disneyland saying: "*I'm tired of the official America. I wanted to see the real America.*" He continued his trip report: "*Like in Russia, there were long, long lines. We chose one that was not so long, only forty-five minutes. It was Pirates of the Caribbean. Then we understand the real secrets of Americans: to find the easiest way to have some decent adventures with happy endings.*"

Scenes from the ride were even featured on a stamp set released by Turks and Calicos Islands in 1985. These re-draw Marc Davis's art from the early 60s in a cartoon style and added some suspect historical connections. The Captain at the Well is said to be Bartholomew Roberts, and for some reason the skeleton atop the pile of treasure is labeled "The Fate of Captain William Kidd". Disney's fiction was already starting to blur with fact.

The collapse of the studio system in the 70s meant that it was harder and harder to find organizations willing to take on the huge cost of filming ocean-going adventures. Pirate films were made, rest assured, but you have never heard of them.

All of this meant that Disney's ride had the cultural stage practically all to itself; for millions, Disneyland's ride-through siege became the one, the **only** point of cultural contact with pirates. So before picking up our story of the ride, let's take a trip through a small gallery tracing the influence of the attraction on subsequent creative visions of buccaneering.

Perhaps the first acknowledgement of the cultural cachet of the attraction came from within its own industry. Bill Tracy was a wildcat attraction designer working the Northeast amusement park industry from his home base in New Jersey.

Tracy was everything Walt Disney was not: a hard-drinking weirdo with limited resources and a feverish imagination. From Tracy's workshop in North Jersey - *it's always New Jersey* - came a constant deluge of paper mâché figures which are equal parts lurid and grotesque, almost outsider art.

As hard as it may be to imagine Tracy sitting down in front of the television with a bottle of scotch to check in on Walt Disney, his work definitely shows an awareness of what Disneyland had on offer. Tracy spent much of the early 60s packaging up "Jungle River" refurbishments for amusement parks looking to spice up their dated log flumes and old mills; in one legendary case he even installed his jungle theme inside an *automatic car wash*.

One Tracy installation, Dracula's Castle in Lagoon Amusement Park[5], begins with a trip past creepy portraits hung on both sides on the ride car and ends with a series of wall crypts with comical epitaphs... strong evidence that Tracy knew the Haunted Mansion well. To have accompanied Bill Tracy to Walt Disney World in its early days would have been a wild time. One wonders if he was ejected from the bar at the Polynesian.

Following the opening of Pirates of the Caribbean at Disneyland, Tracy instantly zeroed in on the attraction's signature image: the merging of pirates and skeletons. Tracy had already been offering pirate attraction themes for years, but following the debut of the Disneyland ride - or, more likely, its showing on national television in January 1968[6]- Tracy's "Pirates Cove" funhouse attractions would be filled with skeletons hoisting bottles and steering ghost ships. This is only the *earliest* hint that Marc Davis' skeleton gags were going to end up stealing the show from the rest of the pirates.

Disney-inflected skeleton helmsman at the Pirates Cove walkthrough attraction at Waldameer Park, Erie, PA. Built by Bill Tracy in 1972. Photo by the author, August 2019.

Back in 1966, when Walt's team loaded into a company station wagon and departed from 1401 Flower Street to make the drive down I-5 to Disneyland, they could not have imagined that their troubled pirate ride would be the defining work in the entire themed entertainment industry.

But time had passed and the zeitgeist had passed Disney by. A new generation was coming of age, one which demanded entertainment of a higher caliber than that which amused the children of the fifties. And just five miles away from WED Enterprises, deep in the bowels of Universal City, Steven Spielberg had already been coronated as the Walt Disney of the 1980s.

What to make of Steven Spielberg? One old theory has it that filmmakers are like tuning forks; every so often one comes along who can vibrate perfectly in tune with the needs of an era. What Walt Disney was for Post-War America, Spielberg was for the 1980s.

Spielberg had grown up in New Jersey - *it's always New Jersey* - as a nerdy outsider. Like most nerds he had fixated quickly upon some hobby that would be his protective talisman in a hostile world; Steve made 8mm movies with toy trains. His parents divorced when he was a teenager, an event he later described as the worst experience of his life. While not exactly the hardscrabble young life of labor that produced Walt Disney, both men would use their childhood traumas to address the needs of a mass audience.

All we have to do is compare the vision of childhood presented in *So Dear To My Heart* and *E.T.* to see the fundamental differences. *So Dear* represents the official, sanctified, basically Victorian conception of childhood as a naive and colorful wonderland; the childhood Walt Disney didn't have and resented having been deprived of.

Spielberg, who grew up with Walt Disney's saccharine childhood imagery elevated to national myth, presents children closer to how they really are: complicated little jerks living in the shadow of an adult world. As critic Art Murphy pointed out in Variety at the time, *E.T.* succeeded while Disney films of 1982 failed because Spielberg recognized the harsh reality of divorce[7] and incorporated it into his fantasy. If Walt Disney were still alive, Murphy contended, he would have changed with the times.

But pure topicality isn't entirely what's going on here. Spielberg, like Disney, mixed and matched cultural touchstones into new and surprising combinations. *Jaws* could have been a simple action picture, but it's actually a character portrait in which the characters happen to be engaged in hunting a huge shark.

Spielberg softened and sanded off the sharp edges from Indiana Jones, who could have been a James Bond parody. At the heart of *Jurassic Park* is the story of a paleontologist who is surprised to discover inside himself the spirit of a father. All of these transformations enliven genre material and, under Spielberg's uncannily savvy direction, punch up emotional content to operatic extremes.

E.T. was *the* monster box office hit of the 80s. At its height, the film was earning Spielberg a cool half-million dollars **a day.** Just as

Walt Disney had founded WED to give him a sandbox he had complete control of, Spielberg took some of that money and founded his own studio to help subsidize his volcanic engendering of content. At Amblin, Spielberg became a one-man entertainment empire. His projects for Amblin often began as films he would have liked to have directed, but couldn't. In 1985, while preparing to film *The Color Purple*, he was executive producing what he described as two "Saturday Matinee kid flicks"[8] - *Young Sherlock Holmes* and *The Goonies*.

Spielberg's Amblin films became outlets for his less responsible impulses as a filmmaker; the side of Spielberg that Molly Haskell deliciously termed the "unofficial Spielberg". The side of Spielberg who delighted in fine-tuning jump scares or spent all night at the gun range with John Milius. Unofficial Spielberg had his knuckles rapped very publicly in summer 1984 for *Gremlins* and *Indiana Jones and the Temple of Doom*; thereafter, his public appearances would be sporadic. *The Goonies* represents one of Unofficial Spielberg's purest anarchic inventions; its absurd flywheel plot plays almost exactly like it's being made up on the fly by a hyperactive seven-year-old.

The Goonies, as almost everyone knows by now, concerns a group of four outcast nerd kids in Astoria Oregon who leave on a pirate treasure hunt the day before their entire neighborhood is set to be foreclosed upon by an obnoxious real estate developer. Along the way they pick up an older brother as well as two high-school girls and run afoul of The Fratellis, a cartoonish gangster family on the run. Traveling underground through a series of booby-trapped caverns, they finally find the pirate gold and save their homes.

The Goonies was written by Chris Columbus, who had caught Spielberg's attention with his script for *Gremlins*. Spielberg and director Joe Dante had turned *Gremlins* into an almost unrecognizable horror satire, but Spielberg kept working with Columbus, eventually becoming something of a mentor.[9]

In order to turn his rambunctious kiddie matinee into reality, Spielberg reached out to director Richard Donner. Donner had been a television director through the 60s, including on the "*Nightmare at*

20,000 Feet" episode of *The Twilight Zone*. In the 1970s Donner had broken through into mainstream movies with *The Omen* and *Superman*.

The film this creative team put together is a one-of-a-kind confection. Almost instantly *The Goonies* became the namer of its own genre: starring a group of kids, a little exciting, a little scary... a Goonies-alike. Some movies, like *The Monster Squad* (1987) and *It* (2017), came close to recapturing that appeal, but few have ever attempted this exact blend of frenzied jeopardy, crazy cartoon logic, and heartfelt emotion.

The film has such obvious Spielbergian themes that the contribution of Richard Donner is all too easy to overlook; the truth is, Richard Donner owns *The Goonies*. In everything from choosing the location in the Pacific Northwest to directing the young cast and tempering some of Columbus' and Spielberg's crazier notions, *The Goonies* works because of what Donner brought to the table. Donner knew that getting fully realized performances out of seven kids was going to be an impossibility and so cannily cast them based on their similarity to the characters; the unfiltered clowning we see on screen is genuine.

To help realize this family atmosphere, the production bought out the entire Thunderbird Motel[10] in Astoria and brought up the entire crew and their families. Parents socialized and baked each other cakes. Donner encouraged the kids to ad-lib, talk over one each other, roughhouse, and not stick to the script. Even if the characters aren't exactly well rounded, the chemistry and energy is infectious and that sense of observing real kids gives the film a center that Columbus' script lacks.

It may be useful to see *The Goonies* as part of an unofficial series of "kiddie peril" adventures by Spielberg. The deep source of all such tales is probably *The Adventures of Tom Sawyer,* where the playtime of Tom and his friends shades seamlessly into terror and adventure. Spielberg himself was no stranger to using children as plot devices to engage audience sympathies; missing children are the engine of the plot in *Close Encounters of the Third Kind, Poltergeist,* and *An American Tail*. Just one year previous, the disappearance of an entire village of children is the central mystery in *Indiana Jones and the Temple of Doom*. *Goonies* almost feels like a flip of the same basic concept as *Temple of Doom*, where the kids become their own heroes.

All of which is to say that *The Goonies* plays nimbly with the differences between adults and children. The kids are the ones to take action in this story; the adults are pictured as sleazy developers or oblivious bystanders. To the Goonies, grown-ups are helpless; would-be Goonie Chester Copperpot was killed by the first booby trap he came across.

The character of Sloth, which on the surface could be a baffling or borderline offensive addition to an already overstuffed pie, is the key to unlocking this film's games with authority. Sloth is a cartoon exaggeration of the kids, an absurdly massive adult with the heart of a child who is such a tragic outsider he's imprisoned by his family, Cinderella-like. There is a secret connection between the kids and Sloth that the adventure uncovers; by the end he has become part of their family.[11]

The only other adult character in the film remotely on the same level as the Goonies is the dead pirate captain One-Eyed Willy. Mikey's home-built Rube Goldberg devices subtly establish a connection between the Goonies and the pirates, who have built their own improbable traps in the caverns beneath Astoria (the Goldberg devices were probably inspired by Mack Sennet's "*Our Gang*" comedies). Once Mikey finally "meets" the skeletal remains of One-Eyed Willy, he discovers that Willy was a deformed outsider, like Sloth. The Goonies are the only ones capable of saving their homes because they are the only ones in town who can *think like pirates*.

This conception of piracy as essentially an extended childhood of irresponsibility tallies well with our modern, apolitical mythology of pirates, a fact that *The Goonies* exploits without making too fine of a point about it. One Eyed Willy as a proxy Goonie gives the film a subtle emotional punch, and at the end of the film when the ancient pirate ship sets sail for the horizon it creates a feeling of catharsis because those childish chaotic energies have been transformed into an image of romance. It's a happy ending for all Goonies everywhere.

The film is also, you know, pretty nakedly inspired by Pirates of the Caribbean at Disneyland. Absolutely nowhere have I been able to find a printed admission of this; the nearest I've come is that the movie is based on "an original idea of Spielberg's".[12] But perhaps in the end nothing more need be said than that it's an adventure that begins at a restaurant, goes underground through a series of caves with skeletons and waterfalls and arrives at a massive indoor pirate ship.

Also consider that in Chris Columbus' script, the final booby trap which releases the imprisoned pirate ship also hoisted the skeleton of One-Eyed Willy through the ceiling where he emerges behind the ship's wheel. Had this been filmed, the movie would have ended with a recreation of the attraction's Signature Image. Spielberg recognized the attraction as a key source of pirate ideas and images and scooped it up into his net of inspirations just as quickly as he did *The Sea-Hawk*. *The Goonies* commemorates the Disneyland attraction's passage into American mythology.

The Goonies publicity still © Warner Brothers. Author's Collection.

In the years since its release, *The Goonies* had graduated from an 80s favorite to something of an enduring classic. The working-class milieu accurately captures much of the vague crappiness of middle-class America, and except for a few very 1985 touches the film could conceivably take place anywhere between 1975 and 1995. Nowhere in the film are things like computers or cell phones; it's the analog world that my generation remembers.

This means that twenty years of kids have been able to identify with *The Goonies* and it's become something of an ark for the entire concept of childhood. If you were a kid in the last decades of the 20th century, there's a good chance you are a Goonie, too.

Astoria, Oregon has become a mecca for nostalgic adults. The drizzly, foggy green world the film conjures up has perhaps done more to raise awareness of the beauty of the Pacific Northwest than any travelogue ever could. Visitors can try to walk up to the *Goonies* house, or visit the jail where the film begins and peer into one of the cells at a costume worn by Ke Huy Quan. Donner's assertion on the location search that they had found a place "*that needed the Goonies to save it*" was accurate in more ways than one.

In 2017, the film was entered into the National Film Registry. In 2019, Pirates of the Caribbean at Disneyland, the basis of so much of the film's setting, returned the compliment by adding a new scene of a skeleton caught in a booby-trap.

The Goonies has become part of the cultural myth of piracy, the only mainstream pirate film of any consequence released between 1950 and 2003. Goonies really are good enough.

And now for something completely different. In 1976 director Roman Polanski sat down with the *Los Angeles Times* and said: "*I feel like doing something very entertaining. I'm a great customer of Disneyland. Every time I go on the pirates ride I think I would like to do a film.*"[13]

It would take more than a decade after the airing of this surprising news for Polanski's pirate film to reach screens, which it ultimately did as a Franco-Tunisian production starring Walter Matthau.

Roman Polanski's Pirates is a fascinating, difficult movie that requires some unpacking, which I will try to do quickly. Polanski conceives of pirates strictly as fairy tale figures, escapees from Saturday matinees and totally divorced from history. The film that helps explain Polanski's relationship to fairy tale material is his 1967 farce *Dance of the Vampires*, which is best described as something like *Into the Woods*, but even bleaker. As such, *Pirates* is another one of Polanski's indigestible comedies of absurdity, alongside cult fare like *Cul de Sac* (1965) and *What?* (1972).

In other words, Polanski's cultural background and his sense of humor were never going to produce anything that mainstream audiences would ever consider an acceptable pirate movie... but bless him for trying anyway, because this movie is capital-W Weird.

Pirates begins with Mattau's Captain Red and his young assistant Frog adrift on a raft in the middle of the ocean; Red is contemplating eating the boy. Lunch is interrupted and they board a Spanish galleon where the primary activity seems to be constant whippings; thrown in the brig, Red spots a massive Aztec throne made of gold that's being transported back to Spain and immediately plots a mutiny. From there the movie keeps getting bigger and crazier through double-crossings, revolutions, and battles until finally Red and Frog find themselves back where they began... on a boat in the middle of the endless sea, only this time with the captain sitting proudly on his huge golden throne. There is food and wine, for now.

The trouble with *Pirates* is that the setup promises audiences one thing and the film delivers something else. Walter Matthau is grossly miscast - Polanski wanted Jack Nicholson - and his presence signals the film to be more of a family adventure, which it absolutely is not.

It's hard to know what to make of Polanski's claims that the film will be "comedy adventure, the kind of thing you dream of as a child". It isn't even a dark fantasy like *The Dark Crystal* or *Time*

Bandits, which were *au courant* in the era. The film has a grimy atmosphere replete with sharply rendered violence and cruelty; in terms of aesthetics it's actually much closer to the 21st century Disney movies than anything made in the 80s. As a result the film falls between two poles, satisfying neither as a pitch-black comedy nor as the lighthearted adventure it wants to be.

But! ... If you *can* overlook that, it's a very interesting creative response to the idea of piracy.

Captain Red and Frog are classic Polanski protagonists, as in his 1958 short *Two Men and a Wardrobe*, where unnamed protagonists struggle to carry the cumbersome piece of furniture from ocean to ocean for no explained reason. Captain Red's greed for the throne is pointless, counterproductive; his pirate crew have already tried to maroon him in the past and he can expect no reward for capturing it. Red is so ineffectual that at one point he presents captives for ransom and is told that the current market prices for nieces of governors is so depressed that they're not worth the trouble! Perhaps the cheerful fatalism of the attraction commanded his attention, for these are uncommonly un-glamorous pirates.

The film is gorgeously mounted, looking like every bit the $40 million that is said to have been invested, but it returned something like $8 million worldwide. When Roger Ebert wrote, " *There hasn't been a pirate movie in a long time, and after Roman Polanski's "Pirates," there may not be another one for a very long time"*, he was right.

The film received a single North American home video release on VHS in the 80s and has fallen into total obscurity since. Polanski's current dire reputation has a lot to do with it; who wants to see a lighthearted adventure comedy from a man better known for being a fugitive from justice? But for viewers longing for a less romanticized version of piracy and willing to be patient, *Pirates* is a peculiar artifact - almost worth taking in for pure weirdness alone.

One last example in our gallery of Disneyland-inflected pirates. It took Steven Spielberg until 1983 to create his own production studio, but George Lucas started off his career that way. Lucasfilm dates back to 1971, when it was organized to be a hub for independent filmmakers based in San Fransisco.

As you may have heard, history didn't pan out that way.

Flash forward to 1984, with *Star Wars* seemingly in the rearview mirror. Swimming in cash, Lucas set up a studio to create video games. The trouble is, Lucasfilm had already cut a deal with Atari for the creation of games like *Raiders of the Lost Ark*. Ron Gilbert, one of the original game division employees, recalled: "*If we had been able to make* Star Wars *games, it's probably all we would have done.*"[14]

Starting as but a single room on the Skywalker Ranch, Lucasfilm Games - better known as LucasArts - had their breakout moment with *Maniac Mansion*, a sendup of horror tropes created by Ron Gilbert. *Maniac Mansion* streamlined the player interface of PC adventure games by inventing the famous action interface. This focuses the experience on solving puzzles and enjoying the environment instead of typing commands; like in *Super Mario Brothers*, you don't need to worry about what you're doing - you just do it. *Maniac Mansion* is frequently hilarious, often subversive, and full of little narrative sidebars and endings locked behind seven different characters. This was a virtual world worth getting lost in.

Ron Gilbert's next creation for LucasArts would be *The Secret of Monkey Island*, a glorious pirate comedy. Starring the unforgettable Guybrush Threepwood as he sets out to become a pirate, *Monkey Island* outdoes itself in self-aware silliness. After mastering the skills of piracy on Melee Island, the undead pirate LeChuck and his crew of skeletons abducts the governor of the island, the lovely Elaine Marley. Threepwood, of course, sets out to rescue her.

After assembling a crew and buying a used boat - which he immediately sinks - Threepwood finds himself marooned on Monkey Island, which doubles as an entrance to Hell. Captain LeChuck plans to marry Governor Marley...

The world the game creates is full of quirky anachronisms, where pirates drink root beer out of Grog vending machines and looting of the governor's mansion is by reservation only. As the story progresses, characters increasingly break the fourth wall, with Threepwood frequently talking back to the player through the computer screen when they command him to make bad choices. Late in the game players encounter a Ben Gunn character, marooned on Monkey Island, who has access to a boat but refuses to leave of his own accord. "*If you're stranded you've GOT to be rescued! It's in the rules!*"

The Secret of Monkey Island is a case of a work taking perfect advantages of the limitations of its format. Smooth scrolling, built into video game consoles at a hardware level, was still impractical for home computers which were really intended first and foremost to crank out a mean spreadsheet. Adventure games were perfect for PCs, in the sense that they could be deep without being exceedingly resource-heavy. *Monkey Island* may be simple, but it is simple and perfect. Extremely important moments or jokes are presented in more realistic but only slightly animated facial portraits. But the bulk of the game plays out with amazingly expressive animated figures. These have just enough detail to be legible but are truly memorable, like the used ship salesman who wears a hideous plaid overcoat and flails his arms constantly.

The funniest scene in the game plays out entirely in the zoomed-out animated sprite view, as Threepwood arrives at Hook Isle via rubber chicken zip line (!) and confronts Meathook, a pirate with two hook hands who is terrified of the parrot he lives with.

The game is so good and the writing is so sharp that we can read everything we need to into the characters in these tiny pixel-art faces, and the results can be devastatingly funny. The main battle mechanic is sword fighting, but you never control Threepwood's arms - instead battles are won by insulting your rivals into submission, a mechanic that would seem to be inspired by the Dread Pirate Roberts in *The Princess Bride*.

Combined with the gorgeous hand-created pixel art scenery in lush 256 colors and Michael Land's calypso-inflected soundtrack - possibly the best pirate theme ever written[15] - and *Secret of Monkey*

Secret of Monkey Island. Taken by the Author in DOSBox.

Island transcends its hardware limitations by making us forget them. With limited colors, rare musical accompaniment, and smart use of animation, *Monkey Island* simply cannot be improved.[16]

The game also very clearly took Pirates of the Caribbean as a starting point, as Gilbert told the LucasArts publicity newsletter *The Adventurer* in 1990:

> *"One of my favorite rides at Disneyland is Pirates of the Caribbean. You get on a little boat and it takes you through a pirate adventure, climaxing with a cannon fight between two big pirate ships. Your boat keeps you moving through the adventure, but I've always wished I could get off and wander around, learn more about the characters, and find a way onto those ships."*

Indeed, the game is replete with the attraction's signature deep blue and bright yellow color scheme, especially in Melee Island. Trips up through the forested interior of the island are awash with silhouetted trees and fireflies, as in the Blue Bayou.

Gilbert zeroed in on pirate skeletons as an idea worth elaborating on, as had Bill Tracy and Steven Spielberg before him. LeChuck's crew of skeleton pirates are indeed very familiar. Also very evocative is a pirate town attached to a fortress, and a few small details such as a bed with a skull headboard.

But it's easy to make too much of this; Pirates is only *one* starting point, and just as much credit goes to Tim Powers' *On Stranger Tides* and Gilbert's detestation of fantasy adventure game tropes. In a way, Monkey Island points not back, but forward to the future of the Pirates of the Caribbean attractions...

......Maybe. That is a story for another chapter.

Despite everything, LucasArts games were never as profitable as those created by Sierra Online and the studio's demise was nearly unavoidable by the late nineties. But LucasArts' template became the industry standard almost immediately, and their verb-based interface banished the old text box system forever. We don't call these *Adventure* games anymore; their user interface was the genre namer. We call them *Point and Click* games, and *Secret of Monkey Island* is the standard bearer which has influenced thousands of developers since. It's the sweet spot where technology, artistry and ambition all "clicked" into a perfect whole.

This small gallery of works inspired by the attraction demonstrates not just that its ideas have been fully dissolved into our *cultural understanding* of pirates, but that these works have also helped ensure the longevity of the attraction. Ideas which were weird abnormalities in the 60s, like starting with a restaurant set in a bayou or caves filled with corpses, keep percolating and trickling down through the culture in new ways, creating a new 20th century mythology of pirates.

Walt Disney's pirates became all of our pirates, and to be a pirate means to have come from Disneyland.

XII. WEIGHT WATCHERS OF THE CARIBBEAN

"The object of their chase will be food."
- *Disneyland spokeswoman Susan Roth, Jan 4 1997*

As the foregoing several hundred pages have suggested, piracy is a pretty flexible narrative construct. Try to nail it down into being just one thing or - god help you - suggest that *your* particular interpretation is grounded in historic reality and pirates will slip out from under your grasp once again. If they're not broken hearted romantics they're childlike innocents, or fast-food mascots, or proprietors of miniature golf courses.

Still, there are some constants, and bad behavior is one of them. Of course, defining bad behavior is even slipperier than trying to define pirates; it's horribly contextual. Everyone wants to see pirates run up a black flag and declare war on the world, but in order for the fantasy to work correctly there has to be a world worth rebelling against in the first place.

That's a razor thin line to walk, because the moment the pirates declare war on you - your values - the fantasy ends. That's the distinction between pirates and terrorists. Stephan Fjellman, always the sociologist, places a pin on that razor line in *Vinyl Leaves* when he points out:

> *"It's not so clear, however, how we are to understand the raping and pillaging in Pirates of the Caribbean. The guidebooks all tell us that the ride is zany and that we will be amused. Well... yes, and no."*[7]

There have always been those who were not amused. Even in some of the earliest published appraisals of the exceptional qualities of the attraction, the specter of disapproval is always somewhere nearby. Rob Morse in "*Rape and Pillage on the Family Plan*" doesn't shy away from this razor edge; it's a disgusting display of vice and also a light entertainment.

Moreover, by the early 90s Disneyland and Walt Disney World had graduated out of their early probationary period and begun to be taken seriously as legitimate cultural forces. It is no accident that Fjellman's *Vinyl Leaves*, the first seriously written book to tackle the theme park question, appears on the scene almost twenty years after Walt Disney World opens.

And if we're going to maybe start taking these places seriously, then suddenly avenues of discussion open that would not if we were simply talking about disposable entertainment. And when we're talking about piracy, that way lies trouble. Perhaps the fiercest shot across the bow came from M. Denise Fraser-Vaselakos, who wrote in her newspaper column WomanSense in October 1993:

> *"Adding to the disgrace of an amusement park ride that sells women as slaves to pirates who rape and pillage, is Disney's perpetuation of the myth that women enjoy rape. One of the women being sold, a heavy-set woman, stood giggling and laughing about her fate. Does Disney World think women enjoy rape? Apparently yes. Does Disney World think heavy women should be grateful to "get a husband" any way they can? Apparently yes."* [18]

Fraser-Vaselakos was not some crank; she is a licensed psychologist with an emphasis on relationship and marriage counseling. WomanSense devoted its columns to advice about divorce, self-esteem, and gender equality, meaning that dissecting the assumptions behind the auction scene was literally her job. And she was not wrong.

In the decades since there's been something of an urban legend built up inside the Disney fan community that changes to the Pirates attractions were initiated in response to "complaints from feminists". Upon finding this article I was initially excited to find perhaps the deepest ancestor of these claims, the smoking gun behind decades of rumors... but I'm actually not all that convinced that this was somehow the shot heard 'round the Disney Studio. The paper

Fraser-Vaselakos wrote for may be a pretty big one in Chicago, but it's also a paper of limited circulation in one city. Fraser-Vaselakos' WomanSense ran intermittently for a few years before tapering off, with no real indication of having made a huge splash. In the pre-viral media universe of the early 90s, she was a voice in the wilderness.

But on the other hand...

The early 90s was a time of changes at Disney parks.[19] There was a time when certain attractions were gender segregated, such as the Enchanted Tiki Room only employing women and Jungle Cruise only employing men. This rule was finally ended in 1993, alongside a handful of other changes at the Hall of Presidents, Jungle Cruise, and American Adventure to better reflect current sensibilities. All of this was coming to a head with *Pocahontas*, embarrassing now but somewhat in the ballpark of progressive for 1995.

Given all of the above, it was probably only a matter of time before someone took a long hard look at Pirates of the Caribbean and decided it was time to make some changes.[20]

It's always interesting how Disney handles these alterations (look, I hope you agree with me that it's interesting, because a lot of the last part of this book is going to be devoted to exactly this). I'm not certain if it's due to some internal deference to Walt Disney... or simply the fact that gradual changes are always received better than drastic changes regardless of merit [21]... but the general approach seems to be to "*change things*" without "*changing anything*".

This often manifests in keeping as much of the original scene staging but changing the context of the characters in the scene, almost as if riders could be caught wondering if anything had changed at all.

In the case of something like the Chase Scene, which was the weakest part of the ride in 1967 and still is today, Imagineering's deference to the "architecture" of the original scene is really puzzling; wouldn't just a new scene of pirates drinking in a tavern be way better? Why continue to pay homage to the rule that *somebody has to be hiding in a barrel*?

Well, in the case of this original wave of changes, the culprit probably was budgetary. Pirates of the Caribbean at Magic Kingdom was patient zero for some cosmetic surgery in 1994.

The updates occurred in May 1994 and they were modest in scope.

The first turntable to the left, with the pirate chasing the pretty señorita, was changed to portray two pirates carrying off a chest of treasure. Next door on the second turntable, the pirate and lady have now switched positions, with the pirate's amorous extended arms now clutching chickens and the lady pursuing him with a pitchfork. Similar changes have been made to turntable four up behind the Pooped Pirate with a lady chasing down a pirate with a rolling pin. All of this means there's no reversal at the end of the scene - no punctuating joke that gave the scene a sense of conclusion.

But the "Pooped Pirate" at the barrel was the real problem in this stretch of the flume and what they ended up doing with him was just strange. In one extended arm, rather improbably pasted to his forearm, was a treasure map, and in the other now appeared a magnifying glass. The lady behind him in the barrel now was holding a very small treasure chest, no larger than a jewelry box.

At first, that was the extent of the changes; Paul Frees' original vocal performance, and the performance of the animatronic figure, was simply chopped down to remove any reference to the scene's original meaning of "a fascinating little old treasure."[22]

If this was a stopgap measure, it was obvious, and within a few months a new dialogue track and animatronic performance was created. This will win no awards for writing but it got the job done:

> "Avast mateys, it be treasure I'm looking for. I been lookin' for the X that marks the spot, but I be seeing no X's about this spot... belay thar ye lubbers, if you be seeing any X's about, shove off!"

This weirdly had the effect of making the girl in the barrel even less important to the scene - why would she be hiding from the Pooped Pirate if he was expressly looking for an "X that marks the spot"? But it does help explain the lingering strangeness that would remain the Chase scene in Florida's hallmark for the next dozen years. In this case, the two guys at the start of the scene were the only swabs aboard who had the right idea and found a treasure chest worth absconding with; all of the remaining pirates are pursuing treasures seemingly hardly worth the effort.

It was *fine, just fine*, as long as you didn't think too hard about it.

Eventually, this lighter touch would prove to be in some ways wiser.

Publicity still © Disney, Author's Collection.

Meanwhile, the World of Motion attraction at EPCOT Center closed in January 1996, and that got Tony Baxter to thinking. John Hench had asked Marc Davis to come back from retirement to help with designs for EPCOT and Tokyo Disneyland, and World of Motion was among the last attractions to open with new Marc Davis jokes and humor. With the attraction closing and ready to be gutted to make way for the GM Test Track ride, perhaps some of those animatronic could find a good home elsewhere - specifically, back home at Disneyland, in the Pirates of the Caribbean. The attraction was about to turn 30, and plans were underway to give the attraction a substantial upgrade to mark the occasion. This would turn out to be the impetus for one of the strangest renovations in Disneyland history.

The 1997 30th anniversary upgrades fell pretty discreetly into two camps: technical embellishments and substantive narrative alterations. Technical upgrades are of course always being looked at, but the 90s was the first time that Disney really began to go in and tinker with the content of these old Walt-era attractions. It's almost as though the comprehensive rethink of Disneyland's basic narrative content that was required to pull off Disneyland Paris created a feedback loop of reconsiderations that has continued to today.

New lighting throughout the "lower grotto" punched up the spooky atmosphere with supernatural greens and reds instead of the original white and blue lights that characterized this area; ever since then it's been a constant project to dial up or down the crazy multicolored lights depending on which team is in charge of the ride at which moment. A few new lighting effects were added, such as some clouds which come together to form a skull. The Paris ride had introduced video projections (run off very exciting *laserdisc technology!*) to add extra life and motion to scenes. One of these, showing the shadows of two men in a brawl, was added to the Burning City... before very quickly moving to the far tower in Bombardment Bay.

Figures sourced from World of Motion finally made the soldiers defending the fortress visible, a nice touch not brought back to any of the other locations. Animatronics were everywhere upgraded; for 1997, the new Auctioneer figure was the most sophisticated robot in any Disney show worldwide. The drunk on the bridge in the Auction scene now tips his bottle upside down and water trickles out onto the heads of riders, a fabulous touch. All of these additions, including a plaque outside the attraction commemorating its legendary design team, were nice embellishments. But once we start looking elsewhere in the attraction, things begin to get... weird.

And it's that Chase scene causing trouble again, and not for the last time! It seems as if every landmark theme park attraction has one of these scenes that doesn't work at all; Big Thunder Mountain had the earthquake, Indiana Jones Adventure had the rat-on-a-log and Harry Potter and the Forbidden Journey has the dementor attack. Attractions seem to work best when they're an escalating series of interesting ideas; this is why Bill Tracy rides can still be exciting while their technical execution is below par. But the trouble with ride-through attractions is that they're pretty much just a series of interesting vignettes; ideally you never break that flowing dream state long enough for riders to say "*hold up, isn't this rape?*".

So in 1997 Imagineering took their first stab at fixing the Chase scene and, understandably, they filled it up with... stuff. *So much stuff.*

The first two turntables to the left upon entering were removed, minimizing the chances of riders seeing the less-than-impressive run animation. A new figure of a befuddled pirate with a plate of food was added here. The two remaining turntables were now home to a pirate chasing some chickens with a pitchfork and a lady with a bottle of rum running away from a thirsty pirate. The Pooped Pirate was now surrounded by food, including a huge ham with a knife in it, more chickens, and a happy, grinning swine. A cat with a fish in its mouth popped out of the barrel.

The Pooped Pirate was now an out-of-control gourmand, waving a drumstick Henry the 8th style and commenting to passing boats:

> "*Ha ha ha! Oh, brush me barnacles, now where be that little old fish dinner I be looking for, eh? If you be hankerin' for a taste of this here bird's*

peg leg, I be willing to share, I be! Hahaha... [to the pig] I be hankering for a fine pork loin... maybe you can help me out a bit, eh?"

Again, this is one of those times where Imagineers being fans of Imagineering arguably didn't help, given that a pirate being a glutton but also offering food to passing boats doesn't entirely add up. Nearby, two pirates now escape with pies from the baker lady, who's chasing them down with her rolling pin. By far the best change to this scene was the relocation of the drunk pirate on the barrel, formerly in the Arsenal, to the courtyard. He was joined by two more pirates hoisting cups to catch streams of rum pouring out of barrels. Unlike most of the rest of these changes described above, he's still there today.

In other words, the whole scene was now about food and drink. I sometimes refer to the 1997 upgrades as the "seven deadly sins" version because adding gluttony and intemperance to the existing roster of vices is an intriguing angle, a "*new idea*" that helps smooth over these rougher edges.

Still, the scene didn't really cohere into the vision it was aiming for. It was hard to appreciate that the design team was reaching for an actual *new idea* here simply because there was so much to absorb.

The way the scenes in Pirates of the Caribbean tend to play out is that riders are oriented into the scene's premise pretty quickly through big, obvious visual clues - like a huge indoor boat - and then are permitted a few moments to "zoom in" on clever details, intricate scenery, or humorous touches. Compare this to the new chase scene which read visually as "a bunch of stuff". It was over before you had really absorbed it, and comprehension was not helped by all of the newly added clucking, oinking and braying which tended to drown out the gourmand pirate's running commentary.

The "food chase" scene may have gotten all of the attention and, uh, commentary, but the **real** interesting change was elsewhere in the ride, at the Upramp section. Two new pirates now appeared at the foot of the Upramp, straining and struggling to haul a huge load of treasure up the hill. A little further along were some dusty skeletons

XII. WEIGHT WATCHERS OF THE CARIBBEAN

who had stabbed each other over a treasure chest, with the echoed refrain of "dead men tell no tales" literalizing the circle closing.

This was very neat, and if you're reading this and never saw it, you're probably imagining something far more impressive than this really was.

The idea of the pirates trying to escape back up to the surface is a fabulous one, but the devil as always is in the details. Because the "lifting pirate" animatronic was repurposed from a guy trying to move an exhausted zebra (you had to be there) from World of Motion, he was connected permanently to a big round shape. This big shape became the sack of treasure, and it never looked quite right.

And *then* there's the fact that you could very clearly see the skeletons just a few feet behind the escaping pirates, and could easily see them from the Arsenal scene; it's not all that big of a ramp. And with the "dead men tell no tales" echoing inside the Arsenal scene along with all of the gunshots and music, the new addition ended up suffering the same sense of cacophony and feature creep that the Food Chase featured.

And about those skeletons... they were clearly the bolted-together plastic type that WED shunned in 1967, which meant that their ability to pose was limited; no custom Adolpho Procopio sculptures here. In the case of the pirate clinging to a treasure chest, the hands of the skeleton weren't convincingly "closed" around the chest, nor was the gesture of the skeleton convincing enough to appear to hoist and support the chest. It looked like a plastic skeleton hanging off a floating treasure chest, which is exactly what it was.[23]

Still, there was now a scene in an area if the attraction which previously had nothing to look at, which in and of itself is an upgrade.

But, you know, here's the thing: we shouldn't be too quick to condemn these efforts to spruce up what was after all a pretty old ride, and we will never see an ambitious and thoughtful refurbishment like this ever again. From genuine efforts to bring new ideas and new humor to the attraction, to treating animatronic figures like resources worthy of preservation, the Imagineering that led this charge is gone.

In the years since, Disney has scrapped beautiful vintage animatronics from Journey Into Imagination, Horizons, Country Bear

Jamboree, Pirates of the Caribbean, Universe of Energy, and America Sings and replaced them with ever more prevalent movie tie ins and projection screens. It's practically crazy talk to speak of a time when there was an actual effort to recover show value and add it to existing attractions, to punch up what was already there in ever more opulent ways.

And that is the true embarrassment - not that pirates are now eating turkey drumsticks and talking to pigs. This was one last hurrah to those traditional Walt-style show values which peaked at Disneyland Paris and Tokyo DisneySea and now have vanished beneath the drowning torrent of mediocrity which is 21st century Disney.

But as I said, this was the *first* and, in some ways, the *last* truly dramatic effort to rethink a classic attraction, and people did not take it well in 1997... not at all.

Disneyland in 1997 was at a crossroads. Since the early 90s the rise of the internet as a daily commodity had begun to spread; the launch of graphical web browsing in December 1994 turned many people's hobbies into more fervent pursuits for worse and worse-er.[24]

There had always been local devotees of Disneyland; in less than a year of the park's opening, something like three-quarters of its visitors were returning locals. For proof, watch *Disneyland After Dark*, an episode of Disneyland that was good enough to release theatrically in Europe. Near the end of the film the Elliot Brothers, the house band at the Plaza Gardens bandstand, ask how many of their audience have been to Disneyland before. Nearly everyone raises their hands. That was in 1962.

In late 1994,[25] former Disney Store head Paul Pressler became President of Disneyland, and his timing could not have been worse. Fans and annual pass-holders had begun organizing online, and they didn't like Mr. Pressler one bit. Amongst his least popular decisions were cutting operating hours and maintenance while adding more merchandise in places it previously was not.

Whether or not Pressler was truly responsible for these changes - the same thing happened at Walt Disney World at the same time - repeat visitors took notice. By 1996, their increasing consternation was getting loud enough for the Los Angeles Times to take notice, which took the form of a front-page article (!).

The Times spent a day with Scott Garner and Al Lutz, who eavesdropped on park radio chatter using a portable scanner, fretted about rumored changes to Great Moments with Mr. Lincoln, and bemoaned the state of Monstro the Whale at Storybook Land. It's like reading Twitter from a quarter century before the medium existed.

The Times sardonically noted, "*If the annual pass-holders are disgruntled they certainly aren't showing it at the gate. Thanks in part to better promotion and a price cut, the number of annual pass-holders has swelled under Pressler's watch to an estimated 200,000*".[26]

You read that right, Paul Pressler invented entitled pass-holders and complaints about budget cuts in one fell swoop, which explains a lot about modern Disney fandom. The mind boggles.

Consider the timing for a second. Tomorrowland at Disneyland closed for a big refresh in 1996. Disneyland announced their second gate as California Adventure in mid-1996. Pirates of the Caribbean reopened from its refurbishment in February 1997. In April 1997, the legendary pass-holder preview of Light Magic took place. It was a succession of disasters that would climax in February 2001 with the opening of Disney's California Adventure, and Pirates got its big refurbishment smack in the middle of these milestones. It was guilt by association, and nobody seemed to be in much of a mood to look objectively at what Imagineering had cooked up.

News of the refurbishment broke on January 4, 1997. The United States had just spent the entirety of summer 1996 doing the "Macarena". Toni Braxton was still wailing from the top 40 about un-breaking her heart. Cassette tapes around the country were still unspooling the soulful sounds of R. Kelly believing he can fly and Seal rhapsodizing about the kiss from a rose on the gray. It must have been

The short lived "Crime Doesn't Pay" coda. Jack and Leon Jensen Collection.

a quiet news day because newsmen began ringing people up to ask their opinion on revisions to fictional, robotic criminals.

Cynthia Graff, president of a weight control clinic in Orange County, opined on the newly food-based shenanigans: "*If it were a skinny woman chasing after the man holding food, I could understand that she may have the hunger. But with an overtly plump woman, then it's the old stereotype of the obese woman out of control. If what Disney is trying to do is bring sensitivity to gender issues, well, substituting food as the solution to the problem may present another problem.*"[27]

Judy Rosener, a professor at University of California Irvine, was more enthusiastic. "*I think it's great. It's Disney taking a nice little step in the direction of a more civil society.*"[28] Demonstrating that the more things change the more they stay the same, Rosener's comments produced an avalanche of hate mail. "*The angriest, ugliest calls and letters and e-mails you ever saw. It's as though I had ruined their whole adult male lives. Chasing women may be entertaining to men but not to women. And just because pirates did such things doesn't mean Disney has to depict it.*"[29]

All of this schadenfreude whipped interest up to a high level. The attraction reopened in March to capacity crowds. The Disneyland Hotel and Disneyland Pacific were entirely sold out. Tony Baxter spoke some good sense to the Associated Press: *"There were a few complaints about the bawdy nature of some of the scenes. Not enough to worry about, really. We just saw an opportunity to change it. We just wanted to shift the focus away from what was overtly sexual. I think it's funnier now, and that's the main thing for us."*

Park goers interviewed at the attraction seemed more sanguine: *"' To be honest, I couldn't really tell what had changed'* said Beth Harke of San Jose, one of the first Disneyland visitors to view the reopened ride. *'I liked it'* said Taylor Gonzales, one of the first riders. So did his big sister Tiffany. *'I didn't object to it before'* said their mom Tracy Gonzales, who brought the children from San Gabriel. *'We did notice the changes, though. I think they did a good job with it."*.

Tricia Tarrach, who flew from Yuba City to see the alterations, had some fun taking the piss out of the whole ordeal. *"Domestic violence, animal cruelty, it's worse than before!"*

In a bizarre postscript to this whole story, in May 2000 Disneyland held a special event inside the park themed to Pirates of the Caribbean featuring merchandise, a panel of Imagineers, and live actors inside the ride.

Disneyland president Cynthia Harris - she who would later go on to open Disney's California Adventure - appeared on a video screen welcoming attendees. As the camera pulled back, Harris was revealed to be locked in the on-ride jail scene. Cue big laugh from the audience.

Later during the exclusive ride through, guests saw her skeleton, complete with name tag, in the same place on ride. I promise I'm not making this up.

After the event the skeleton was hung up inside the first jail cell to the right, where it remains to this day. Talk about something Disney would never allow today!

The "seven deadly sins" version of Pirates would end up lasting less than nine years. Many of the Captain Jack Sparrow changes, especially in California, would end up walking back a lot of these ambitious ideas; the Chase scene would revert to closer to its classic staging, the Upramp lift hill at the end of the ride is now once again a quiet break at the end of the experience - even the multicolored lights in the grotto would revert to blue and white.

But say what you will, there was at least a *direct conceptual link* back to the attraction's original conception of pirates as bad news. If Disney really wanted to get rid of the pirates being horny skirt-chasers, then the Auction scene would have been a better place to start than the Chase scene. And the whole circular structure of doom was expanded and underlined; you couldn't mistake this for an approving depiction of criminality.

As we shall see, each subsequent change to the attraction would increasingly lose sight of this fact.

In the end it was, of all people, Paul Pressler who had the best line about the whole fiasco. He said: "*There is very little that is "politically correct" about* Pirates of the Caribbean. *In fact, in order to be politically correct, we would probably have to close down the whole ride.*"

XIII. RAIDERS OF THE CURSED GENRE

This is the tale of Captain Jack Sparrow
A pirate so brave on the seven seas
Mystical quest to the isle of Tortuga
Raven locks sway on the ocean breeze
- Michael Bolton

Back in movie land... By 1995 the time was right for another crack at the pirate genre, and everyone in Hollywood seemed to feel it. The first company to take a stab at it, to the woe of everyone involved, was Carolco Pictures with *Cutthroat Island*.

Cutthroat Island appears to have been a passion project by producer-director Renny Harlan, who is rumored to have spent some $1 million of his own money on script re-writes. Harlan is clearly having a ball orchestrating all of the onscreen madness, with stunts, slow motion explosions, and gorgeous images of clippers at sea all cut to the sweeping sounds of John Debney's score. It's shot on exotic locations with incredible full-sized vessels, their decks animated by seemingly hundreds of extras. In wide shots of the vessels the rigging is filled with stunt persons swinging around on ropes for no apparent reason, as if the ship is some huge sailor equivalent of a McDonald's PlayPlace. It's all incredibly silly.

Cutthroat Island stars Geena Davis as pirate queen Morgan Adams on a quest for a legendary island where huge amounts of gold are said to be hidden. This turns out to be a scavenger hunt involving a map tattooed on her father's scalp (!), Matthew Modine as a pirate who can read Latin (?!), and Frank Langella in full *Masters of the Universe* cheese mode (!!) as the evil Black Dawg. The plot is so convoluted that the interesting core idea of an adventure starring a lady pirate is totally sunk in the torrents of excess that characterize 90s action extravaganzas; I've never heard anybody bring up *Cutthroat Island* as an example of an action picture with a female protagonist, which is telling.

Renny Harlan was married to Davis at the time, and *Cutthroat Island* is his multi-million dollar attempt to turn her into an action star, but sadly she is the weakest part of the movie.

Geena Davis is cute as a button in *Beetlejuice* and *A League of Their Own*, but here she simply doesn't convince as a cunning pirate leader. There's multiple moments where the plot requires Davis' character to double-cross characters, and at no moment are we convinced that Morgan Adams is some sort of Machiavellian schemer four steps ahead of everyone else. It's the sort of role that would have required a Sigourney Weaver or Carrie Fisher to carry off well. And without a strong central character to hold audience interest, all of the convoluted crossings and double crossing quickly tire.

Despite being nearly two hours of solid action, *Cutthroat Island* is curiously dull. Every single place Geena Davis and Matthew Modine go turns into some kind of brawl or chase, as if they're cursed by pyrotechnicians and stunt coordinators to be forever swept up in expensive looking action sequences. Upon leaving another location reduced to rubble, Modine quips: "*Congratulations, madam. There's another town you've destroyed.*"

The ham is sliced extra thick all around. *Cutthroat Island* is the kind of 90s action picture where everything is exploding all of the time; early in the film you assume this has reached its crescendo when a candle-lit chandelier crashes into a wooden table and somehow produces a fireball, but no! Frank Lagella's "evil pirate ship" explodes at least one hundred times before finally blowing apart in spectacular fashion; as it sinks, the seas churn as if it's still exploding underwater.

Despite all of the wisecracks, explosions, and human scalps stuffed down ladies' pants, even *Cutthroat Island* cannot pass up a nod to Pirates of the Caribbean.

Exploring a dark cave, Geena Davis and Matthew Modine come across a skeleton with a sword through its chest accompanied by a crab. Modine turns to Davis and comments, "dead men tell no tales." *Yeah.*

Less than two months later, Walt Disney Pictures released *Muppet Treasure Island*. The timing makes it seem almost as if the Muppets are intentionally sending up Harlan's bloated blockbuster, but it's just one of those fascinating synchronicities. The production was inspired by the modest success of *The Muppet Christmas Carol*, a non-competitor at the Christmas 1992 box office which has none the less become something of a classic on video.

Muppet Christmas Carol worked because the Muppets counterbalanced the Charles Dickens story while remaining true to the material; the parts of the Dickens story that needed to be played straight were played straight, and the Muppet frivolity was a welcome counter-shade where it appeared. But it almost feels as if somebody went to Jim Henson Productions and told them to take it easy on the scary stuff this time around. All of the tense highlights of Stevenson's story - the arrival of Blind Pew, the mutiny, the face-off with Israel Hands - are downplayed or removed, as are any action scenes, leaving the Muppets with little to do but stand around and tell jokes. It's a deeply silly film, with conga lines, and Hawaiian shirted tourists, and Miss Piggy as Ben Gunn.

And yet, and yet!!

Every so often the film rattles awake to remind us that this is a pirate movie, and gives a few delicious glimpses of the sort of fun we could be having. The film begins with a gorgeous sweeping model shot of Treasure Island backed by spine-tingling music from Hans Zimmer which very much seems to be a premonition of *Curse of the Black Pearl*. In one brief segment, Tim Curry as Long John Silver has a torchlit monologue on a beach with no Muppets in sight, and with Zimmer's atmospheric music rumbling beneath his sonorous words the effect is electrifying. Tim Curry is dream casting as Long John Silver, but his commanding performance is marooned in a film that doesn't actually require it.

But perhaps the most important thing about *Muppet Treasure Island* is that it was successful.

It wasn't a run-away success, but it out-earned *Muppet Christmas Carol* at the box office and was discovered by an audience on video. And so of all things, *Muppet Treasure Island* broke the curse on pirate movies by demonstrating that, yes, you could make money on these things. Somebody at Disney took notice.

By the early 2000s, a handful of executives at Walt Disney Pictures were seriously discussing a new screen pirate epic. These were Production VP Brigham Taylor, Creative Executive Michael Haines, and Josh Harmon on story development. These three had apparently worked out a very basic outline involving a young couple getting caught up in a feud between two pirates, one evil and one not-so-evil.

Despite the *Cutthroat Islands* of the world, it was a good... maybe even inevitable idea for Disney. As Taylor noted, "*[There was] a reason to pursue a pirate movie... nobody has gotten it right, and we have the best title out there.*"[31] The executive team produced a page and a half memo and went shopping for screenwriters.

They ended up picking Jay Wolpert, screenwriter of their recent version of *The Count of Monte Cristo*, who wrote the script in straightforward swashbuckling style aboard his sailboat to get into the spirit of the adventure. His script was then picked up and revised by Stuart Beattie, who apparently did a huge amount of pirate research before embarking on the draft. As Beattie put it, "*Pirates was an idea conceived by the Disney executives and they brought us writers in to work on assignment.*"

The screenplay that Wolpert and Beattie jointly produced involves Elizabeth Swann, daughter of the Governor of Jamaica, who is in a star-crossed romance with Will Turner, a blacksmith. Elizabeth is captured for ransom by Captain Blackheart, a pirate in league with Commander Norrington, a captain of the guard who wants to overthrow the government of Jamaica and become the new governor. Will Turner is aided in his quest to save Elizabeth by Jack Sparrow, a heroic pirate whose ship has been stolen by Captain Blackheart. In the end Blackheart and Norrington are defeated in a final raid on Port Royal.

XIII. RAIDERS OF THE CURSED GENRE

At this point Disney approached Ted Elliot and Terry Rossio, screenwriting partners who had recently completed work on Disney Feature Animation's ill-fated *Treasure Planet*. More to the point they had worked on *The Mask of Zorro* starring Antonio Banderas, a smash hit from a few seasons before.

Unbeknownst to Disney, Ted and Terry had been waiting for just such an assignment to fall into their lap; they had come up with an idea to merge the two threads of pirate narratives back in the early 1990s after completing work on *Aladdin*.

Let's pause for a moment to unpack this. Back at the start of this book we separately explored the two dominant threads of pirate stories, what I called the Pirate Gothic and Pirate Romance. The Pirate Gothic came first, in things like *The Money-Diggers*, *The Gold-Bug*, and *Treasure Island*. Pirates of the Caribbean at Disneyland is Pirate Gothic; arguably, so is *The Goonies* and *Roman Polanski's Pirates*. These are stories where pirates are villains or ghosts. Pirate Romance, on the other hand, begins with Lord Byron's *The Corsair* and gave us *The Black Pirate, Captain Blood, and Cutthroat Island*. These are stories where pirates are heroic - probably since the 1970s a bit more on the side of anti-heroic - but none-the-less they are the characters we are supposed to be invested in. Most pirate films since the 1920s have actually been in the romantic mode, unless they are positioned as an adaptation of *Treasure Island*.

As Terry Rossio put it, "*Our approach was to literalize the supernatural, then make a Golden Age of Hollywood movie that happens to have these supernatural and Gothic elements in it.*"[33]

Their version condenses the Wolpert-Beattie script into the first act. The climatic attack on the town is moved up to become an inciting incident, swollen with hints of the unearthly. One of the cleverest things about the final screenplay is that by switching midway from Wolpert-Beattie to Elliot-Rossio, it allows the film to play as a series of thrilling surprises.

The writers and executive team had been given a tour of Pirates of the Caribbean by Marty Sklar and Tony Baxter, but just as Steven Spielberg, Roman Polanski, and Ron Gilbert before them had found, the ride is more a series of environments than an actual narrative. As Brigham Taylor pointed out, "*We didn't get a narrative from the ride, but we did get a backdrop, a milieu.*"[34] The Elliot-Rossio half of the story uniquely keys in on the haunted caverns sequence, but it also flips our expectations on the sort of movie we're *actually watching* at the one-hour mark.

We *expect* Blackheart - now named Captain Barbossa - and his crew to be villains, but they're actually victims. We expect pirates to be stealing treasure, but these pirates are actually *returning* treasure. If we've been on the Disneyland attraction we've already been prepared for a pirate adventure which turns into a ghost story, but the reversals in the center section of the film fly so dense and fast that the film basically reboots itself halfway through into a more interesting version of itself. It's a marvelous group effort of writing, and it took every step on the ladder to make it as good as it is.

On the strength of this new supernatural script, Jerry Bruckheimer and Johnny Depp signed aboard. Bruckheimer had produced three of Disney's biggest hits in history up to this point: *Con-Air*, *Armageddon* and, uh, *Coyote Ugly*. For Depp, this film would prove to be the stepping stone from an actor of interest to a genuine box office star. Since the early 90s Depp had been receiving attention for flashy, offbeat performances in movies like *Edward Scissorhands, Fear and Loathing in Los Vegas* and *Benny & Joon*. The mere presence of Johnny Depp on the poster of a movie called *Pirates of the Caribbean* cued audiences to get ready for something unique, and Depp did not disappoint.

But just as important was the choice of Gore Verbinski as director. Verbinski was best known for the 1999 version of *The Ring*, but it's his weird, gothic *MouseHunt* from 1997 that's a true preview of what he would bring to *Pirates of the Caribbean*. Verbinski actually signed on after Johnny Depp had agreed to the job but before Elliot & Rossio had delivered their draft, and jumped right into pre-production based on a story outline. Verbinski told him: "*This could be the end of our careers... but let's have fun.*"

This ball of wax was getting big, and fast. None of these choices were safe choices - an overlong and unconventional screenplay, a well-known character actor instead of an action star, and a director ready to amp up the gothic horror, all riding on a $140 million budget in a genre better known for disaster at sea.

Even with Dick Cook as head of Walt Disney Pictures in the corner of Bruckheimer and Verbinski, the setup was giving Disney CEO Michael Eisner hives. Dick Cook had pulled the plug on a previous makeup job for Jack Sparrow that saw every tooth in his mouth capped with gold. It would take all of Bruckheimer's producing acumen to steer this one into port.

Production began without a Will Turner; Orlando Bloom signed on immediately coming off *Lord of the Rings* and one day before he shot his first scene. A Caribbean village was constructed facing the ocean in Palos Verdes West of Los Angeles; the remainder of the "Port Royale" location was shot on the historic European Village set at Universal Studios. Johnny Depp rode into film history atop the mast of a sinking skiff.

Publicity still © Disney, Author's Collection

Already the executive team was in a panic over the performance that would give them one of their most viable profit centers in history. Nobody had actually seen Depp performing the character until he showed up on set to act the role, and they weren't sure they liked what they were getting.

Johnny Depp recalled overhearing Michael Eisner bellowing "*Goddamnit Johnny Depp's ruining the film! Is he drunk? Is he gay?*"[35] Bruckheimer, Depp, and the executives convened at a meeting. Depp said: "*Look, you do your thing, this is mine. This is my circle, and you're not allowed in my circle.*"[36] Ultimately Brigham Taylor ran a few rushes for Dick Cook, who agreed to stand behind the creative team.[37]

Production continued to spiral. Once the crew moved out of Hollywood and to the Caribbean location on St. Vincent, they were contending with locations spread over nearly forty miles of open water. Verbinski recalled: "*It's all true what they say about shooting on water. Everything that can go wrong will go wrong. That's just the way it works.*"[38]

Geoffrey Rush elaborated: "*You would be waiting to do a really substantial, meaty, dialogue-driven scene on the deck, and then the wind would change and the smoke would blow in the wrong direction... you'd have to wait for seven boats to come around. It was painstaking.*" Amazingly, Disney pulled the plug on the movie twice due to cost overruns.[39]

The post-production period was just as crazy. Verbinski had something like fourteen weeks to finish a film with hundreds of effects shots. Preview posters were circulated with the film advertised simply as "*Pirates of the Caribbean*". The poster showed nothing of the cast, simply the attraction's signature image of a skeleton at a ship's wheel. That was enough.

Bruckheimer disliked the musical score turned in by *Back to the Future* composer Alan Silvestri and asked Hans Zimmer to step in. Zimmer was already committed to *The Last Samurai* so he ended up collaborating with Klaus Badelt. "*The first film was very collaborative and a great panic, because it was a last-minute rescore*", he told Soundtrack.net in 2006.[40]

Continuing executive nervousness about the film may be spotted in the fact that the film originally carried no Walt Disney Pictures logo; the title simply pops up amidst a flurry of rendered CGI embers. Michel Eisner didn't even want to call the movie *Pirates of the Caribbean*. The final poster was an unexciting mish-mash of actor faces and a moonlit pirate ship. Absolutely nothing about the marketing of the film gave any indication it would be anything but a disaster.

But then Disney actually let people see the thing.

After an audience preview the film acquired a subtitle, *The Curse of the Black Pearl*, all the better to leave the door open for a potential sequel. Disney sprung for a movie premiere at Disneyland on June 28, 2003, with the film projected on a massive screen erected on Tom Sawyer Island and gigantic stadium seating built ringing the Rivers of America.

I was visiting Disneyland for the very first time in late June 2003 and falling in love with Walt Disney's baby; a colossal scaffolding being built on the front doorstep of the attraction seemed to me to be an ominous portent. Disneyland closed early and stars walked down the red carpet on Main Street USA; I walked over to California Adventure.

Nobody expected the film to actually be good. But then people began seeing it.

The film opened wide on July 9 and it was a slow burner. I saw it once in a nearly empty theater, then twice more with successively larger and larger audiences. There was absolutely no reason to expect a movie based on an amusement park ride to turn out as well as it did, but word got around. It may have been the most expensive Disney film yet made, but it was also their biggest hit yet. Despite a suspect concept, a bad poster, an ungainly title and a mediocre trailer, people showed up and kept showing up. The film whose release Disney very nearly botched turned out to be their first blockbuster film franchise.

Curse of the Black Pearl begins with a ship lost in a foggy sea. Young Elizabeth Swann stands aboard the deck, eerily chanting "*A Pirate's Life For Me*" into the open ocean. She's excited at the notion of meeting some pirates. This unexpected, spooky cold open instantly sets expectations for something unique, but it also begins the film at the level of a child's understanding of piracy. We, like Elizabeth, grow up to discover there's more to the story than simply high seas adventure. But the film still starts where *audiences* do, opening a door and inviting us to step through it.

Every single component of this film was timed amazingly well. The *Lord of the Rings* and *Harry Potter* film franchises had begun, improbably enough, within a month of each other in 2001. Sword and sorcery genres were suddenly the hottest thing around, and here Disney was sitting on this supernaturally tinged pirate film with "*the best title out there*".

To be a pirate was to be from Disneyland, and a film positioned with the title of *the* touchstone pirate media work of the 20th century perfectly set audience expectations.

For 2003, the cast could not have been better. Orlando Bloom was hot - literally. His role as Legolas in *Fellowship of the* Ring had earned him some admirers, but upon the release of *The Two Towers* in December 2002 Legolas fandom went into overdrive as Bloom surfed down a staircase on a shield into the hearts of filmgoers everywhere. *Curse of the Black Pearl* appeared in theaters six months after *The Two Towers* and six months before *Return of the King*. In *Pirates*, Orlando Bloom benefits from having much more to do than Legolas. He's allowed to show his natural brown hair and brown eyes, and combined with an easy onscreen confidence - gained from surviving the filmmaking equivalent of Tolkien boot camp - Will Turner turns *Curse of the Black Pearl* into one of the best leading man showcases since the days of Errol Flynn.

Kiera Knightley had appeared in the hit comedy *Bend It Like Beckham* in 2002 but her role as Elizabeth Swann is the glue that holds the film together. Elizabeth is a pirate enthusiast who never seems out of her depth amongst the gruesome buccaneers. She already knows the term "parley" when the crew of the Black Pearl attacks Port Royal and can run circles around Barbossa on the technicalities of the pirate code. Elizabeth invents a strategy to surprise the Black Pearl with a dangerous keel-haul and cannon volley. She "has read about" Jack Sparrow, fends off his advances, drinks the pirate under the table (!) then engineers their rescue from a desert island. Is it any wonder that she ends up marrying a pirate?

And then there's Jack Sparrow. Jack Sparrow is the perfect pirate for the 21st century. He's a double outsider; the colonial government sees him as a pirate and pirates see him as incompetent. He's an operator; constantly playing both sides against each other - as Johnny Depp puts it, "running between the raindrops". But his goal isn't wealth (Barbossa) or prestige (Norrington) - it's freedom, symbolized in his need for a ship. Jack Sparrow became an iconic character overnight, but he needs all of these supporting characters to make good sense of his arc, and there's a reason why subsequent Jack Sparrow adventures are a case of diminishing returns.

One of the secrets to the film's success is the way it explodes character conflicts in previous pirate adventures into separate characters. If you go back to films like *Captain Blood* and *The Black Swan*, most of the narrative spends its time spinning its wheels trying to explain why a heroic character is engaged in obviously criminal activity. You would think that in a post-*Godfather* world somebody would have risen to the challenge of making a good movie out of the old pirate stories, but as we have seen most of these opportunities were squandered.

So *Curse of the Black Pearl* gives us an apprentice blacksmith who goes a-pirating against his better judgement and a damsel in distress who rescues herself. This inverts the old-fashioned movie template we see in Romantic Pirate stories, updating them for modern audiences who think they know all the tricks.

But it adds to this a parallel set of pirates who express the moral ambiguity of the pirate archetype. Jack Sparrow and Captain Barbossa are equally self-centered and scheming, but align along different moral axes: the "chaotic neutral" trickster pirate and the "lawful evil" villain pirate. By providing all of these different "takes" on the morality of piracy, *Curse of the Black Pearl* actually solves the problem with pirate stories since time immemorial. At the end, even the forces of law on Jamaica concede that sometimes piracy is justified.

But if you're going to fly a jolly roger and declare war on the world, there needs to be something worth rebelling against. *Cutthroat Island* and *Roman Polanski's Pirates* did innovate by depicting an unjust ruling class in the Caribbean, but really only *The Goonies* gave us a status quo worth fighting by pitting their pirate-kiddies against sleazy real estate developers. The colonial government embodied by Commander Norrington isn't merely dense and unimaginative, its hypocritical. Jack Sparrow saves Elizabeth Swann without hesitation at the start of the film and is rewarded for his efforts by being sent to jail. *Black Pearl*'s vision of pirates vs colonial governments turns the film into something like a snobs vs slobs comedy, like the warring fraternities in *Animal House*.

But the film's games with authority go deeper. Having encountered an unjust social situation at Port Royal, we follow Jack Sparrow and Will Turner to Tortuga, a cartoonish pirate universe filled with references to the attraction. But the trip to Tortuga signifies more than Will Turner's deepening involvement in piracy, it's the door for us, the audience, to step through into the shadow world of criminal activity. If the film began with a child's excitement at the idea of pirates, proceeds into the sun-dappled world of Jamaica but still within the relative safety of official civilization, Tortuga is where there's no turning back. All of the rest of the film involves double and triple crosses not with the pirates as an external threat bombarding the town, but between warring factions of pirates themselves. At Tortuga, we join the crew.

And about that cursed gold - it's Aztec gold. As Barbossa says, "*One of 882 identical pieces they delivered in a stone chest to Cortez himself. Blood money paid to stem the slaughter he wreaked upon them with his armies. But the greed of Cortez was insatiable. So the heathen gods placed upon the gold a terrible curse.*"

In this sense, the film paints the horror unleashed upon the world not to be piracy, but to be Colonialism itself. This tallies fabulously well with modern attitudes towards the geo-political climate of the era, and makes good story sense to both acknowledge this fact and to turn our knowledge of this historical injustice into a fantasy of retribution.[41]

All of this is held together by Gore Verbinski's excellent direction. The film is paced about as rapidly as *Cutthroat Island*, but that film's flurry of explosions seem cut together from cameras pointed any which way to capture the incredibly expensive mania. Verbinski has a classical streak to his aesthetics which favors wide angles and symmetrical compositions. He has a knack for picking out tiny details which enhance our understanding of the situation; when the sword fight in the blacksmith shop goes up into the rafters he picks out a close angle on feet struggling to find steady footing, then a wide shot pointing up towards the rafters to emphasize the danger of the height. As a result the scene doesn't feel like Will Turner and Jack Sparrow are re-enacting a scene from *Crouching Tiger Hidden Dragon* for the fun of it; it really feels like the fight has taken on a new and dangerous dimension. All of this may seem like the basics of what the director is there to do, but our modern glut of fantasy-action films all shot with the same tedious handheld look demonstrates that it really does make a difference when a committed filmmaker is behind the camera.

Whereas Renny Harlan spread the action so thick over *Cutthroat Island* you could barely move, Verbinski and Bruckheimer achieve fabulous effects by saving their big action effects for very good character moments. Both films have scenes where pirate ships pull up alongside each other and blast cannons; Harlan's is a nonsensical mess of expensive looking coverage whereas Verbinski goes in close to catch character moments. It's the difference between a scene about explosions and a scene about strategy. When Barbossa strides forward as the mainsail of *The Dauntless* crumbles and barely misses him, in-theater audiences cheered. As Rossio and Elliot put it, it's an action movie where "*everything stays on a personal level*".[42]

Looking over the above, if anything it feels like I've over-praised the film... but very few modern popular films are as well put together or get as much right as this one. *Curse of the Black Pearl* is an example of how corporate filmmaking is ideally supposed to work

- a staggeringly ironic fact given how vehemently Eisner wanted to kill the picture. Subsequent sequels have lost the zest and savor of this original entry, but really part of that is due to the way *Black Pearl* uses up everything useful from the well of inspirations. It delivers a bravura old-fashioned movie sword fight at 25 minutes. At 30 minutes, a pirate raid that would end any other action film begins. This movie has parrots, monkeys, keel-hauling, walking the plank, rum swilling, marooning on desert islands, huge caches of treasure, ships set ablaze, and that's saying nothing for a clever and well-developed story. There was precious little left for the next four entries.

Audiences rewarded this film because it was great fun, and those who missed it in theaters caught up with it on home video. As with all other aspects of this production, in this arena the film was fabulously well timed. DVD had been simmering away in the background since 1997, but by 2003 it was becoming the standard entertainment format. DVDs were made using a well-established technology and so the economics of scale worked quickly in the format's favor. Once studios began packaging new movies with value added features and selling titles for less than $20, it became an attractive alternative to the home rental market.

Early 2000s teenagers - I was one of them - ran out and snapped up copies of this film like candy, and we traded them amongst each other, inevitably inspiring others to do the same. It certainly felt like everyone I knew at that time owned a copy of this movie.

And really *Black Pearl* is a perfect film for watching at home on DVD; it looked fabulous on those new widescreen monitors and when the film drags you can go make a sandwich. The film is said to be the eighth best-selling DVD of all time, which feels just about right; even today thrift stores seem to be well-stocked with copies.

Very rarely, a film comes along made by the right people at exactly the right time which blows the doors off. *Curse of the Black Pearl* is one of those. As Jack Sparrow said, it acted at exactly the "opportune moment".

XIII. RAIDERS OF THE CURSED GENRE 277

This ragged poster, located in the attraction gift shop in Florida, was the sum total in-park advertising presence for one of Disney's most important hit films in its history. Taken by the Author in 2004.

I began working at Pirates of the Caribbean at Magic Kingdom in early 2005. Those were different days, both at Magic Kingdom and at Pirates. The newest attraction at the park was Stitch's Great Escape, and Stitch made the announcements on the monorails as they pulled up to Magic Kingdom. Attendance was still unsteady after the terror attacks; most days you could get on Big Thunder Mountain or Haunted Mansion with perhaps a 25-minute wait, tops. Maintenance was more of a platonic ideal than a day-to-day reality. Disney was treading water. Pirates of the Caribbean had a queue that almost never extended out its front doors into the entrance plaza. We had a sign that we would manually spin to display a number; most of the time it was permanently set at "15 minutes".

At night, Caribbean Plaza emptied out, and the memory of standing amidst those stuccoed columns and listening to the steel drum music is one of the most blissful in my career in Operations.

At night I would walk Colin Campbell's delightful queue, sweeping up trash and listening to the George Bruns "Pirates Arcade" music. Every so often a small throng of tourists would come inching down those cold stone corridors and I could scare them. The ride was so quiet that we would take wheelchair groups down the Port side queue, turn on the Load station just for them, load them in their own boat, then fold up the wheelchair and walk it around the building to Unload.

At Pirates, everyone's least favorite position to work is Unload. Unlike at Disneyland or Disneyland Paris, you're stuck alone in a sub-basement waiting for your position to be bumped to the next in the rotation; at night those rotations got pretty slow and it was not uncommon to lose an hour of your time down there. Most boats were coming in empty, meaning your job mainly consisted of standing upright and pressing a green button. Every so often some tourists would float in on their boats and you could tell them to gather their items and step out to their left.

As the first live person encountered once exiting the attraction, at Unload you heard and saw some pretty interesting things. One fellow got off the ride late one night and asked how many live actors were in the ride; he refused to believe me when I said none. One night, the Cast Members in the control room saw on the closed circuit monitors a couple alone in their boat going at it pretty strong; we got a group of Cast Members and Managers together and clapped and cheered the horrified pair as the boat pulled into the Unload station. And then there was the night a boat pulled into the station and its sole occupant, an elderly woman, had expired during the ride.

But the main thing you heard at Unload in 2005 was always the same. The boats would return to the station, everyone would stand, and somebody near to your control console would exclaim: "***Where's Johnny Depp??***".

The question was never "Where is Captain Jack Sparrow", it was always "Where's Johnny Depp??". I hated that, because it felt like it was every few boats and there was never a good answer. All you could do was stand there and apologize.

Little did we all know that very soon we would be all be getting Johnny Depp... and how.

XIV. JULY 2006: RECHRISTENING

I was told to report bright and early at 7 am on the morning of July 7, 2006.

It was a hot day, hot in the way only Florida in July can be, with clear skies and no wind. The humidity hung around you like weights. Pirates of the Caribbean was re-opening the very same morning that the movie sequel, *Dead Man's Chest*, was going into wide release, and all of us who had worked there were going to be re-trained to work the ride. Pirates of the Caribbean in Florida was re-born in a pressure cooker of humidity, crowds, and hype.[43]

Rumors of the addition of Captain Jack Sparrow had swirled since the release of *Curse of the Black Pearl*, and Disney made official what everyone suspected with a press release on February 3, 2006.[44] The phrase repeated over and over was "First the theme park attraction inspired the movie -- now the movie is inspiring the attraction." We employees were encouraged to actually say this to guests, verbatim.

Magic Kingdom's Pirates closed on March 1, then reopened on April 1 with few noticeable changes. This was done because Easter fell on the 16th, and the week of Easter is always one of the busiest of the year. The attraction then closed again on May 1 to get its new additions ready for July 7. I worked the attraction that April, and besides some new lighting, much of the work was out of guest sight at that time. The only noteworthy change was that Disney had replaced all of the skeletons on the beach[45] in Dead Man's Cove with new models.[46]

In late June, Disney brought all of their employees trained to work Pirates into a classroom where Imagineering described the work that was being done and trained us on the correct terminology that we were expected to use. We were forbidden from referring to "Johnny Depp", only to "Captain Jack Sparrow" (title mandatory). We were given additional historical information on the age and location of the fortress at the front of the attraction, the Castillo del Morro. We were also encouraged to develop our own "pirate personae" and really play up the buccaneering atmosphere. Merchandise agreed to allow us to poach plastic swords from their supply as needed.

It's hard to convey the atmosphere of excitement all of this carried with it. The popularity of *Curse of the Black Pearl* had only grown on home video. It became customary among Pirates Cast Members to go into the Pirate Shop at the exit of the ride and buy one of the Aztec Gold Medallion replicas Disney had been doing a brisk business in since 2004. However, this tchotchke wasn't actually part of the official costume, meaning anybody who wanted to wear this at work had to do so *under their work shirt*. And here was Disney not only encouraging us to personalize our work appearance,[47] but giving us carte blanche to do things like wave around plastic swords and refer to guests as bloody land lubbers. Every day was to be Talk Like a Pirate Day.

Pirates of the Caribbean has never been one of the attractions with a lot of cachet inside Disney's work culture. If you are backstage wearing Jungle Cruise khaki or a Haunted Manson maid dress, you feel like royalty. If you walk into the Mousekateeria[48] dressed in those silly pirate pajamas, nobody cares - you may as well be one of the people who works food service in Fantasyland. A lot of the cast at Pirates of the Caribbean were excited by this new sense of prestige, and it wasn't uncommon to see such things as custom made pirate hats, bandanas, and swords. Our ride was finally getting some recognition, and it was riding the hype of one of the most anticipated movies of the summer.

To help guests find the attraction, a new ship's mast attraction sign was buried in the planter out front. At the top is a crow's nest where a skeleton peers through a sight-glass, searching for unknown adventures. On that hot morning of July 7, stepping through the Pirates Gate to see this new marquee and hearing the Hans Zimmer movie music rumbling through the speakers of Caribbean Plaza was one of the most exciting things I remember as a Cast Member.

We were brought inside to the Load Area to learn our new control console. It felt like every single boat that left the station that morning did so to thunderous cheers. Many of the boats were loaded with fans who had tickets for the first showing of *Dead Man's Chest* at the AMC Downtown Disney later that day.

In my memory, that day was pretty much the climax of excitement for the adventures of Captain Jack Sparrow. A lot of that has to do with the fact that *Dead Man's Chest* is a pretty bad movie, a 2.5-hour commercial for the next installment.

But we didn't know that on that hot morning, and many of us wouldn't find that out until the coming days and weeks. But for now, let's hop into one of those little boats and see what $700 million-plus in revenue has bought our classic attraction.

The attraction shortly before its conversion. Taken by the author, January 2005.

Since Imagineering designs attractions primarily with an eye for Disneyland in California, I'll discuss how this refurbishment played out at the original attraction before jumping back to Florida. As always the Florida version was the afterthought.

Anybody queueing up for Pirates of the Caribbean at Disneyland would end up waiting quite a long time to see any noteworthy changes to the ride. The changes up through the two downramps were minimal, even subtle. Dead Man's Cove had a new, somber version of *A Pirate's Life For Me* playing. With reedy flutes and spooky echoed wind, it keys well into the tone of this area. Elsewhere in the caverns, new props were added, including a skeleton chess match in the bar scene and a parrot skeleton - complete with matching nightcap - to the Captain's Quarters. In the Treasure Room, the inevitable stone coffin of Aztec gold was added to the scene. In the days when *Curse of the Black Pearl* was still fresh, riders would often excitedly point this out to their companions.

The first big addition occurred in the Transition Tunnel. Gone was the classic Paul Frees "no fear have ye" narration - the narration that inspired the linchpin of the film, I'd like to point out - and in its place was a new, triple-A Imagineering illusion: the Davy Jones waterfall.

This was one of those cases where a Disney illusion ended up being adopted and cloned by everyone else pretty much instantly. It was a thin layer of chilled, falling mist which appeared to be a waterfall thanks to a rear-facing digital projection; Davy Jones, the new big baddie of the series, would appear to break through the layer of falling water to issue forth admonishments. *"Ah, but they do tell tales - so says I, Davy Jones!"*

Unlike the version of this effect which has appeared at weddings and regional haunted houses in the years since, Disney's version had a few subtle grace notes. To begin with, the falling mist and the shimmering highlights of the waterfall projection combined to create a pretty good illusion that your boat really was headed straight towards a solid sheet of water. Below the mist screen Disney had bubbles in the water which agitated the surface. When the mist fell all the way to the water's surface, the mist spreading over the water and the churning effect made a pretty convincing illusion that you were about to get soaked. For the first few years, many guests would cover their heads. However, keeping the mist sufficiently refrigerated to fall all the way to the flume and allowing enough space between boats for the effect to properly reset proved to be simply too much. After the first few years the mist curtain rarely looked its best. However, in 2006, this was a great effect, very memorable.

The boats then headed into Bombardment Bay, another of this refurbishment's most impressive changes. The Klaus Badelt movie track "*The Medallion Calls*" now filled this room, making one of the attraction's real highlights even more impressive. Captain Barbossa now stood on the deck of the pirate ship, replacing the original "Blackbeard" captain. More subtly, the original "soldier" dialogue tracks were entirely redone. The soldiers are now voiced by actual native Spanish speakers, without any of the "Speedy Gonzales" voices used in 1967. This is a good change, and rarely commented on.

Around the corner in the Well Scene, the new additions take a turn for the weird. The first Jack Sparrow audio-animatronic figure appears here, hiding behind a pair of dress forms. Apparently during the production of the refurbishment Imagineering asked Johnny Depp where Jack Sparrow would hide from Barbossa; his answer of "inside the Redhead's skirt" could not be used.

Instead, artist Chris Turner came up with a visual gag where Jack Sparrow would seem to be wearing a dress, but then would actually be revealed to be hiding behind a dress-form. It's a good joke, a quick visual read and in-character... especially here in Anaheim where the figure is staged behind the dress so it really does look like his head is connected to the mannequin's body.

Less successful is the new dialogue recorded for all three of the revised scenes. The most obvious problem is that all of the pirates are constantly referring to the copyright-enforceable term of "Captain Jack Sparrow", and do so every few seconds. This is noticeable enough that even regular guests comment on it.

But the real issue is that a lot of the zest of X. Atencio's dialogue is gone. No offense to show writer Michael Sprout, but there's simply no comparison.

Photo by Andy Castro.

Take just a few examples:

> *"By gum he'll talk, or do a fine dance at rope's end! Be that clear, signor?"*

Becomes

> *"Where be Captain Jack Sparrow? Speak up, do d'ye fancy a swim with Davy Jones?"*

Or

> *"Surrender, ye lilly-livered lubbers! Another broadside and ye goes down with the tide!"*

Becomes

> *"It's Captain Jack Sparrow we're after, and a fortune in gold!"*

Again, Atencio's script has never been topped, but it seems strange not to keep at least most of this delightfully purple pirate talk. Much of the entertainment value of the attraction was found in these lines, and without them the attraction feels like it becomes a game of "spot Johnny Depp".

This same on-the-nose dialogue also infected the next changed scene, the Chase scene. A lot of the changes made in 1997 were undone; each turntable went back to its classic arrangement of one pirate and one maiden per table. The staging of each of these was simplified, with maidens chasing pirates absconding with food. The confused gentleman with the plate of food, his horse and goat companions, the extra crates of chickens, and all of the piles of food were removed, a rare case of addition by subtraction. The Pooped Pirate now holds a key and examines a treasure map, very close indeed to the revised staging at Magic Kingdom in 1994. Captain Jack now pops out of the barrel behind him to spy on the map.[49]

This is one of those cases where we must admit that, unless one is dead set against the idea of Jack Sparrow being in the ride, this is a significant improvement over **any** version of this scene that's been here before. The Jack Sparrow figure in the barrel is startlingly, almost bafflingly lifelike, and hiding in a barrel is a great funny place for the character to pop up next.

All of the remaining changes in Anaheim were clustered at the end of the ride. The "pirates escaping uphill" scene installed in 1997 was removed, with the spot at the bottom of the hill now given over to a treasury where we discover that Jack has lifted the treasure map and found the treasure. The fact that the treasury is feet away from an arsenal which is on the verge of exploding doesn't make much of an impression. This is another fabulous animatronic, who rocks back and forth seated in a throne and gets his own reprise of *"A Pirate's Life For Me"*. Positioned as he is at the bottom of the ramp where we wait to be lifted back upstairs, he is successful at keeping riders entertained much more than any other scene that has been in that space. As we are lifted back to the surface, Jack's singing transitions to an upbeat version of *"Yo Ho"* played on Davy Jones' submerged organ as the villain makes some final remarks that we have been lucky to escape.

For a corporate mandated overlay, in Anaheim these changes work pretty well, or at least don't do egregious harm. They don't interrupt the "deepening dream state" which is the attraction's most salient characteristic; Davy Jones bookends the raid on the town, and following the progress of Jack Sparrow through the town to the treasure adds a nice little bow to the ride. As project lead Mary Rogers told author Michael Singer, "*We were very sensitive that we were going to go in and touch that classic story... we really wanted to make sure that the things we did to enhance the experience didn't feel like we were just putting [Captain Jack Sparrow] into the attraction just because we could.*" Writer Michael Sprout elaborated: "*The pirates are still attacking the town, we just gave them a little more pointed reason.*"[50]

And yet, *and yet.*

These are still characters imported into a fifty-year-old ride that was built with a different set of expectations and values around piracy.

In classic Pirates of the Caribbean, pirates are Bad News. When I was a little kid being brought to Magic Kingdom, the idea that I was going to meet pirates inside that big building in Adventureland was scary. Even in the 1997 "seven deadly sins" version the pirates were still depicted as criminals who will get their just desserts - whether that be exploding in a burning warehouse, being stabbed over a chest of gold, or slowly dying in a cave full of pilfered treasure. That's *why* the ride begins with Dead Men Tell No Tales.

But the movie characters are built around the very different expectations of more recent audiences, audiences for whom the notion of an "antihero" is a commonplace one. This audience has grown up accustomed to films where the main characters may be not all that sympathetic and where evil is not always punished. For this audience, it makes sense to present pirates not as criminals, but as fantastical creatures from a storybook come to life.

And by simply doing that one thing, introducing characters from a different moral universe, then the attraction is already backing away from the position that the ride was designed under - that pirates are Bad News. It's also the moment when you then open up the possibility for debate of the merits of their actions.

That's when you start losing the heart of the ride and why the mere presence of Jack Sparrow seems to fundamentally change it. If *Curse of the Black Pearl* is fresh in your mind then all of these changes seem logical, but that movie is twenty years old now and all of these alterations have continued to muddle up what the ride seems to be saying. Are we supposed to admire the pirates? Are pirates bad guys?

New attraction marquee. Taken by the author, August 2006.

And as for Florida?

Most upsetting was the removal of a lot of stuff that made the Florida ride unique. The Talking Skull at the downramp was removed. All of the lovely pirate animatronics from the Treasury finale were removed, a pointless waste. George Bruns' Pirate Overture now plays through the queue, stepping on the carefully designed spooky atmosphere. And, worst of all, Peg-Leg Parrot out front was removed and has not been seen since. Like I've said, that bird was probably the best thing about the whole ride.

But it wasn't all bad. The new opening, with Davy Jones appearing in the waterfall, was much better than what was there before, and actually provided some of the flavor of the Talking Skull at Disneyland; the sense of a supernatural gatekeeper warning you not to proceed. The tunnel at the bottom of the downramp saw the removal of the truncated "*no fear have ye*" narration, which was replaced with a snatch of movie soundtrack building excitement for the big Bombardment Bay scene.

The new ending, with Jack in the Treasury, does add a sense of narrative closure to the attraction that the original version lacked. The new scene creates a little pocket of subdued action after so much over the top spectacle, and everything from the upbeat music to the soothing blue color of the scene helps cue riders that they have reached the end of a journey. The new ending puts a nice bow on the ride and allows you space to digest what you've just experienced.[51]

And you know? Even without a talking parrot out front, unique ending, and cannons firing on the facade, the popularity of the attraction *soared*. The old days of pirates being a quiet job were long gone, and our queue was packed from morning to night. On the day the attraction reopened to guests, the line for it began at the Swiss Family Treehouse.

It became normal for Pirates operations to break records on daily efficiency. One summer we were challenged to "race" Rock n' Roller Coaster to see who could move more crowds for the month of July. It felt like every few weeks Management was "treating" us to a catered lunch,[52] as thanks for breaking yet another record.

The enthusiasm of July 2006 evaporated pretty quickly. Merchandise revoked our ability to take swords because they were being lost more often than not. Our jobs became an endless cattle drive to fill and dispatch those boats. Tempers frayed under the pressure.

As a friend of mine commented one day in the break room, the Peg-Leg Parrot was the only one of us who had enough sense to leave before the movie overlay opened.

XV. CAPTAIN JACK GOES DOWN WITH THE SHIP

But Disney was just getting started on milking Captain Jack.

On January 26, 2007,[53] Disney announced the addition of a "Pirate's Lair" to Tom Sawyer Island at Disneyland. Disney's official reasoning for the IP injection was built on the flimsiest of rationales - Tom and Huck pretending to be pirates in *The Adventures of Tom Sawyer*. Back in the real world, this was done because Tom Sawyer Island was a poorly-attended attraction and because the Jack Sparrow character meeting in New Orleans Square was regularly mobbed. The intention was to utilize the existing Fantasmic! stage facing New Orleans Square for a daytime stunt show which could be enjoyed from across the river, as well as incentivizing guests to take the raft journey across the river to meet Captain Jack.

The "new" island opened on May 25, 2007 to coincide with the release of the third film. To be fair to Imagineering and Disneyland, they put in a good effort to make this work. A lot of the deteriorating elements around the 1956 attraction were spruced up and refurbished. The "Fort Wilderness" stockade at the rear of the island had been closed up and rotting away in the elements since the 90s; it was rebuilt as a new structure (Still off-limits to exploration, but at least something was done). Old cave structures were rebuilt into shipwrecks, and the "Smuggler's Cove" area was now home to a very neat interactive area where water can be pumped out of tidal pools to reveal skeletons.

The centerpiece of the island was Dead Man's Grotto, a new version of the Injun Joe's Cave walk-through attraction. This simple cave experience dated back to 1956 and had changed very little in fifty years. Imagineering turned this into an atmospheric walk-through haunted house with some very good illusions (even a jump scare!). At the end of the cavern was an effect devised for the attraction overlay but never used, of a moving pirate who transforms into a skeleton when the moonlight shines on him. This was considered for the "transition tunnel" before Davy Jones moved in; as a Cast Member I saw documents referring to a "skeleton transformation in Crow's Nest" intended for the Florida ride.

When the attraction was new Disney made good on their promise of "*opportunities to search for buried treasure while encountering live pirates*" as the island was alive with pirate actors, including a pirate band and Captain Jack meeting back by the Fort. Many of these performers were quite good, commandeering Tom Sawyer Island rafts and improvising fun interactions.

But the stunt show was never a large draw; in the end its stunts consisted of a slide down a zip-line and some tame sword fighting. The performers ended up lasting a mere summer. Once the show was cut, all of the island's actors went with it, and a lot of the life went out of the place. When I was a Disneyland local in 2012 and 2013, Dead Man's Grotto was simply closed off more often than not. Today, Pirate's Lair on Tom Sawyer Island is much the way it was before the overlay: a quiet place where you can explore the island with perhaps at most a few dozen others. Most of the attractions and exhibits found therein are best described as quaint.

Also in May 2007, Tokyo Disneyland premiered their version of Pirates of the Caribbean with the movie overlay. This hewed pretty close to what was done at Disneyland the year prior, with the addition of the "Dead Man's Chest" which contains the beating heart of Davy Jones. Tokyo already had a more spacious version of the Arsenal scene, so figures were moved around to make way for a more elaborate version of the Treasury finale.

All through this period the Jack Sparrow was flying fast and thick in a way that is hard to comprehend. At this distance it all seems bizarre and almost quaint, like a jerky silent film of somebody hand cranking a Model T. But it's important to remember that *Dead Man's Chest* and *At World's End* were the highest grossing films of 2006 and 2007, and *Dead Man's Chest* set a record for fastest film to top $1 billion at the box office. In a world before Disney owned Pixar, Lucasfilm and Marvel they were literally making money at a pace the company never had seen in its history.

If *Curse of the Black Pearl* gave Disney their first blockbuster franchise, *Dead Man's Chest* transformed them into the bloated behemoth we know today.

This silly old boat ride made that possible.

Disney doubled down on both Pirates and Princesses in 2009.

The exit of the attraction in Florida has always led into a shop, the first such attraction anywhere to do so. In the early days this was much more of an evocative space, filled with the sort of souvenirs Disney used to stock for atmosphere rather than any real conviction they would be strong sellers - silk flowers, serapes, wind chimes, etc. The **real** merchandise was off to the side in the "House of Treasure" shop, which is where you could buy your plastic pirate swords, play guns, and other items. This was amongst the most evocative retail spaces in Magic Kingdom, with a vaulted ceiling and its own secluded courtyard with a trickling fountain at the exit.

Through the 90s the Plaza del Sol had become increasingly cluttered with t-shirt racks and the like, until finally the arrival of Paul Pressler as head of Parks & Resorts had resulted in a very aggressive push of the merchandise out of these quaint interior spaces and directly into guest line of sight.

Main Street USA became strewn with merchandise carts in what had previously been open space. The House of Treasure and its nearby shop, Lafitte's, were closed and turned into stock rooms, which is how they remained for ten years. At last the House of Treasure was converted in The Pirates' League, only the latest outpost of the Princess Dress Industrial Complex at Walt Disney World.

To understand the Pirates' League, we need to go back to the Bibbidi Bobbidi Boutique, a princess "makeover" experience (think: face paint and some basic hair styling) which was the surprise hit of a 2006 refresh of the World of Disney store. Given Disney's laser focus on Pirates and Princesses in this era, it was an inevitable step to open a pirate version of the experience.

If the Bibbidi Bobbidi Boutique was basically just some mirrors, curtains and salon chairs, The Pirates' League was a fully themed experience from door to door. Supposedly once an office of the East India Company, the interior was replete with rich woodwork, intricate carving, pirate flags, nautical maps, and a door which had been blown off its hinges by cannon fire. Young pirates, mermaids - or, inevitably, pirate princesses - were presented with a small gift and escorted into Captain Jack's hidden "treasure room" where secret compartments were opened to present children with crew medallions. Finally, the kids were instructed to peek out of a peep hole to see if the coast was clear before they exited through a hidden door and back out into the Magic Kingdom. It was all very cute, and unlike the Bibbidi Bobbidi Boutique it was a bust almost from day one.

I can well remember that day in June 2009 when The Pirates' League finally opened and we had to kindly ask a merchandise cast member not to stand in the Unload area of the attraction and hand out flyers promoting the experience. They relocated to the top of the Speed Ramp near the shop, of which there was no end of grumbling from ride operations managers that day.

The whole concept of the League was to join a secret society, which meant the whole experience took place behind closed doors, which limited its exposure to the general park going public. One initial plan was to offer an Adventureland treasure hunt to pirate recruits, which never materialized - after short-lived attempts to organize a daily "pirate parade" through Adventureland, Merchandise settled for simply offering reserved seating to the wildly popular Captain Jack Sparrow's Pirate Tutorial show. Prices were reduced from $50 to $30, something that almost never happens at Walt Disney World. Eventually one of the doors looking into the League from the Gift Shop was left often as a sort of enticement to passersby. After staggering along for over a decade, the experience closed with the rest of Walt Disney World in March 2020 and never reopened.

All through this period, a subtle change was occurring in Caribbean Plaza. The area had originally been constructed to be a tourist's idea of the Caribbean, all bright colors, tropical flowers and colorful tile. In 2006 an unusually heavy level of grunge was applied to the attraction facade, not just water stains but powder burns and antiquing, making the attraction appear much more age beaten than it previously had been. The ship's mast marquee only reinforced the notion of age and disarray.

"Jump Scare" effect in Dead Man's Cove walkthrough experience on Tom Sawyer Island. Taken by the author, November 2011.

When the old steel drum bandstand was rebuilt into a stage for the Pirate Tutorial show, the level of clutter and grunge only increased. The original bandstand had been picturesque with baskets of hanging flowers, but the new stage was covered in nautical detritus. All of this changed the character of Caribbean Plaza to something a little less friendly.

The Pirates' League continued this, with details like East India Company plaques "painted over" by pirates, and a marquee that looked like it had been the side of a sailing vessel, complete with a gun port and cannon. The boxes, barrels, and ship parts strewn across Caribbean Plaza created the unfortunate impression that some enormous ship floating in the sky had exploded, littering timber everywhere.

The whole notion of pirates using ship salvage in unusual ways is so endemic to modern pirate mythology that nobody much seems to question it, but the tradition actually comes from a different genre closely tied to pirates: the Robinsonade.

This book so far has steered well clear of the Robinsonade - it's already long enough - but for much of the nineteenth century the genre was something of piracy's more respectable brother. The source is of course *Robinson Crusoe* by Daniel Dafoe. There's nautical detail and pirates aplenty in Dafoe's novel, including a group of mutineers who end up being Crusoe's ticket off his tropical island. This is the chief reason Dafoe has long been suspected as the author standing behind the nom de plume of Captain Charles Johnson, the author of *The General History of Pirates*. There's really no evidence for this, but it shows how the two genres have been linked from the start.

Robinson Crusoe's scavenging trips to the wreck of the slave ship inaugurated a tradition in adventure literature of reformulating ships into structures that were not ships. The most famous of these is of course *The Swiss Family Robinson* from 1812, with its house built in the branches of a huge tree.[54]

By the time of Washington Irving and *The Money-Diggers* the ideas of piracy and nautical salvage were already converging; one character in that book lives in a shack "*rudely constructed of fragments of wrecks and drift-wood*". It is no accident that Adventure Isle in Disneyland Paris is a Robinsonade on the south side and a pirate hideout on the north; Disney literalizes how both narrative archetypes reside in the same mythic territory.

The use of salvage in pirate iconography speaks to their romanticized resourcefulness, making do with what's available in an inhospitable environment. It's sort of telling that this sort of ship-salvage aesthetic is often tied to whimsical or positive depictions of piracy, whereas negative depictions of piracy always are dressed up in the pomp of 18th century finery.

So it's logical that these different design teams would hone in on the "nautical salvage" motif once given the precedent of the "black sail" attraction marquee from 2006, even if it means the original design intent of the area was being lost. Originally, Caribbean Plaza represented the orderly world that the pirates attack, the world of the colonial residents. Today it better represents the world of the pirates, but moreover it takes as a given that we, the park goers, should be comfortable imagining ourselves to be pirates. After all that is the whole ethos of the Captain Jack Sparrow Pirate Tutorial, The Pirates League, and the Pirate and Princess Parties... "join the crew, a pirate's life for you".

Are pirates bad guys? Are we?

By 2011, Captain Jack was back on theater screens.

In one of the strangest examples of recursive inspiration in history, Disney had purchased the rights to Tim Powers' *On Stranger Tides*. This 1987 book was inspired by the attraction and gone on to influence Ron Gilbert in the creation of *Secret of Monkey Island*. The book... or if we're being honest, just its title and premise... was then turned back into the latest adventure of Captain Jack Sparrow. To commemorate this event, Disney updated the Davy Jones waterfall effect to alternate between Davy Jones and the new villain, Blackbeard.[55]

The Pirates-related additions which occurred next year in 2012 must be the strangest on record. There must have been some goof juice being passed around the Imagineering offices.

In October 2012, mermaids were added to the Grotto scene in Florida. The mermaid scene was the most memorable one in *On Stranger Tides*, and for a short time it looked as though Disney was poised to add "spooky mermaids" to their permanent bestiary. The mermaid effect consisted of digital projection onto the surface of the ride flume's water; as the boats passed, images of mermaids could be briefly seen swimming alongside the boats. Their tail-fins would even kick up little splashes of water as they vanished into the "depths".

This was pretty neat, but the trouble is that the mermaids seemed to be about 18 inches from head to tail, making it seem as though your boat were being swarmed with Barbie dolls - perhaps escaped from the Emporium.[56] Dead Man's Cove also received a new skeleton. It was the skeleton of a mermaid, lying dead with her hands tied above her head to the hull of a boat. The somber "Yo Ho" music from 2006 was replaced with an echoed vocal track of the mermaid song "Jolly Sailor Boy".

This is a case where I have to hand it to Imagineering, because if the goal was to make the beach scene scary again, they absolutely succeeded. This was the sort of morbid content that Disney hadn't even tried to approach since the days of Disneyland Paris. The mermaid skeleton was unnerving and brutal, especially in a park which - let's not forget - had a family-friendly dark ride based on *The Little Mermaid* across the park.

But the mermaid projection effect never seemed to work reliably, and not that many riders seemed to notice them when they *were* working. Back in 1973 when WED restructured Pirates of the Caribbean and cut the caverns, they effectively cut the ghost story aspect out of the ride. Yes, it's there, but it's never been the overriding impression the ride in Florida gave. I think the confusion of riders speaks to this apparent contradiction. It would be like if suddenly Cinderella was hanging out with centaurs in Fantasyland. Yes, the Fairy Godmother is a supernatural entity, but where did the centaurs come from?

Regardless, the skeleton and "Jolly Sailor Boy" song flew the coop in 2018. It may have had something to do with Imagineers being traditionalists, it may have had something to do with guest complaints, or it may have had something to do with the fourth and fifth Pirates films combined still earning less in the United States than *Dead Man's Chest* did.[57] I never made my mind up if the mermaid skeleton was good or bad, and the prop ended up lasting only six years before being removed. But I did love the pure creepiness of the whole thing, in a way that was wholly and entirely foreign to modern Disney.

That same year, in Winter 2012, Jack Sparrow was set on course to rescue a sinking ship elsewhere at Walt Disney World. It would turn out to be a death by misadventure. Having been to Tortuga, Isla de Muerta, the belly of a kraken, purgatory and the far east, Captain Jack would discover true hell when he ventured to Walt Disney World's most troubled theme park... Disney's Hollywood Studios.

Now to be fair, *The Legend of Captain Jack Sparrow* was the nearest anything occupying this cursed little corner of the park had come to being a proper attraction, having previously housed collections of movie props and projected movie trailers.[58] The exterior of this new attraction had a huge skull mural, and the interior was as richly dressed as space would allow. The attraction was hosted by the skull from the movie poster, maybe the only time a movie tie-in attraction was hosted by a graphic design element. Visitors entered and faced a large stone door, repurposed from a previous exhibit. Above it was the movie skull, who came to life and repeated some warmed-over lines from X Atencio's downramp skull script at Disneyland. Visitors then entered a large room with the hull of a ship, rocks, candles, skeletons, and a rear screen showing a view of the ocean and crashing waves. This was just about the neatest thing the attraction had to offer.

The Legend of Captain Jack Sparrow turned out to be a series of audience participation gags the likes of which Disney has used to pester tourists in pre-shows since time immemorial. Weirdly, the best gag was the first one, where some menacing projected skeleton pirates were defeated by a small child holding up a, um, skeleton key. Likewise the kraken was banished by shouting and some spooky mermaids defeated by, uh, stomping feet. I think you can see why people hated this already.

Once Jack Sparrow appeared on the bow of the ship, the energy level actually dropped even more. After some lame gags involving cannon fire and a pistol shot bouncing around the room, the show ended just as the Pirate Tutorial show at Magic Kingdom had... with a Yo-Ho singalong.

Unless you were there, it's hard to convey just how badly this thing bombed with audiences. Despite being a mere 8-minute standing room show, the hostility in the room was evident and only increased as the show went on. Upon its opening on the week of Thanksgiving 2012, Cast Members were informed that the show was the lowest-rated single attraction in the history of Walt Disney World. Despite efforts to speed up the show and reduce awkwardness, the show closed for good in October 2014, having lasted less than two years.[59]

It's hard to say how something so trivial warranted such a violent reaction. In this era of Hollywood Studios, crowds had ballooned faster than the park could actually accommodate, which was the entire reason such an unpromising space had been pressed into service in the first place. But maybe the answer lies next door, at Toy Story Mania, which opened in 2008. A ride-thru video game with very modest thrill elements, it was so popular that Disney actually built an extra version of the ride next door to its original footprint to handle demand. Guests who wandered over to Toy Story and found the lines too long frequently bounced over to Captain Jack, causing queues to swell to as much as 45 minutes. With such a short, low-capacity attraction as the "reward" for such a long wait, guests were understandably angry. In the end, the attraction was so reviled that Disney felt it better to leave it closed and lose the capacity than keep it open.

In the end the 2006 refurbishment to the classic ride turned out to be the capstone of the Captain's career, with an awkward goodbye that went on longer than anyone wanted. The rum was all gone.

XVI. PIRATES ACROSS THE HORIZON

The Legend of Captain Jack Sparrow wasn't just a boondoggle, it marked the end of a half-decade of escalating Jack Sparrow presence in the parks. In his 2005 book *Pirates of the Caribbean: From the Magic Kingdom to the Movies*, Disney writer Jason Surrell could speak of Jack Sparrow as "the first iconic movie character of the new millennium" and his words weren't *too* much of an exaggeration. By the time The Legend of Captain Jack Sparrow limped to its ignominious end, audiences were more excited for Iron Man; Jack Sparrow felt like a party goer still crashed on your patio a day later. The show demonstrated that the mere presence of the Captain was no guarantee of success, and its poor reception looks to have soured Disney Parks & Resorts on further dalliances with the brand.

In the years since, Imagineering has started to claw the Pirates of the Caribbean attraction back from being a promotional tool for the movie studio. In 2015, Pirates at Magic Kingdom finally received an overdue top to bottom refresh, touching nearly every part of the ride and really making it shine. Animatronic figures were rebuilt with new advanced eyes, teeth, and skin that makes them look even more convincingly human. New costumes, lighting, and set dressing makes the ride seem almost like it was built yesterday. Imagineering even added some themed scents to the attraction. Even if it's the short version, the Magic Kingdom ride has a very high level of technical polish which has not faded a decade later.

The Talking Skull was finally returned to the Florida ride in 2017 under the guise of an on-ride flash photo. This brand-new figure is great, with far more detail than the original skull had. He even goes to sleep and starts snoring if the ride breaks down.

Arriving fashionably late, Disneyland Paris finally got their movie characters in 2017. Installed a full decade after the peak of Jack Sparrow mania, these film additions seem to have been afforded a bit more space to be rationally considered. The good news is that almost all of these changes are improvements. The bad news is that they break the logic of the Paris show, which was the best thing about it.

In this new version, Jack Sparrow makes his grand entry into the attraction by popping out of a barrel in the Chase scene, then reappears in the Treasure room downstairs, displacing the original skeleton at the top of the treasure pile. I'm fairly certain this place was chosen because the realistic figure can now be seen from the Disneyland Railroad, where viewed from on high looking down into the treasure cache it is an impressive sight.

The other interesting addition was a full-body Captain Barbossa animatronic in the Grotto scene, where he is perfectly positioned to upstage the Hurricane Lagoon helmsman. That's bad news for the ships-wheel skeleton but at least it's a cool representation of Barbossa, who hoists a lantern then transforms in a skeleton during a lightning flash.

Sadly this totally negates the time travel aspect of the attraction, where we first come across evidence of the battle which blew up the garrison then travel back to see it happen. Perhaps treating everything we see while on the ride as purely and simply "pirate stuff" reflects the way most riders view it, but making the time loop clear and linear was *the defining feature* of the Paris ride - the reason it was possible to discuss it as a potential best version.

The *other **other*** noteworthy change was in the Auction scene. Instead of auctioning women the pirates are now auctioning town valuables, with the famous Redhead now converted to be a pirate wench. The women tied up in a line are now a co-ed group of villagers in nightgowns carrying precious items to the auction block. The Redhead oversees the proceedings with a huge rifle; the hecklers across the way are now vying to bid on her firearm.

Marc Davis would probably say that the staging of this new scene makes no sense; why the villagers are bringing their valuables to the block is counter-intuitive to the logic of a pirate raid. At least they're clearly being forced, dressed in nightgowns with jackets thrown over top. Of course then we have to account for what the average foc'sle swab would do with, say, a crystal chandelier, but at least the scene is written to indicate that they're more interested in Redd's gun than fancy paintings.[60]

Imagineering probably wanted to turn their assignment to re-jigger the Auction scene into a bit more of an upgrade once the changes began to make their way over to Disneyland and Walt Disney World. In Paris, the money was being spent on more urgent changes elsewhere, so much of the new Auction was basically a prop refresh. In Florida and California, the choice was made to go in for an entirely new Redhead figure and make her more a part of the scene. This wasn't a bad idea, but the execution is another matter.

The new Pirate Redd character - who travels with a gun in every hand - has her foot jauntily up on a box and joins the hecklers in their demands that rum be brought to the auction block. The rotund lady on the auction block is now auctioning chickens and has a great new "worried" face. All of this creates opportunities for some decent wordplay:

> "Do I hear ten? A hen for a ten? ...Strike your feathers, dearie, show 'em your flock.."

Redd and the chickens are good, but sadly somebody went totally overboard in redoing the tied-up villagers, who now are bringing forth a bust, a chandelier, a painting, and for some terrible reason a *grandfather clock*. All of them are now dressed in eighteenth century finery of ruffles and silk, complete with powdered wigs.

Films and popular culture have been using powdered wigs as symbols of impotent authority for a hundred years, for instance the moment in *The Black Swan* where Henry Morgan removes his powdered wig and throws it down on a table to punctuate his decision to renounce his governorship. In this sense the powdered wigs and absurd grandfather clock seem to be intended to mock the victims; something the original scene, faults and all, did not do. Are pirates bad guys?

As for Pirate Redd, she belongs to a long lineage of lady pirates which stretches all the way back to the advent of the pirate myth.

The notion of female pirates has existed for as long as pirates have; Anne Bonny and Mary Read - who sailed in the crew of Jack Rackham - were the most famous. As with all other historical pirates, there's scant evidence of the actual lives of Bonny and Read - we don't even know if they were actually hanged after their trial by jury in Jamaica. We have multiple accounts of them a-pirating in the crew of Rackham, as recorded at said trial. Dorothy Thomas, whose canoe was robbed and overturned by the Rackham sloop, reports:

> *"The two women, prisoners at the bar, were then on board said sloop, and wore men's jackets, and long trousers, and handkerchiefs tied about their heads; and that each of them had a machete and a pistol in their hands."*[351]

Whereas two French captives who had the opportunity to observe Read and Bonny for multiple days reported:

> *"When they saw any vessel, gave chase, or attacked, they wore men's clothes; and at other times, they wore women's clothes. They did not seem to be kept, or detained by force, but of their own free will and consent."*

And certainly most who saw the Rackham sloop seemed to be in no doubt of the gender of the two women, for in the arrest warrant for the pirate crew issued by Nassau governor Woodes Rogers in September 1720 it is plainly stated:

> "Whereas [Jack] Rakham, George Featherstone, John Davis, Andrew Gibson, John Howell, Noah Patrick, and two women by name Ann Fulford alias Bonny and Mary Read, did on the 22nd of August last, combine together to enter on board, take, steal, and run-away with out of this road of Providence, a certain sloop called the William, burden about 12 tons, mounted with 4 great guns and 2 swivel ones..."[68]

Charles Johnson in the *General History of Pirates* takes the basics of these historical facts and lays on the fiction quite thick. Johnson invents entire backstories for the women, then engineers a "meet cute" where they are both disguised as men and uncover each other's secret gender.

There may be no evidence for the true histories of Bonny and Read, but there is ample evidence for a theme in popular culture of women disguising themselves as men, as anybody who has seen Shakespeare's *As You Like It* will recall. One early combination of crossdressing and piracy occurs in a play called *A Christian Turned Turk*, from 1612, and historian Neal Rennie notes that about a quarter of all plays performed on English stages after the Restoration involved women cross-dressing as men. Johnson fit his scanty historical information to a popular narrative of the time, and the combination of history and myth is so dense that few authors or story-tellers since have been able to resist it.

What is it about the female pirate? It could be that if pirates are deviants, then female pirates are double deviants - or triple deviants, if we add the juicy rumors that Read and Bonny were lovers. Again, there's absolutely no evidence for this, but it may tie into an existing tendency to conceptualize pirates as socialists, or confederated homosexuals - after all, once you've already got one type of rebellion, it's easy to add more. Or it could be that the lady pirate is simply and purely another manifestation of the deadly female, a character who has remained in our culture from Lady Macbeth to Mrs. Lovett and Catwoman.

And persist the Lady Pirate has, from the 1867 book *The Pirate Queen* to Ruth, the pirate wench in Gilbert and Sullivan's *Pirates of Penzance*. In 1945, RKO released *The Spanish Main* with Paul Henreid, where actress Binnie Barnes portrayed Anne Bonny. In 1951, 20th Century Fox's *Anne of the West Indies* sees Bonny as an independent pirate captain mentored by Blackbeard. *Cutthroat Island* starred a lady pirate, and Disney's filmed pirate adventures have always included a least a few women amongst the crew. Anamaria joins Captain Jack aboard the Interceptor as revenge for his stealing and sinking of her pirate skiff, and Elizabeth Swann's progression from dainty governess to pirate participant is tracked by her wardrobe changes. Like the historical Bonny and Read, she has to slip out of her dress and wear sailor's garb to join in on the action in the third act. And let's not forget Elaine Marley from *Secret of Monkey Island*, who manages to combine pirate, action hero, and governor of the island into one package!

Marc Davis, never one to turn down an opportunity to draw a pretty lady, zeroed in on Bonny and Read instantly upon being given the Rogue's Gallery assignment and turned out a number of highly evocative concept drawings in 1961. Upon opening in 1967, only a painted portrait of Bonny and Read in the attraction's entrance foyer remained.

All of which is to say that some sort of change to the Auction scene was long overdue. Even X Atencio, a generation younger than Walt, expressed some reservations about the scene during ride development, and certainly modern audiences acclimated to a certain degree of gender diversity in their action-adventure escapism were only going to see the obvious ugly in a joke centered around treating women like livestock. But moreover, given that so much of the corporate messaging surrounding Pirates of the Caribbean and Captain Jack Sparrow hinges on the notion of "joining the crew" - given that Disney was simultaneously selling Pirate Princess makeovers and dresses to little girls on the doorstep of an attraction where women were jokingly being auctioned as "brides" - the change better aligns the attraction with modern audience expectations of entertainment.

Leaving the debated actions of fictionalized criminals behind and turning to the new scene itself, I like it. I think Marc's instincts were right and having a lady pirate in the ride does add something to the experience. I slightly prefer the more understated version in Paris, but Redd is already becoming as much of a fan favorite as the Redhead was. It's a pirate's life for everyone - whether you like it or not.

High seas piracy, as a genre, shows few signs of slowing down. Halloween displays still feature undead pirates cavorting through shipwrecks and speedboats still fly pirate flags on placid inland lakes. Everyone from Abbot and Costello to the Harlem Globetrotters and Garfield the Cat have met pirates. *Sea of Thieves* for Microsoft operating systems is one of the most successful video games of the past five years, and received a Jack Sparrow expansion in Summer 2021. This contained a full recreation of the Florida attraction, including a recreation of the original Bombardment scene - 1967 dialogue and all.

Looking to the tourism industry, pirate museums operate in Nassau, Salem, Cape Cod, and St Augustine. You can dine at two Pirate's Adventure Dinner Theaters in Florida and California, take a tour of New Orleans' French Quarter with a pirate actor, or set sail on buccaneer ships from Charleston, Hilton Head, Virginia Beach, Martha's Vineyard, Dominican Republic, St. Thomas, and Cancun. Romantic hedonists can even honeymoon on the Isles of Shoals, New Hampshire, "where Blackbeard honeymooned" (the mind boggles).

Once you include bars, miniature golf courses, marinas and maritime tours there are many more people employed in exploiting pirate legends than there were actual pirates on the high seas during the brief "Golden Age of Piracy".

Disney Cruise Line has operated a "Pirates Day at Sea" on their Caribbean cruises for nearly fifteen years, a night climaxing in a stage show and fireworks. The Disney Wish, premiering in 2022, features an expanded "Parlay Party" featuring a live rock group where Captain Redd sings " *We're Not Gonna Take It*" and banters with Jack Sparrow. With classic rock added to the already heady mix of Disney and lady pirate mythology, this cultural historian's cup runneth over.

Jack Sparrow, as a cultural institution, has entered a comfortable middle age. The bohemian Captain Jack "look" - eyeliner, dreadlocks, red banana and beads - is now as common a signifier of piracy as Robert Newton's squinting eye and rolled "*ar*"s or Blackbeard's burning fuses. It's become not uncommon for productions of *The Pirates of Penzance* to cast the "Pirate King" as a Jack Sparrow type character. Put on a red bandana and waggle your arms around weirdly and everyone will know who you are riffing on. He has, in short, ascended to the Mount Olympus of pirate infamy and now reposes comfortably alongside Edward Teach and Long John Silver as one of our culture's ideal pirates.

Even so, the Jack Sparrow cinematic adventures have encountered less than smooth waters in the United States in the years since the release of the first sequel. The $650 million reception to *Curse of the Black Pearl* was pretty evenly split between the United States and the rest of the world, and *Dead Man's Chest* surpassed that everywhere. But each subsequent entry has seen diminishing interest in the United States. *On Stranger Tides* made nearly 75% of its money overseas, and was greeted with polite but unenthusiastic interest stateside.[63]

The reasons of this could be many, but maybe the largest issue is simple Jack Sparrow burnout. Following *At World's End*, Johnny Depp became something of a required accessory for Hollywood studios looking to launch a mainstream fantasy-adventure franchise: *Alice in Wonderland*, *The Lone Ranger*, *Dark Shadows*, *Fantastic Beasts*... even as the Invisible Man in Universal's infamous "Dark Universe". Each of these roles was increasingly seen as acting weird simply to be weird, and as Depp himself has become more and more associated with litigation, studios have begun to back away.

In season two of *The Good Place*, an advertisement in a train station in that show's version of Hell is for "*Pirates of the Caribbean 6: The Haunted Crow's Nest Or Something, Who Gives a Crap*". The joke struck a chord on social media and went viral, despite being a detail in the background of a single shot.

That's a movie series with a bad reputation.

The Disney films and attraction have spread the mythology of piracy far and wide beyond its origin in the English-speaking world. Japan showed some resistance to Western pirate genre upon receiving their own version of Pirates of the Caribbean in 1983. But a generation on, and the idea has taken root in local culture. The 2002 video game *The Legend of Zelda: Wind Waker* was entirely predicated on familiarity with the pirate myths, complete with eyepatches and treasure chests. But we need look no further than *One Piece*, a massive media franchise which was still only growing in popularity when *Curse of the Black Pearl* hit theaters. *One Piece*'s animated television show has been broadcast continually since 1999, has produced over a thousand episodes, and begat **ten** feature films. With that kind of success and recognition, we can no longer say that pirates are exclusively a Western mythology.

Shanghai Disneyland opened in June 2016 with a mammoth area devoted to *Pirates of the Caribbean* the film franchise. This area includes a stunt show, numerous interactive exhibits, and the park's signature attraction Pirates of the Caribbean: Battle for the Sunken Treasure. This a modern, top-drawer, state of the art ride featuring boats which are moved around with magnets. They can speed up, slow down, move sideways or backwards, and go up and down hills. The attraction involves Jack Sparrow - who for some reason is initially disguised as a skeleton - sending you on a mission to distract Davy Jones so he can steal treasure sunken in a graveyard of lost ships. The attraction is full of touches and references to the legacy attractions, including a skeleton version of the jail scene and a queue-line recreation of the Captain's Quarters.

But comparing it to the classic attractions really isn't fair, given the entirely different intention and audience base for this ride. It's a modern theme park action ride, tied into a modern film franchise, keyed to the audience expectations of what that means.

For what it is, it's very good, and when you put it against other similar recent Disney rides like Mystic Manor and Rise of the

Resistance, it's obviously one of the better ones. It does, however, fall outside the magnitude of this book.

The "Battle for the Sunken Treasure" attraction sits inside a massive area, Treasure Cove, entirely devoted to the Jack Sparrow universe. It's richly detailed and opulent, but it doesn't really resemble the films in any meaningful way, with whimsical architecture and vibrant colors. From my perspective this area is totally lacking the romance and conviction of New Orleans Square or Caribbean Plaza. I *like* beginning in some semblance of historical reality and then, like the Goonies, slipping sideways into fantasy... but maybe the audience in China doesn't care about that. Maybe for them starting in total fantasy better represents their cultural orientation towards piracy. Perhaps some future writer will use my work here as a stepping stone to discussing the film franchise's impact on East Asian culture.

You know, the thing is, movies used to expect their audiences to *know things*. Whether this be elements of day-to-day life or other media, the makers of so many Hollywood movies counted on their audiences to be media literate. This is how Walt Disney could base an entire ride around a series of riffs on the "idea of pirates", or Richard Donner could include an allusion to *The Sea Hawk* secure in the knowledge that at least *somebody* out there had, like Sloth, seen it on TV. So much of the effect of these older films is dependent on these assumptions, assumptions which are no longer taken for granted.

Audiences no longer have cheap and easy access to these classic films, which once aired regularly on television or were low-priced rentals in video stores. Similarly, filmmakers can no longer count on their audience having access to a common pool of ideas and experiences. You can't make jokes about Martin Van Buren when half of your audience is in China or India. This has resulted in films that explain absolutely everything constantly, but also films which are increasingly insular, like sealed bubbles.

So let's attack this question from a different angle. Consider this: why is *Curse of the Black Pearl* commonly held as the best entry in the series? Why has the impact of the subsequent films less fully felt in the United States? What is it that that first film had that the others didn't?

As I pointed out in my chapter on that film, it used up all of the tropes - there was little left in pirate lore for the remaining films to draw upon, which means they had to start spinning their own universe. And Americans increasingly tuned out. The thing that *Curse of the Black Pearl* does is it takes concepts which float freely in American culture and gives them back to viewers in surprising and exciting forms. This is the same thing that the Disneyland attraction managed in 1967.

As demonstrated by the fact that there could be a public debate on the actions of robotic, fictional criminals, in North America we are pirate traditionalists. Blackbeard and Jean Laffitte are archetypal Wild Colonial Boys. This may account for the fact that the first film, which is very much attuned to exploiting awareness of these traditional stories and images, captured our imagination in the way that none since have.

But if you haven't grown up with a "pirate tradition", then the Jack Sparrow films are a wild adventure in an exotic culture - a Western one. Where we look at pirates and humor ourselves that we see some echo of an actual historic event, a Chinese audience doesn't have that context and likely doesn't care. They enjoy pirates the way we in the West enjoy ninjas - cool bad guys with cool accessories.

2024 marks three hundred years since the publication of *The General History of the Pirates*; in effect, we are now entering our third century of pirate mythology and its plane of influence is only growing. As we have seen, it is a genre subject to constant reinvention to meet the needs of its public, as pirates have gone from genuine threats to sources of easy wealth then on into childhood delights, light opera comedies, undead skeletons and even strange squid-men.

Through all of this, starting in 1950 with *Treasure Island* and continuing to the present day, Disney has "owned" the idea of pirates in a way that no other single cultural entity has. Even that great brand ambassador of rum - Captain Morgan - is drawn to look as if he stepped out of the Disneyland ride. Pirates of the Caribbean is the "name brand" in theme park rides, evoked by Ian Malcolm in Jurassic

Park: "*But John, If the Pirates of the Caribbean breaks down, the pirates don't eat the tourists!*"

It's been axiomatic to declare piracy a dead genre since Errol Flynn hung up his rapier, but just like our pirate skeleton endlessly turning his ship's wheel in a musty basement in Anaheim, there's life in these scoundrels yet. Piracy, as always, awaits its next reinvention. Perhaps some overseas culture will see the life we are missing and re-export pirates back to us in some new way, the same way Sergio Leone westerns responded to American horse operas and have now replaced them in our cultural memory.

And as long as the world needs rebels, miscreants, and outcasts I suspect the pirate will be with us, forever riding alongside us in their pirate sloops over the horizon. As Howard Pyle wrote in his *Book of Pirates*:

> "*Ye Pirate Bold -- It is not because of his life of adventure and daring that I admire this one of my favorite heroes; nor is it because of blowing winds nor blue ocean nor balmy islands which he knew so well; nor is it because of gold he spent nor treasure he hid. He was a man who knew his own mind and what he wanted.*"

NOTES

Part One

1. Pirate Alley: A history of the New Orleans street and its name(s) https://www.nola.com/archive/article_4dde2d84-9782-59fb-aaa9-afd5bea481bd.html
2. Rennie, pg. 23
3. For more on this see *Under the Black Flag*, Chapter 11
4. Rennie, pg. 10
5. General History, Chapter 3
6. Johnson, pg. 82
7. The Boston News Letter, Feb 23 - Mar 2, 1719
8. I have no idea where the fifteen wives came from, unless folklore is mixing up Blackbeard and Bluebeard. The Shoals are rocky outcroppings with no real topsoil in which to bury treasure, but that hasn't stopped them from marketing themselves to tourists as being where "Blackbeard spent his honeymoon", which is admittedly a good sell.
9. I've spent so much time reading about pirates in preparation for this book that I can tell you that this sort of pirate-mixing is dirt common. I'm currently inclined towards thinking that this sort of human inclination towards building an ideal, composite outlaw is how the English-speaking world developed the Robin Hood tradition.
10. Cordingly, pg. 272
11. Irving has Ichabod Crane go on to become a lawyer and politician, which tells us pretty much everything we need to know of Irving's opinion of him.
12. Much of this chapter's information is owed to Rennie, who has a greater capacity for Romantic fiction than I.
13. Fenimore Cooper's greatest contribution to literature was his *Leatherstocking Tales*, starring Natty Bumppo, frontiersman. These novels migrated from the bookshelf to the nursery over the course of their popular lifespan, making James Fenimore Cooper the reason J. M. Barrie included Native Americans in Neverland.

Part Two

1. Kaufman, pg. 200
2. All previous efforts at this trick had been in black and white, using a combination of optical printers and visual tricks. Probably the most effective had been Schlessinger's Porky Pig short *You Ought To Be in Pictures*, which re-photographed frame enlargements with animation cels laid over top.
3. Gabler, pg. 432
4. "Piercing the Perce Pearce Mystery", *Walt's People Volume 12*
5. Ghez, pg. 56-58
6. Snow, pg. 96
7. Building A Company, pg. 169
8. Maltin, pg. 89
9. Schuster is mistaken here. The *So Dear To My Heart* depot is copied pretty directly from the December 1946 edition of Model Railroader, where it is identified as "Flag Depot in use on the Pottsville Branch of the Lehigh Valley RR" - meaning its original was an obscure and apparently lost little structure in eastern Pennsylvania. Ward Kimball added the depot to his backyard Grizzly Flats railroad after filming was completed. John Lasseter purchased the original building and water tower and had the whole thing moved up to the Lasseter Family Winery in Sonoma Valley, where it won a preservation award in 2012. The structure burned in the 2017 California wild fires. Thanks to Scot Lawrence for doing the research I could not and tracking down the provenance of the original depot, see his work here: https://scotlawrence.github.io/grizzlyflats/index.html
10. This makes Ken Andersen the original Imagineer; Walt would proceed to cherry-pick talent from his animation studio and put them on his personal payroll in the build-up to beginning work on Disneyland. The old animation guard hated this practice; they referred to WED Enterprises as "Cannibal Island", where talent goes off to and is never seen again.
11. Thomas, pg. 224
12. Gabler, pg. 468
13. Time Magazine, Jan 7, 1946
14. Variety, May 1949
15. Gabler, pg. 470
16. Adamson, pg. 168

17. Singer, pg. 22
18. London Evening Standard, September 28 1949
19. The same Don DeFore who would one day open the Silver Banjo Barbecue at Disneyland, incidentally!
20. Adamson, pg. 170
21. Adamson, pg. 171
22. Singer, pg. 22
23. This delicious story comes from Mark Penrose's Robert Newton biography; I've been unable to verify it myself, but sometimes good stories cannot go unrepeated.
24. Variety, July 1950
25. There are two known silent versions of *Treasure Island*, from 1918 and 1920, both lost. The 1920 version was directed by Maurice Tourneur, father of *Out of the Past* director Jacques Tourneur and one of the best talents of his era - I'd give a lot to see that one.
26. Adamson, pg. 176
27. As quoted in Ghez, page 64
28. Ghez, pg. 65
29. Gabler, pg. 438
30. E Ticket, Issue 21, pg. 18
31. Bossert, pg. 41
32. The Fritos location is noteworthy in that, according to legend, a line cook dropped some hot tortilla chips into a bag of taco seasoning, gifting the world the legacy of Doritos.
33. Surrell, pg. 15
34. Tellingly, Freedomland in New York City opened with a ride called "*Buccaneer*" in its New Orleans section. Freedomland was the brain child of C.V. Wood, a wily Texan whose own hucksterish energy is hugely responsible for Disneyland opening on time and the only man in history to have a severe enough falling out with Walt to be totally expunged from official company record. Wood lifted ideas and corporate partners wholesale from Disneyland, such as a highway of the future ride and a fried chicken restaurant in a southern plantation. Freedomland folded in 1964 and the *Buccaneer* ride was moved to Cedar Point, leading to generations of Ohioans who have long harbored dark suspicions that Walt Disney lifted the idea for *Pirates of the Caribbean* from *Buccaneer*. But given the once-close association between Walt and Wood, it's even more likely that Wood heard Walt discussing his ideas and thought it was a good idea, too.

35. Pierce, pg. 90
36. Wood's ventures, most especially his hiring of Randall Duell and management of the design of Six Flags Over Texas is what gave us the modern regional amusement park. Disney fans tend to sniff at these ventures but they are as essential to the growth of the theme park industry as Disneyland was. Readers interested in following C.V. Wood down the rabbit hole should check out the books by Robert McLaughlin for Images of Modern America on Freedomland and Pleasure Island, as well as Barry Hill's essential book Imagineering An American Dreamscape.
37. Hurlbut, incredibly, designed, funded, and partially engineered the attraction himself. Even Walt Disney was impressed.
38. I recognize that I'm flying in the face of 60 years of official Disney history by placing the work on the Pirates ride system before the development of the Small World boat system, but you'll have to trust me here that this is the real deal. Besides, it makes more sense - Ed and Karl were brought in in the first place because Disney couldn't build an acceptable boat system with a lift hill and drop. The official version - which conveniently excludes Bud Hurlbut and Six Flags - would have you believe that the ride system for some reason regressed to a simpler form for Small World before re-evolving closer to the original Arrow log flume worked, complete with submerged wheels and chain dogs. The only reason Small World used the flume system is because it's easier to disassemble and move a water flume back to Disneyland than it is to move a flooded building.
39. The 1964 Small World "submerged trough" ride system would be used on the 1971 Jungle Cruise at Magic Kingdom, and copied for Tokyo, a fascinating holdover of a very strange boat guidance system.
40. D23 Expo 2017, Panel: "Pirates of the Caribbean, 50 Years of Swashbuckling Adventures in Disney Parks"
41. Interview with David Oneal, Extinct Attractions Club
42. Moore, pg. 44
43. Martin, pg. 26
44. And about George Bruns: in collaborations it's impossible to say who suggested what and when, but Bruns had already composed music that used the term "yo ho". His music for the 1961 Disney short *The Saga of Windwagon Smith* is an inspired mixture of high seas and high plains, and similarly uses "yo ho ho" as part of a repetitive choral hook. I'm not saying that's where it came from, but the precedent is intriguing.

45. Wathel's harness can be seen in the Disneyland episode Disney Goes to the World's Fair. It proved to be as impractical as it looks on television.
46. Tom Morris, Interview, December 2022
47. A couple of sources indicate that trouble with the down ramp kicking up too much water delayed the ride; I think these people are conflating events that occurred before and after the attraction opening. Hey, it was a long time ago!
48. E Ticket, Winter 1996, pg. 32
49. Interview with David Oneal, Extinct Attractions Club
50. Boag was wearing a costume taken off the Auctioneer figure, Alice Davis noted with horror!
51. Surrell, pg. 68
52. This used to spell out the attraction's name in fiber optics.
53. Interested parties can read Marc's capsule histories of these famous pirates in *Marc Davis in His Own Words*, pg. 249
54. According to Ryan Dudley, current owner of The Cellar, Gene White apparently not only served time in Folsom Prison but began swinging an axe around when the restaurant's original owner, Louis Schnelli informed him that his project was behind schedule! Per Chris Merritt, Bud Hurlbut also had to enlist family members to finish White's job on the Timber Mountain Log Ride. Class act!
55. *Camptown Races* was published in 1850, 25 years after the supposed death of Jean Laffite and some 120 years after the end of the Golden Age of Piracy, for those who wish to ascribe a time period to the Blue Bayou tableau.
56. This is according to the memories of 'Jaime Maas' in private correspondence. Based on internal reference photos taken by WDI, both "old man" figures seem to have been manufactured in sequence alongside the figures for the Florida pirates attraction.
57. This is an idea that stretches all the way back to the walk-though attraction version, where the entrance door that leads down to the museum always seemed to have a jolly roger above it.
58. Merritt, pg. 248
59. Subsequent commentators have expended much ink (and bandwidth) attempting to link this to actual oceangoing sea shanties, although it's most likely simply to have sprung out of Stevenson's imagination.
60. Younger, pg. 318
61. Interview with David Oneal, Extinct Attractions Club

62. This observation comes from Jack Jensen's marvelous piece on Pirates of the Caribbean for The E Ticket magazine in 1999
63. Actually, in 1967 the figure didn't turn his wheel at all; you can see this for yourself in the Disneyland television special "*From the Pirates of the Caribbean to the World of Tomorrow*". It seems that the turning motion debuted at Florida's Pirates and was brought back West at some later point.
64. The lowered ceiling here is due to the return ramp from the end of the attraction crossing literally above the scene; the support column is disguised as a ship's mast.
65. My favorite appearance of this running gag is in Marc's unrealized attraction *Adventure House* for Fort Wilderness; a bear asleep in a bed slumbers below a motto reading "Many Brave Souls Are Asleep In The Deep"!
66. See animator Andreas Deja's marvelous recollection of Alfonse's here: http://andreasdeja.blogspot.com/2020/07/alfonses-restautant.html
67. Rennie, pg. 46
68. Surrell, pg. 87
69. Merritt, pg. 275-8
70. Merritt, pg. 304
71. Surrell, pg. 80
72. Younger, pg. 121
73. The E Ticket, Number 31
74. Surrell, pg. 80
75. Interview with Bloody Good Horror, http://www.bloodygoodhorror.com/bgh/interviews/bgh-investigates-the-poltergeist-curse-with-craig-reardon
76. Charles Hilliger, June 15 1988, https://www.latimes.com/archives/la-xpm-1988-06-15-fi-4276-story.html
77. Interview with Bloody Good Horror, http://www.bloodygoodhorror.com/bgh/interviews/bgh-investigates-the-poltergeist-curse-with-craig-reardon
78. https://earzup-podcast.com/2013/11/real-skeletons-disneyland/
79. Ellms has the date of the earthquake as 1658, but some accounts change the date to 1638, which is the date of the most famous New England earthquake. W.T. Brigham does note a 1658 quake in his 1869 "*Historical Notes on the Earthquakes of New England*", meaning the earlier date may be a conflation. See this resource at: https://quod.lib.umich.edu/m/moa/AGJ1409.0001.001

80. See Joseph Citro, *Weird New England*, pg.128
81. For more on 19th century Spiritualism, see my book *Boundless Realm*, Part II, Chapter 9.
82. Knott's Preserved, pg.109
83. Merritt, pg. 26
84. https://goldenageofpiracy.org/history/buccaneering-era/sack-of-campeche-1663.php
85. This story corresponds well with what I've read in published writings on Morgan, but this is a case where we are going to have to trust the considerably well-organized piracy internet community on these matters. 'Golden Age of Piracy' is an excellent starting point, although I wish it were better sourced: https://goldenageofpiracy.org/history/buccaneering-era/sack-of-panama-1670.php
86. Hollywood films of the era didn't credit the entirety of those who worked on a film, usually simply the department head in charge of the unit.
87. A favorite hidden detail: As you enter the Auction scene, if you look behind you and to your left you will see a little transitional piece of architecture, a small balcony with a lantern hanging inside it. There's small, child-size chairs with their legs sawed off sitting up on the balcony, and the whole thing is painted dark brown and black to avoid bouncing too much light and thus attracting undue attention. You have to look for it.
88. The Chase's status as an issue predates the opening of the attraction; if you look at Claude Coats' layout art you'll notice that the "Pooped Pirate" figure was added at some point to give the scene a bit more life.
89. Curtis, Kindle location 366
90. Kindle location 414
91. Rums like this are still produced today and, much as with those individuals who love blue cheese, the "rum stink" is indeed a potent addiction. Modern pirates should seek out the nectarous Smith and Cross, an estery Jamaican rum aged on London docks and bottled at 100 proof - a very good taste of what the American colonists were lusting for in the decades leading up to those heady "Days of '76".
92. This is why Cuban rums are very light and Jamaican rums are very dark - the Spanish-Speaking colonies preferred a lighter spirit and so employed a column still, a device unknown in the eighteenth century.
93. Wayne, Kindle location 531
94. pg. 245

95. This tendency reached its apex in Country Bear Jamboree five years later, where a coonskin cap perched atop a stovepipe hat turns out to be a living, singing raccoon.
96. pg. 24
97. This is an actual thing made by *VeggieTales*, you're welcome.
98. Anderson is not officially credited but we know for sure he was working on similar concepts for Haunted Mansion. I think what happened here is that these early concepts were headed up by Bruce Bushman; it looks much more like his work than that of Anderson. Bushman left Disney in the late 50s and thus was excluded from a lot of official histories; he died in 1972, leaving the floor open for Anderson to tell the stories. Bushman's departure actually explains why the project was halted and re-assigned to Marc Davis a year later. Don't blame Anderson, by the way; the man was recalling things for a project he wasn't fully on that happened decades prior and he had two strokes in one week in 1962. I'm not sure I could recall the details fully either.
99. For what it's worth, I worked at Pirates in Florida, and the fire effect is on a separate switch, which would seem to validate the story.
100.   Johnson, *Wonderland*, pg. 160
101.   For copious detail on all of this see Erkki Huhtamo's *Illusions in Motion*, chapter 7.
102.   Hat tip to historian Barbara Rimkunas for this delicious irony, see https://exeterhistory.blogspot.com/2019/03/the-conflagration-of-moscow-exeter.html
103.   pg.11
104.   Interview with David Oneal, Extinct Attractions Club
105.   Moore, pg. 44
106.   The one-two punch of Pirates of the Caribbean and The Haunted Mansion would boost Disneyland's attendance from 6 million to 9 million in three short years. As Alice Davis later said, it was the ride that saved Disneyland.

Part Three

1. Flower, pg. 51
2. Building a Company, pg. 303
3. Realityland, pg. 63
4. Marc Davis In His Own Words, pg. 493
5. Marc Davis In His Own Words, pg. 511

6. This gag would seem to be lifted from Sergio Leone's *For A Few Dollars More*. Nobody can never accuse Marc Davis of having a limited range of tastes!
7. DACs, or Digital Animation Control, was a centralized room below Fantasyland which contained all of the looping bin tapes which contained the instructions to move the Audio-Animatronics figures at Walt Disney World.
8. Surrell, pg. 53
9. *The "E" Ticket*, Number 30, 1998
10. Disney Report, *Orlandoland Magazine*, Feb 1972
11. https://www.disneydocs.net/_files/ugd/5db718_c37acba1f6324de09858786f989bf996.pdf
12. Even today, kitchen installation is the most expensive portion of opening a restaurant. This fact delayed the return of the Adventureland Veranda for almost a decade.
13. Marc Davis in his Own Words, pg. 534
14. Surrell, pg. 54
15. Tampa Tribune, April 16 1972
16. For a point of comparison, the Haunted Mansion cost $6.5m in 1969 and Space Mountain cost $15m in 1975. The price of Pirates of the Caribbean in Disneyland is difficult to discern because the cost of the whole New Orleans Square area was budgeted as part of the project; Disney reported that cost to be $18m and compared it to the $17m price tag to build the whole of Disneyland in 1955. Regardless, claims that Disney spent less than half the budget of the original to build the Florida ride are grossly exaggerated.
17. One wonders if this was as much an effort to save headaches as it was an early example of "viral" marketing.
18. Orlando Sentinel, Oct 29 1973
19. You can see Yale's white robe in his publicity shots for Haunted Mansion; it looks more like a lab coat to me.
20. Pat Burke Interview, Alain Littaye, https://disneyandmore.blogspot.com/2009/07/d-grand-interview-of-wdi-imagineer-pat.html
21. Marc went back and removed several first nations stereotypes from the attraction concept in 1974 but this failed to get the show moving again.
22. This effect still works today; it's one reason Splash Mountain and Big Thunder mountain feel so much more massive at Magic Kingdom than they do at Disneyland.

23. And this is still pretty much where most of them come from.
24. I'm looking at you, Avatar boat ride.
25. Okay look, I know that this concept is literally as old as amusement parks, going back to the Chute-the-Chutes at Coney Island. But my point is that for people in that particular time and place, unless they had been to Six Flags Over Texas, this was new and exciting stuff.
26. This from an internal memo shared with me by Michael Crawford, thank you!
27. Marc Davis in His Own Words, p.323
28. WED went to some trouble to source period accurate wavy glass for the Tavern in Liberty Square, although elsewhere in Liberty Square they used stock windows - perhaps deciding that nobody would be lingering around them long enough to notice.
29. When I worked at the ride in the early 2000s this scene was done up in amber light. However lighting diagrams I examined from 1973 indicated green light for both the caverns and Dead Man's Cove, which would have established a stronger mystery atmosphere. Years later I was finally able to see Marc's concept art for this scene and he specified green lights; vindication!
30. This same skull went missing in the 2006 Captain Jack Sparrow refurbishment, finally returning in a much more lavish and nicely sculpted version in 2017. This was done as part of the installation of an on-ride flash photo, but regardless it's great to finally have this character back in the ride.
31. This is where boats are taken off the main track to be brought backstage for repair work; in the bad old days before Jack Sparrow we liked to do this during ride operation for lack of other things to do!
32. One of the Amazon reviews of my first book complained that the author "will always use a big word when a small one will do." Whenever I read this particular remark around "perambulation" during editing I imagine that reader throwing my new book out a window in disgust.
33. pg. 28
34. Interview with David Oneal, Extinct Attractions Club
35. If you want to see Disney Imagineers repeating it, you can check out Disney+'s amazingly gross "Behind the Attraction" series.
36. http://tezukainenglish.com/wp/?page_id=3039
37. Bossert, pg. 115
38. Quoted in Raz, pg. 160

39. Much of the detail here comes from OLC's own public history, accessed at http://www.olc.co.jp/en/company/history/history01.html. Even if the researcher's desire for thoroughness is a little suspicious of the tidy story, I also wish Disney were even one-tenth as good at presenting their own history.
40. Interview, *The Progress City Radio Hour Episode 7*
41. pg. 218
42. Sklar attributes the design of the park to Dick Kline, who seems to have also worked on Fort Wilderness. Page 225
43. I lack the language skills to prove this but I suspect Disney has incorrectly transliterated "Teichiro Hori" on their internal documents as he seems to have no film credits to his name on the Western internet. Toho is among the best documented Japanese studios amongst Western fans, so this raises red flags for me.
44. Although this whole point does beg the question: why did they bother with the train tunnel in Florida at all? Why not just build the attraction behind the existing railroad tracks if saving money was such a big concern? And while we're at it, why build the Florida version in such a bizarre and pointy building? If saving money was the concern, why not just build it in a huge box?
45. I make it seem in this chapter as if Japan had absolutely no idea what a Western pirate was, but this is manifestly untrue. To begin with, one of the most popular party games in Japan is "Pop Up Pirate", which has been on the market since the 1970s. If Japanese children were really so ignorant on pirates, it didn't show here. There's also lots and lots of pirate-themed Japanese video games from the 1980s, including Pirate Pete, Pirate Ship Higemaru, The Goonies, and Captain Silver. The last of these provides a fascinating case of different cultures not knowing the "rules" of a myth and producing something that sounds hilariously wrong to our ears. Japanese people love to use English and will often just grab any old English that's sitting around, which is how the main protagonist of Captain Silver ended up being named "Jim Ackroyd". Ackroyd is a Scottish, not English surname and is instantly recognizable as a goof to native English speakers. The character was renamed to the more appropriately piratical "Jim Avery" for the US release.
46. Grover, pg. 186; these numbers would seem to come direct from Dick Nunis.
47. Masters, pg. 282
48. Associated Press, Dec 20 1985

49. Baltimore Sun, April 13 1992
50. Dunlop, pg.166
51. This regulated aspect of the experience can strike one as either an immense relief or entirely sinister. The authors of *Inside the Mouse* - to cite one memorable example - can never quite get over the latter reaction, as if the adults who accompany their children on the Autopia are never again free to make bad decisions while driving.
52. Amusingly, all of this visual signposting still did not save the Parisian pirates from the same fate as Orlando, where visitors still didn't get the point and a jolly roger was run up from the fort's highest point to get the idea across. Paris even hung a pirate flag from the front entrance to Adventureland for a few years, demonstrating that even cultured continental types can't find their way around a theme park.
53. Don't be like me and assume that fireflies don't exist in the Caribbean; they do and are called peenie-wallies.
54. Disneyland Paris From Sketch To Reality, pg. 165
55. Masters, pg. 280
56. Masters, pg. 279
57. Stewart, pg. 130

Part Four

1. "Disneyland Magical Fantasy Defies Description", May 17 1980
2. "Rape and Pillage on the Family Plan", Dec 4 1983
3. June 8, 1980
4. "Sharansky Finds Magic in Kingdom", Newsday, June 1 1988
5. Lagoon Amusement Park, incidentally, provided the summer job of Nolan Bushnell - the visionary weirdo who went on to found Atari and Chuck E Cheese on the basis of his experience working at the park. It's all connected...
6. Disney A-Z lists the air date as January 21.
7. The American divorce rate had peaked in 1981 - NY Times, March 7 1985, https://www.nytimes.com/1985/03/07/garden/decline-in-divorce-is-first-in-20-years.html
8. McBride, location 8498
9. Columbus himself would turn out to be a gifted director of young actors in *Adventures in Babysitting*, *Home Alone*, *Mrs. Doubtfire*, and his *Harry Potter* films.
10. Today the Riverwalk Inn

11. The Fratellis could be seen as sort of bridges between kids and adults, dysfunctional squabbling adults who still need their mother. After all what are mobsters in the mind of children - and Walt Disney - but modern pirates?
12. Christie, location 2737
13. Los Angeles Times Calendar, April 11, 1976, pg. 41
14. Retro Gamer, Issue 116
15. Yes, you heard me. Go home, Hans Zimmer.
16. To prove this, LucasArts shipped a Special Edition in 2009 with redrawn art, voice acted lines and wall-to-wall music and effects which simply cannot capture the zest of the original. The art is better in smaller resolution, the lines are funnier when you read them in your head. Or at least, that's this author's blistering hot take.
17. Fjellman, pg. 257
18. Daily Southtown, Oct 28 1993
19. In case you need a refresher on why, it's worth remembering that the 90s may have been the playground of The Fresh Prince of Bel-Air and the Ninja Turtles, but it also saw the LA Riots, the OJ Simpson murder trial, and the Michael Jackson scandals.
20. And in the event that you think this is some new development, I'm here to tell you that you are sadly misinformed. Twenty years before these mid-90s changes, old old school Disneyland fans suffered their own slings and arrows as African American cast members were finally allowed to join Operations and Guest Relations in the late 60s, having previously been limited to Food Service and Custodial roles. Elsewhere, a "speedy Gonzales" accented Mexican was altered to become a Texan in America Sings, and the Carousel of Progress proudly proclaimed that "Now Is the Time" for gender equality. One fact in the favor of Fraser-Vaselakos' article having made its way into the upper halls of Disney management is a curious event that supposedly occurred in the late 70s. It's A Small World initially included a visual gag where a pair of African boys were seen laughing with a hyena. A South African guest wrote a letter to Disney informing them that Africans culturally consider hyenas to be unclean creatures and that depicting African children cavorting with them could possibly cause objection. Disney removed the scene on both coasts, replacing the tableau with a line of three boys with crossed arms singing. This happened so early that it's very difficult to find evidence that the scene was even ever there.

21. I'm gonna name this "Nolte's Law of Ghostbusters", it's now official because it's in print. Sorry, that's the rules.
22. I couldn't believe this when I found it, here: https://youtu.be/8ItmTO4ap-w
23. Recently Disney has tried to do this gag again at the Battle for Sunken Treasure attraction in Shanghai; this time the classic skeleton pinned to the cave wall is stabbing another guy in the back over an open chest of treasure. It's an actual new piece of sculpture, and much more impressive in detail and posing, but doesn't really look that much better than what WDI came up with here in 1997. Let's call the whole thing off?
24. That's a bold statement for somebody who wrote this book to write, but I ask you: have you *seen* Facebook recently?
25. Los Angeles Times, Nov 20, 1994
26. Los Angeles Times, Sept 12, 1996
27. Cynthia here seems to be referring to the fact that the final turntable briefly had the escaping pirates holding a ham. It seems pretty clear to me that the pirates - not the lady - want the ham, but then again Cynthia here is simply doing her best to respond to some lunatic asking her questions about Disneyland over the phone.
28. Los Angeles Times, Jan 4 1997
29. Associated Press, March 8 1997
30. McBride, location 6770
31. Surrell, pg. 114
32. DVD Audio Commentary
33. Surrell, pg. 117
34. Surrell, pg. 115
35. Vanity Fair Interview, November 9 2015
36. Stewart, pg. 438
37. A lot of this comes from official sources endorsed by Disney; it's fascinating what a corporation will own up to when unconventional choices net them a billion-dollar payday. Would all of this information have come out had the film been anything less than a sensation?
38. Surrell, pg. 135
39. Singer, pg. 92
40. https://www.soundtrack.net/content/article/?id=205
41. *Roman Polanski's Pirates* actually toyed with this concept briefly. In an exciting scene, an old Spanish gentleman lays in bed rambling incoherently about a curse placed upon the gold Aztec throne currently

being transported back to Spain. But *Pirates* never goes anywhere with this idea, because the only curse Polanski believes in is terrible behavior.
42. DVD Audio commentary
43. WDWMagic, online since the Clinton administration, was very helpful in jogging my memory of the exact dates of all of this, https://www.wdwmagic.com/attractions/pirates-of-the-caribbean.htm
44. Bizarrely, this was positioned to be part of the 50th anniversary celebration of Disneyland; nothing says a historical anniversary like adding modern characters to the park's best ride!
45. About those skeletons. At one point the plan was to have the center skeleton, with the sword in his back, be animated to some degree. When the figure was installed for the April 2006 soft open, instead of being flopped on the beach in the way a skeleton actually would be his head was raised and turned as if he was looking back at the sword. I think the plan was to have this figure raise his head, turn it to look at the boat, and say something. Regardless, the fact that this skeleton is "lifting his head" instead of appearing to be dead only in Florida has always driven me absolutely crazy. In recent years his head has been rotated so he is no longer looking back at the sword, but it still looks silly. And I'd bet those of you who read *Boundless Realm* thought I was taking it easy on the nit-pick complaining this time!
46. Another another note on the skeletons. Back in 2005 I had traipsed up on the beach, gone right up to the guy pinned to the wall, and decided that the skeleton was plastic. Since doing the research for this book I'm no longer convinced that those original 1973 bones were plastic ones. And I'm just saying, Pirates at Magic Kingdom is famous for being haunted, and has been since it opened.
47. Back in the days when things like tattoos and even nail polish were forbidden, this was a big deal!
48. The Mousekateeria is the cast commissary located below Fantasyland. Yes it really is called that.
49. Here's the sort of thing chapter end notes exist for: every single version of the "Pooped Pirate" is a lil' different. The original 1967 figure was leaning on a barrel, meaning he could only gesture with his left hand because his right hand was affixed to the rim of the barrel. The 1973 version was sitting on the floor and therefore could wobble back and forth while gesturing with both hands. Paris regressed to the leaning-on-the-barrel look, because they were traditionalists. In 2006, Anaheim got a brand-new version of the Pooped Pirate, which is far closer to the 1973

Orlando look, but because he's staged up on top of a tall barrel instead of sitting on the floor, there's extra barrels all around him, including under his resting foot. I think Tokyo has the best version of the new scene, with a chest he got the treasure map from and extra baskets of wine strewn about. But every version is different, something I never even considered until writing this book.

50. Singer, pg. 64
51. Yes, that sense of closure comes at the expense of five now-removed unique Audio Animatronic figures, but honestly I always found Marc Davis' intention of providing a lot to look at while waiting to disembark to be a solution in search of a problem.
52. These catered lunches always came from Sonny's BBQ and never failed to make me sick.
53. https://disneygeek.com/news/releases/2007/2007_01_26_newattractions.html
54. In the original German the family isn't actually named Robinson; the title means something like "*The Swiss Robinson Crusoe*"
55. Weirdly, after several years the mist screen effect reverted to only featuring Davy Jones while Blackbeard continued to narrate at the exit. Make up your minds, Disney!!
56. I've always wondered if the effect was devised for California, where the higher ceiling in the grotto would have resulted in a larger projected image on the water surface.
57. Go ahead, check my sources here: https://www.boxofficemojo.com/release/rl4083713537/, and https://www.boxofficemojo.com/title/tt1790809/, and https://www.boxofficemojo.com/release/rl4117267969/
58. You must really be a glutton for punishment for coming to this note for more information, but here we go. Hollywood Studios... once upon a time, The Disney-MGM Studios... was envisioned as an operating movie studio with a ticketed theme park tour attached. All of this was experienced on a combination tram tour and walking exhibit that took several hours. The working studio aspect never really came to be, so much so that it's kind of inaccurate to say it ever was a real studio. You can read my book *The Hidden History of Walt Disney World* for more details. The most popular part of the studio tram tour was Catastrophe Canyon, so much so that Disney split the thing in half, presenting the tram half and the walking half as separate attractions. This left Disney with a "special effects tour" past soundstages with standing but

inoperable sets for The All-New Mickey Mouse Club and Star Search and a post-production exhibit that nobody cared to see. Starting in 1996, Disney attempted to solve this problem by further subdividing the Effects Tour into smaller attractions. The soundstages now hosted sets from *Tarzan: The Epic Adventures* and the live-action *101 Dalmatians*. What was previously the Post-Production exhibit became a rotating "Behind the Scenes of..." walkthrough attraction. Films promoted in this space were, as far as I can determine, *The Hunchback of Notre Dame*, *George of the Jungle*, and *Armageddon*. Again, I promise I'm not making this up. Disney's big promotional push for 2001 was the "100 Years of Magic" celebration, supposedly marking the centennial of Walt Disney's birth. Previous promotions had focused on the Magic Kingdom (Remember the Magic) and Epcot (Millenium Celebration), so Disney-MGM had the honor of being the park that received the attention this time. The attention consisted of a huge metal wizard hat plopped down in front of the Chinese Theater, the park's central icon. There was a desire to create a Walt Disney history exhibit to make good on the premise of the celebration, but money was tight and so part of the traveling "Architecture of Reassurance" museum exhibit was brought in. The whole thing was called One Man's Dream and it occupied some, but not all, of the previous "Behind the Scenes..." attraction. We're focused on the space left over once One Man's Dream was installed, a subdivision of a subdivision of the exit of an opening day attraction. It was basically two big rooms. Since 2003 these two remaining rooms had hosted three "attractions", promoting *The Haunted Mansion* (2003), *The Lion, the Witch and the Wardrobe* (2005), and *Prince Caspian* (2008). Disney never made the third film in the planned Narnia trilogy, and the Prince Caspian attraction closed in 2011.

59. Which is still a year more than the disastrous tenure of Bob Chapek as Disney CEO in 2022, just saying.
60. A little further along the way the sword duelists have also gone co-ed, with the handsome Errol Flynn-type now an eye-patched lady pirate and the "wide eyed damsel" removed. My suggestion here would have been to keep the aggressor pirate and converted the Errol Flynn and damsel figures into Pintel and Ragetti, which would have been appropriate for their characters in the films as well as added a pretty good laugh to the scene.
61. Quoted by Rennie, pg. 65

62. https://www.postandcourier.com/gov-woodes-rogers-pirate-proclamation-in-the-boston-gazette/pdf_d53297f8-dd54-11e8-a5bb-f382533ea96d.html
63. https://www.boxofficemojo.com/release/rl4117267969/

Bibliography

Adamson, Joe. Byron Haskin: A Directors Guild of America Oral History. Metuchen, NJ, Scarecrow Press. 1984.

"Anyone for Yo-Ho-Ho?" Life Magazine, September 15, 1967.

Arrington, Joseph Earl. John Maelzel, Master Showman of Automata and Panoramas. Philadelphia, Philadelphia Historical Society. 1960.

Berry, Jeff. Beachbum Berry's Potions of the Caribbean. Cocktail Kingdom. 2013.

Bill Tracy Project, The. 2008 - 2013, http://ochh.net/tracyindex.html

Bossert, David A. Claude Coats: Walt Disney's Imagineer. Los Angles, The Old Mill Press. 2021.

Bradley, Elizabeth. Knickerbocker: The Myth Behind New York. New York, Rivergate Books. 2009.

Bright, Randy, Disneyland Inside Story. New York, Harry N. Abrams. 1987.

Brown, Stuart. "RetroAhoy: The Secret of Monkey Island". YouTube, video documentary. May 18 2018 https://www.youtube.com/watch?v=9F9ahZQ7oP0

"Captain Blood (1924)." Silent Era: Progressive Silent Film List, 30 Nov. 2008, www.silentera.com/PSFL/data/C/CaptainBlood1924.html.

Christie, James. You're The Director, You Figure It Out: The Life and Films of Richard Donner. BearManor Media. 2010.

Cordingly, David. Under the Black Flag: The Romance and the Reality of Life Among the Pirates. Random House. 2006.

Curtis, Wayne. And A Bottle of Rum: A History of the New World in Ten Cocktails. Revised and Updated Edition. New York, Broadway Books, Random House. 2018.

Daveland. (2007, June). Daveland Disneyland Photo Index. https://www.davelandweb.com/disneyland/

Dunlop, Beth. Building a Dream, The Art of Disney Architecture. Harry N. Abrams. 1996.

Eco, Umberto. Travels in Hyperreality. Mariner Books, translated by William Weaver. 2014.

Ellis, Lindsay. "Dead Genres Tell No Tales". Video commentary. 2017. https:/nebula.app/videos/lindsay-ellis-pirates-of-the-caribbean-dead-genres-tell-no-tales

Ellms, Charles. The Pirate's Own Book. Sanborn & Carter, 1837. Digital Edition by Project Gutenberg, Accessed June 2020.

"Embargo Act." Encyclopædia Britannica, Encyclopædia Britannica, Inc., 21 June 2019, www.britannica.com/topic/Embargo-Act.

Extinct Attractions Club: Pirates of the Caribbean. Documentary. Directed by David Oneal. 2005.

Fanning, Jim. Did You Know? 12 Blue-Ribbon Facts About Walt Disney's So Dear to My Heart. D23. 19 June 2019. https://d23.com/did-you-know-12-blue-ribbon-facts-about-walt-disneys-so-dear-to-my-heart/

Fjellman, Stephen M. Vinyl Leaves: Walt Disney World and America. First Edition, Routledge. 1992.

Flower, Joe. Prince of the Magic Kingdom. First Edition, Wiley & Sons. 1991.

Gabler, Neal. Walt Disney: The Triumph of the American Imagination. First Edition, Vintage Press. 2007.

Ghez, Didier. Walt's People Volume 12. Xlibris. 2012.

Gordon, Bruce and Mumford, David. Disneyland: The Nickel Tour. Los Angeles, Camphor Tree. 2000.

Grover, Ron. The Disney Touch: How a Daring Management Team Revived an Entertainment Empire. Homewood, IL. Business One Irwin. 1991.

Haskell, Molly. From Reverence to Rape: The Treatment of Women in the Movies. Third Edition. University of Chicago Press. 2016.

_____ Steven Spielberg: A Life in Films. Jewish Lives Series. Yale University Press. 2017.

Hass, Charlie. "Disneyland is Good For You" New West Magazine, 4 December 1978.

Hench, John. Designing Disney. New York, Disney Editions. 2003.

History of Disney Theme Parks in Documents. 2013 - 2022, https://www.disneydocs.net

Hollis, Richard and Sibley, Brian. The Disney Studio Story. New York, Crown. 1988.

Huhtamo, Erkki. Illusions in Motion. Cambridge, The MIT Press. 2013.

The Imagineering Story. Directed by Leslie Iwerks. Disney+, 2019.

Irving, Washington. "The Money Diggers", Tales of a Traveller. Carey and Lea, 1824. Digital Edition by Amazon. Accessed June 2020

Isackes, Richard M and Maness, Karen L. The Art of the Hollywood Backdrop. Regan Arts, 2016.

Jansen, Leon J. and Jack E. "A Marc Davis Pirates Sketchbook" "More Gems From This Disney Treasure" The "E" Ticket, Fall 1999.

_____ "Art of Pirates of the Caribbean... A Hunt For Buried Treasure" The "E" Ticket, Summer 2007.

_____ "Designing Disneyland with Marc Davis" The "E" Ticket, Summer 1989.

_____ "A Talk with Marvin Davis" The "E" Ticket, Winter 1997.

_____ "Walt Disney's Sculptor Blaine Gibson" The "E" Ticket, Spring 1995.

_____ "Wathel Rogers and Audio-Animatronics" The "E" Ticket, Winter 1996.

Johnson, Captain Charles. A General History of the Pyrates. Second Edition. London, T. Warner, 1724. Digital Edition by Project Gutenberg, Accessed July 2020.

Johnson, Steven. Wonderland: How Play Made the Modern World. New York, Riverhead Books. 2016.

Kaufman, J. B. South of the Border with Disney. New York, Disney Editions. 2009.

Kingsley, Charles. At Last: A Christmas in the West Indies. Digital edition by Gutenberg; Accessed April 2023.

Kurtti, Jeff. Walt Disney's Imagineering Legends. New York, Disney Editions. 2008.

Laff in the Dark - The World of Dark Ride and Funhouse Amusements. 1998 - 2021, https://laffinthedark.com

Leonard, Richard. "Chicago Railroad Fair 1948-1949: Guide Books, Photos, and Other Items." RailArchive.Net, Mar. 2006, www.railarchive.net/rrfair/index.html.

LMG Vids. "Pirates of the Caribbean Ride: But It's Recorded at Every Angle POV" YouTube, video documentation. Feb 22 2020, https://youtu.be/pg8C-VSWabk

Marling, Karal Ann. Designing Disney's Theme Parks: The Architecture of Reassurance. Flammarion. 1998.

Martin, Stacia. The Sounds of Disneyland. Walt Disney Records. 2005.

Masters, Kim. Keys to the Kingdom: How Michael Eisner Lost His Grip. William Morrow. 2000.

McBride, Joseph. Steven Spielberg: A Biography. Second Edition. University of Mississippi Press. 2011.

Merritt, Christopher and Lynxwiler, J. Eric. Knott's Preserved. Revised Edition. Santa Monica, Angel City Press. 2015.

Merritt, Christopher and Doctor, Pete. Marc Davis In His Own Words: Imagineering the Disney Theme Parks. Disney Editions. 2019

Maltin, Leonard. The Disney Films. New York, Crown Publishers. 1973.

McDonald, John. "Now the Bankers Come to Disney". Fortune Magazine, May 1966.

Moore, Charles. Los Angeles: The City Observed. Santa Monica, Hennessey + Ignallis, 1998, 1984.

Moruzzi, Peter. Classic Dining, Discovering America's Finest Mid-Century Restaurants. Gibbs Smith. 2012.

Nueman, Robert. From Hollywood to Disneyland. McFarland, 2022.

Oriental Land Company History Oriental Land Co., Ltd., http://www.olc.co.jp/en/company/history.html.

Penrose, Mark. Apologise Later, The Biography of Robert Newton. Lulu Press. 2016.

Pierce, Todd James. Three Years in Wonderland. University of Mississippi Press. 2016.

"Pirates of the Caribbean Behind the Scenes". Disneyland Special Event. Panel. June 2000. Video provided by Michael Crawford.

Poe, Edgar Allan. "The Gold Bug", Tales of Mystery and Imagination. New York, Tudor Publishing. 1933.

Powers, Tim. On Stranger Tides. New York, Ace Books. 1987.

Raz, Aviad E. Riding the Black Ship: Japan and Tokyo Disneyland. Harvard East Asian Monographs. 1999.

Rennie, Neil. Treasure Neverland: Real and Imaginary Pirates. Oxford, Oxford University Press. 2016.

Retro Gamer Magazine, "LucasArts: A Celebration", Issue 116, May 2013.

Sanna, Antonio, et al. Pirates in History and Popular Culture. McFarland, 2018.

Singer, Michael. Disney Pirates: The Definitive Collector's Anthology. New York, Disney Editions. 2017.

Sklar, Marty. Dream It! Do It! My Half-Century Creating Disney's Magic Kingdoms. New York, Disney Editions. 2013.

Snow, Richard. Disney's Land. New York, Scribner. 2019.

Stevenson, Robert Louis. Treasure Island. London, Cassell and Company. 1883.

Stewart, James R. Disney War. Simon & Schuster. 2005.

Surrell, Jason. Pirates of the Caribbean: From The Magic Kingdom to the Movies. New York, Disney Editions. 2005.

Thomas, Bob. Building A Company. New York, Disney Editions. 1998.

_____ Walt Disney: An American Original. New York, Disney Editions. 1994.

Walt Disney's Pirates of the Caribbean - The Story of the Robust Adventure in Disneyland and Walt Disney World. Walt Disney Productions Souvenir Book. 1973.

Walt Disney World - The First Decade. Walt Disney Productions Souvenir Book. 1981.

Yardwood, Jack. Spilling the Secrets of the Canceled Curse of Monkey Island Movie. Polygon. 21 Feb 2021. https://www.polygon.com/features/2021/2/21/22291761/curse-of-monkey-island-movie-lucasfilm-spielberg-canceled

Younger, David. Theme Park Design & The Art of Themed Entertainment. Inklingwood Press. 2016.

Filmography

The Black Pirate. Directed by Albert Parker. United Artists, 1926.

The Black Swan. Directed by Henry King. Twentieth Century Fox, 1942.

Captain Blood. Directed by Michael Curtiz. Warner Brothers, 1935

Cutthroat Island. Directed by Renny Harlan. Carolco, 1995.

The Devil-Ship Pirates. Directed by Don Sharp. Hammer Films, 1964.

From the Pirates of the Caribbean to the World of Tomorrow. Directed by Hamilton Luske, Walt Disney Productions, 1968.

The Goonies. Directed by Richard Donner. Warner Brothers, 1985.

A High Wind in Jamaica. Directed by Alexander Mackendrick. Twentieth Century-Fox, 1965.

Hook. Directed by Steven Spielberg. Tristar Pictures, 1991.

Muppet Treasure Island. Directed by Brian Henson. Walt Disney Pictures, 1996.

Peter Pan. Directed by Herbert Brenon. Paramount Pictures, 1924.

Peter Pan. Directed by Clyde Geronimi, Wilfred Jackson and Hamilton Luske. Walt Disney Productions, 1953.

The Pirate Movie. Directed by Ken Annakin. Joseph Hamilton International Productions, 1982.

The Pirates of Blood River. Directed by John Gilling. Hammer Films, 1962.

Pirates of the Caribbean: The Curse of the Black Pearl. Directed by Gore Verbinski. Walt Disney Pictures, 2003.

The Pirates of Penzance. Directed by Wilford Leach. Universal Pictures, 1983.

Roman Polanski's Pirates. Directed by Roman Polanski. Cathargo Films, Accent-Cominco, 1986.

The Sea Hawk. Directed by Michael Curtiz. Warner Brothers, 1942.

Scalawag. Directed by Kirk Douglas. Paramount Pictures, 1973.

Swashbuckler. Directed by James Goldstone. Universal Pictures, 1976.

Treasure Island. Directed by Victor Fleming. Metro-Goldwyn-Mayer, 1934.

Treasure Island. Directed by Byron Haskin. Walt Disney Productions, 1950.

Treasure Island. Directed by Fraiser Clarke Heston. Turner Pictures, 1990.

ALSO BY FOXX NOLTE

Boundless Realm:
Deep Explorations Inside Disney's Haunted Mansion

The Hidden History of
Walt Disney World

ALSO FROM INKLINGWOOD PRESS

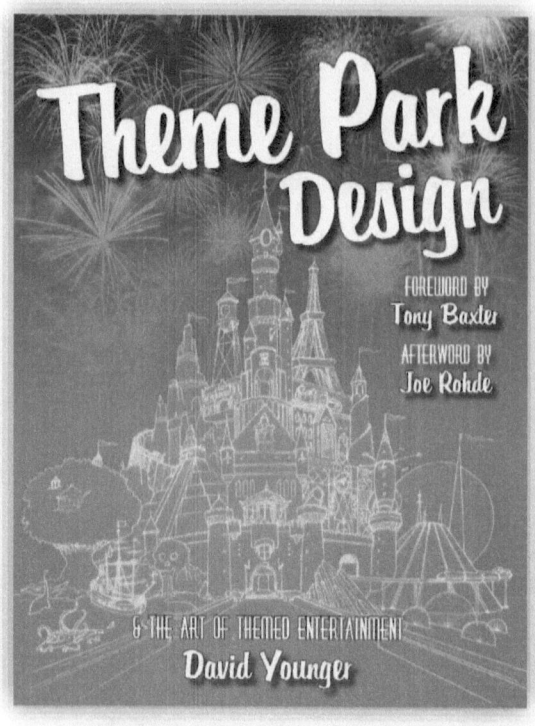

Over the past century, theme parks have created worlds where pirates still loot Caribbean towns, where daring adventurers explore booby-trapped temples, and where superheroes swing from New York skyscrapers - and allowed us to step into them too. This is a book about how to design those fantastic places, and the ingenuity that goes into their creation.

This is a handbook for the practicing designer, a textbook for the aspiring student, and a behind the scenes guidebook for the theme park fan, building on hundreds of interviews with accomplished designers from Walt Disney Imagineering, Universal Creative, Merlin Entertainments, and more. *Theme Park Design & The Art of Themed Entertainment* explores everything from the stories, themes, and characters that theme parks bring to life, to the business models, processes, and techniques that allow them to do it.

From rocket ships to roller coasters, fairy tales to fireworks shows, and dinosaurs to dark rides, never before has a book dived so deep into the art form of themed entertainment.

Written by David Younger
Foreword by Tony Baxter, Afterword by Joe Rohde

"This is the most thorough book on theme park design I have ever seen. One that quotes real designers with priceless knowledge."
Peter Alexander, lead designer of Universal Studios Florida

"This book captures in one document the greatest collection of turning points, philosophies, and ground rules that have sprung to life since the birth of the theme park. I can't imagine a person contemplating a role in themed entertainment not coming out of this immersive experience inside David Younger's mind without the equivalent of a Master's Degree in the psychology of the themed experience."
Tony Baxter, lead designer of Disneyland Paris

"David Younger has created one of the finest studies of the themed entertainment industry ever attempted. It is a comprehensive and thoughtful analysis of every aspect of this most complex design discipline from the micro to the macro levels without once becoming heavy handed. Congratulations on providing both the novice and the grizzled veteran with this wonderful compendium!"
Steve Kirk, lead designer of Tokyo DisneySea

"Authoritative, entertaining, and fascinating, *Theme Park Design* is a themed entertainment aficionado's dream. David Younger has created a one-of-a-kind work that is both a scrupulously researched reference and a jolly good read; an excellent encyclopedia on its subject, and a 'bathtub book' one can open to any page and have a wonderful time exploring."
Jeff Kurtti, lead designer of The Walt Disney Family Museum

"The art of theme park design involves more alchemy than it does art or science, and much of the secret sauce resides behind the obvious surface. Perhaps that's why so little has been written about the subject, let alone anything of practical value. David Younger's book is the first to break down many of these illusive and temporal theories into distinct, understandable, and enlightening observations."
Tom Morris, lead designer of Hong Kong Disneyland

"Expertise is real, and, at least in part, quantifiable, as David Younger's magnum opus demonstrates. By amassing the communal knowledge of this disparate and diverse group into a single opus, David Younger has provided us all with a landmark in our intellectual space."
Joe Rohde, lead designer of Disney's Animal Kingdom

www.ThemeParkDesignBook.com

www.ingramcontent.com/pod-product-compliance
Lightning Source LLC
Chambersburg PA
CBHW020135130526
44590CB00039B/175